SUBACUTE CARE SERVICES

The Evolving Opportunities & Challenges

SUBACUTE CARE SERVICES

The Evolving Opportunities & Challenges

Marshall W. Kelly

A Healthcare 2000 Publication

IRWIN
Professional Publishing®
Chicago, London, Singapore

HEALTHCARE
FINANCIAL
MANAGEMENT
ASSOCIATION

A Healthcare 2000 Publication

IRWIN
Professional Publishing®

© Richard D. Irwin, a Times Mirror Higher Education Group, Inc. company, 1996

Irwin Professional Book Team

Publisher:	Wayne McGuirt
Acquisitions editor:	Kris Rynne
Marketing manager:	Cindy Ledwith
Managing editor:	Kevin Thornton
Project editor:	Jean Lou Hess
Production supervisor:	Dina L. Treadaway
Prepress buyer:	Jon Christopher
Manager, direct marketing:	Rebecca S. Gordon
Compositor:	Lisa King
Typeface:	11/13 Times Roman
Printer:	Maple Vail

Times Mirror
Higher Education Group

ISBN: 1-55738-621-8

Library of Congress Cataloging-in-Publication Data

Subacute care services : the evolving opportunities & challenges /
   [edited by] Marshall W. Kelly.
       p.   cm.
   "A Healthcare 2000 publication".
   Includes index.
   ISBN: 1-55738-621-8
   1. Subacute care facilities—United States.   I. Kelly, Marshall
W.
   RA975.C64S83   1996
   362.1—dc20   95–24869

Printed in the United States of America
1 2 3 4 5 6 7 8 9 0 MV 2 1 0 9 8 7 6 5

Contributing Authors

Linda Berezny

Ms. Berezny is a consultant with Therapy Management Innovations, Inc., where she assists rehabilitation services, develops or expands subacute rehabilitation programs, and provides the needed tools and processes for therapists to adapt to the managed care environment.

Prior to joining TMI, Ms. Berezny presided over her own business, which offered clinical staffing, management, and consultation to the first physical therapists' preferred provider organization.

Ms. Berezny attended Boston-Bouvré College at Northeastern University, where she graduated as a physical therapist. She belongs to the Individual Case Management Association, American Subacute Care Association, and the American Physical Therapy Association (APTA). She has served on various committees and executive boards of specialty sections within the APTA and in her local district and chapter.

Harry Dalsey

Mr. Dalsey is president of Specialty Care Management (SCM), which develops and manages physician organizations, specialty physician groups, Medicaid managed care programs, and disease carve-outs.

Prior to joining SCM, Mr. Dalsey, as vice president of Chi Systems, established Michigan Health Systems and Midlands Health Network. These hospital networks were vehicles for product development, sales, new business development, and acquisition. Also while with Chi Systems, Mr. Dalsey worked as a consultant with a broad spectrum of healthcare providers, such as university teaching hospitals, specialty hospitals, and physicians, on business planning, corporate development, marketing, and establishing new services, joint ventures, and networks.

Mr. Dalsey received his JD from Detroit College of Law, his masters of public health from the University of Michigan, and a bachelor of arts from Knox College.

Jane E. McGeough Danzl

Ms. Jane McGeough Danzl is the current director of nursing at Integrated Health Services at Brentwood in Burbank, Illinois. She has over 15 years of hospital management experience in surgical intensive care and the emergency department.

She received her diploma in nursing from St. Francis School of Nursing, LaCrosse, Wisconsin, and her bachelor of science in nursing from Lewis University in Romeoville, Illinois. Ms. Danzl is a certified critical care nurse, a licensed nursing home administrator, trauma nurse specialist, and basic life support instructor-trainer. An active member of several regional and national nursing organizations, Ms. Danzl lives in Oaklawn, Illinois.

Burton Grebin

Dr. Burton Grebin is the president and CEO of St. Mary's Hospital for Children, Bayside, NY, and Friedman Rehabilitation for Children, Ossining, NY. In addition, Dr. Grebin is an associate professor of clinical pediatrics at the College of Physicians and Surgeons, Columbia University, and an associate attending pediatrician, Columbia Presbyterian Medical Center, New York City. He received his MD degree from New York Medical College.

Dr. Grebin is a member of the board of governors, Greater New York Hospital Association, and a member of the board of trustees, National Association of Children's Hospitals and Related Institutions. In 1990, the Healthcare Association of New York State presented him with its Distinguished Service Award.

Janet Howells

Ms. Howells is a vice president with Therapy Management Innovations, Inc. She is responsible for rehabilitation management consulting services to national chains of skilled nursing facilities, including strategic planning and operational and reimbursement consulting for rehabilitation services. Ms. Howells holds bachelor of science and master of science degrees in physical therapy from Ohio State University.

Ms. Howells was the director of rehabilitation services for Doctors Hospitals in Columbus, Ohio, and co-director of cardiac rehabilitation services. She has published in *Clinical Management* and has co-authored a chapter in *Improving Care in the Nursing Home*.

Ms. Howells is an active member of the American Physical Therapy Association, in which she currently serves as the chief delegate for the Ohio chapter. She was the chairman of the Ohio Physical Therapy Reimbursement Committee from 1988–1991 and was appointed to the Professional Technical Advisory Group of the Joint Commission on Accreditation of Health Care Organizations, Long-Term Care Division.

Stuart C. Kaplan

Stuart C. Kaplan is the executive vice president of St. Mary's Hospital for Children, Bayside, NY, and Friedman Rehabilitation Institute for Children, Ossining, NY, where, as chief operating officer, he is responsible for continuing development/implementation of the strategic plan and of program, policy, and financial initiatives. He is also a member of the board of directors of each organization.

Mr. Kaplan is a member of both the American Subacute Care Association and the National Association of Children's Hospitals and Related Institutions, where he has chaired and been a member of a number of program planning committees. He received his MBA degree from Bernard M. Baruch College—Mount Sinai School of Medicine.

Linda A. Megan

Linda A. Megan has had over 13 years in healthcare sales, marketing, and strategic planning. Currently working as vice president for Rehab Partners, a consulting and development company based in New York City, she has worked with a number of healthcare providers in developing specialty programs. In addition to the client work, she has written certificate of need applications for skilled nursing and subacute programs for submission in a number of states.

Her experience includes the marketing of pharmaceuticals for Johnson & Johnson and Whitehall Laboratories. Ms. Megan also served as physician liaison and development officer for Curative Rehabilitation Center within the Milwaukee Regional Medical Campus and as director of marketing for Northwest Neurological Center and Lakeview Transitional Center in Milwaukee, Wisconsin.

Ms. Megan has a bachelor's degree from Indiana University and credits toward a certificate in management from Marquette University. She currently lives in New York City.

Stephen H. Press

Stephen H. Press rejoined Meditrust as vice president of acquisitions in October 1993. He had served in that capacity from 1987 to 1989. Mr. Press, an attorney and member of the New York State Bar Association, has extensive experience in the nursing home and retirement industry. In his current role with Meditrust, he develops new subacute investment opportunities.

Prior to joining the company, Mr. Press was vice president of development and regulatory affairs for Integrated Health Services, Inc., a medical services company that provides subacute care to geriatric patients. His responsibilities included both the acquisition and development of additional sites for the provision of subacute care and dealing with regulatory and legislative issues on the state and federal levels. Earlier, Mr. Press was vice president of regulatory affairs and communications for the American Health Care Association, initiating a national effort to develop the long-term care insurance market. He was also the director of medical care administration for the State of Connecticut, where he supervised the state Medicaid program, including rate setting and provider relations. Mr. Press is a graduate of Fordham Law School and lives with his family in Newton, Massachusetts.

Kenneth F. Raupach

Mr. Raupach is president and chief executive officer of AmCorps, Inc., a national healthcare management and consulting firm. He earned his bachelor of science degree in health services management from National University in San Diego, California. Prior to founding AmCorps, Mr. Raupach served as senior vice president of operations for Integrated Health Services, an international subacute and skilled provider.

In addition to counseling clients on specialty product development and operation, Mr. Raupach conducts seminars for healthcare corporations, industry associations, and trade journals.

Gary W. Singleton

Gary W. Singleton has been senior vice president–strategic planning and development of Integrated Health Services (IHS) since July 1989. He is responsible for the development of the company's national network of medical specialty units. He is also a board member of the International Subacute Healthcare Association and speaks frequently on the emerging subacute care industry.

Prior to joining IHS, Gary was executive vice president and chief operating officer of Rehabilitation Institute, Inc., a 175-bed specialty hospital located in Detroit.

Gary received his BS and MA degrees from the University of Illinois and received a PhD from Wayne State University.

J. Mark Waxman

Currently a principal in Weissburg & Aronson, Inc., specializing in the representation of healthcare providers and systems, Mr. Waxman is a graduate of the University of California, San Diego, and the University of California at Berkeley (Boalt Hall) Law School. He is a former member of the National Health Lawyers Association Board of Directors.

Acknowledgments

I want to thank my close personal friends who have helped me understand and grow with the industry. Some of them have helped write this book. So I will publicly thank Linda, David, Steve, Bob, and the other contributors for their efforts. I also thank my other friends who have taught me what I know; these include Larry, Jan, Sue, Bill, Mary Cay Lori, Lana, Stephanie, Joyce, Heather, Bob, Jennifer, Dennis, Joe, Bob, and Aaron.

I would also like to thank the State of New York healthcare officials who I have learned from: Linda, Diane, Ellen, Bill, and Brian. Going through the process has been rigorous and I believe that it has improved my focus. Of course there are many people in the field who I have learned from, been inspired by, and have disagreed with. I hope they permit me the license to interpret their ideas without acknowledgment.

There are many others I need to thank for their support, but I need to acknowledge my friend and associate Linda Megan, for without her help, persistence, and kindness this project would never have been accomplished. My thanks also to Kristine Rynne for asking me to write this book.

The sins of this book, the content, the omissions, and the inaccuracies are my responsibility and mine alone. Lastly, thank you, the reader, for taking the time to engage your mind with ours. I hope it was a helpful experience.

Contents

## Chapter 1

Introduction

Subacute Care Services

Marshall W. Kelly

President, Rehab Partners, Inc.

I chose to call this book *Subacute Care Services: The Evolving Opportunities and Challenges* primarily because the approaches and implementation of subacute services will change as the industry matures and as the design of the healthcare delivery system emerges.

Therefore, although I and the contributing authors will touch on many specifics, the focus and intent of the book is not on the "how to" but on the "why" type of information. We have focused on the issues faced and the choices made by a variety of providers. Providers and managers will need to understand not the next step but the reason for the next step. Not to have this background is not to be prepared, for there are no right "answers"; there are only "good choices." I hope this book will help prepare you for making the right decisions.

QUALIFIERS

This book is by no means comprehensive. At the very least, there are enough issues not addressed in this publication to fill several other books. There are also regional differences, cultural differences, company biases, and unique approaches that are probably not addressed in this book. This book reflects the set of experiences of the authors and should not discourage providers who will be taking different or new approaches; in fact, I believe that the industry will be evolving rapidly and today's solutions are tomorrow's history.

HEALTHCARE REFORM

In many ways, the evolution of subacute services parallels the issues and timing of the healthcare reform initiatives being discussed by those in government and the marketplace. The focus is on cost containment, the integration of delivery systems, the cost structure of inpatient services, and the emphasis on market-driven healthcare reform. As these concerns have become the influences of the design of the healthcare system, the growth and evolution of the subacute level of services has accelerated.

As healthcare reform initiatives take place, there will be a new alignment of the service delivery system. The incentives inherent in this system will certainly affect financial incentives, power structures, and acceptance of the subacute level of care.

To understand what subacute services will be in the near future (maybe even next year), it is important to study the issues involved in the approaches that freestanding nursing home facilities, hospitals, and companies have taken to design and implement their programs. Therefore, it is these issues that this book explores and focuses on.

A SHORT HISTORY OF SUBACUTE SERVICES

Freestanding Nursing Facilities: The Beginnings

Simplisticly stated, subacute programs involve high-acuity patients and exceptional funding streams. They were initiated in several nursing homes, but primarily in the Northeast United States and California. The motives for initiation were the difficult-to-place specialty populations combined with a desire for higher revenues on a per-bed basis.

The subacute services in the Northeast started with specialty programs (mostly traumatic brain injury rehabilitation programs) in nursing homes funded by out-of-state exceptional Medicaid rates. These programs were fed by many states. For many state Medicaid directors, it was easier to develop exceptional rates out of state than to create new differentiating funding levels in state. This patient population had significantly higher nursing and therapy needs and longer lengths of stays than were associated with stays in hospitals.

These programs were started by two companies—Greenery and New Medico. It is ironic that although these two companies were pioneers, they did not expand their patient populations and therefore were not significant players in the evolving subacute horizon.

In other locales like California and South Florida, adventuresome nursing home operators were pushing the limits of what had traditionally been patient populations in skilled nursing facilities. They found that managed care organizations would pay for services done in nursing homes and that some of the more enterprising operators tested the limits of the Medicare program through the Medicare atypical exception process. For the most part, this was done by individual operators who were eager to pursue their visions.

Once a critical mass of patients was achieved in these units, these providers actively marketed other payor streams. Since the service delivery, particularly to brain-injured individuals, involved relatively new service modalities, and the patient populations were young adults and children, the market and the funding streams were new to the long-term care setting. Consequently, for the first time, a nursing home was paid according to charges like a hospital setting, not on a cost basis like routine Medicaid or Medicare funding streams, or private pay, which had the market discipline of competing with other nursing homes. Higher profit margins than were previously thought possible were available.

The financial opportunity of subacute services was born. And as healthcare providers know, the overwhelming majority of changes in healthcare come in relation to reimbursement incentive changes. The possibility of a charge-based structure with a savings over a higher-cost structure (the hospital) opened up an opportunity for long-term care providers.

These providers went down this path for several reasons. Their programmatic flexibility had been severely limited by the low payment by Medicaid programs. They responded by focusing on other funding streams and the beginning of focused specialty programs. Their experience was not replicated, however, until several entrepreneurs with access to a larger resource pool acquired the vision of taking these models in multiple sites.

These pioneers also overcame another major issue—that of credibility. Whether a skilled nursing facility could provide services to a high-acuity patient population was a major issue to families and referral sources. By staffing appropriately, redesigning the facility both clinically and physically, marketing the facility assertively, and documenting outcomes, they would prove the case for these services and the sites of the services.

A little later, companies discovered the advantages of operating under a chronic care hospital licensure. Although they did not see themselves as subacute companies, their hospitals provided services to similar patient populations. The investment community eagerly embraced these companies because investors understood the placement issues involved with this population. This provided a climate for receptivity for subacute companies that were about to enter the public markets and gain access to significant amounts of capital to stimulate growth.

Several CEOs picked up on these examples and the investment environment and took advantage of the growth opportunities. Integrated Health Services was the first of these companies to go public, followed closely by Mariner, Mediplex, MCR, Horizon, Genesis, Sun, Hillhaven, and so forth; and they were well received.

Wall Street embraced the concept of subacute services for several simple reasons. Primarily it was perceived as a low-risk strategy because subacute services brought higher revenues to long-term care companies, which could always return to long-term care services if they were not successful. Long-term care was perceived favorably primarily because of the demographics, the limited availability of beds, and the return of a favorable business cycle in the industry. The primary reason for the downturn was the scarcity of professional personnel and the accompanying inflation of salaries for those people.

The access to capital to the formerly pure long-term care companies accelerated the development of subacute services through a rapid expansion of sites, resources for program and evaluation development, and significantly increased market valuations. This capital access was the primary reason for the rapid widespread development of subacute services, a development that was probably faster than that of any programmatic type of service delivery ever. Another reason was that the barriers to entry for facilities to convert to subacute services were relatively low. The physical plants required for conversion to subacute care were available, whereas new facilities had to be built for the rehabilitation and psychiatric industries.

Clinical, managerial, and financial technical knowledge became available primarily through seminars and a rapidly expanding population of personnel experienced in the field. The financial rewards for providing subacute services became widely known and were reinforced by publicly traded companies' high multiples in the stock markets. Capital for purchasing facilities, converting operations, and funding cash flow issues were made available from the public markets in the form of debt and equity placements, real estate investment trusts (REITS), venture capital, and mezzanine financing.

In 1994, trade associations were formed, multiple seminars with large audiences were held, the flow of literature increased, newsletters were published, and multiple consolidations of companies were completed.

The acute hospital community started its initial reaction to the presence in the marketplace. In some markets, hospitals started to look to subacute services to include in their continuums of care. In the states where there were few barriers (particularly no certificate of need processes) to the easy conversion of hospitals' licensed beds to subacute services, hospitals rapidly relicensed beds. This was clearly evidenced in California, where many hospitals have converted beds.

Subacute services were inevitable once dieases-related groupings (DRGs) were implemented. Payment of services was based upon a diagnosis and was a fixed figure. The reason was to control open-ended costs, and the incentives were to discharge patients from hospitals to an alternative service delivery, like home healthcare. Subacute services allowed earlier discharge dates from hospital licensures for patients who still required inpatient services.

In the states where there is no certificate of need barrier, many hospitals relicensed some or all of their medical/surgical licensed beds to a skilled nursing licensure, called transitional care or subacute units, that provide care to many of the patients previously treated in medical/surgical beds. The service delivery staffing, location, and focus is probably no different from the past patterns; the only difference is licensure.

But a key question was and is: Will subacute services have an important presence in the integrated service delivery system necessitated by global capitation, which is becoming the dominant financial paradigm in the market-based healthcare reform initiatives occurring across the country? At least initially, the answer is a resounding positive presence for subacute services. In fact, the extent of the presence in a mature, integrated market is heightened significantly.

Unfortunately for many providers who have subacute services, the ultimate choice for the location and ownership of the site of the service is at the discretion of the organization that accepts the capitation risk. Many hospitals in particular, if they are the system integrator, will select the site to their best advantage, and this might not include the current provider in the area.

Whatever the ultimate disposition of subacute services will be, and whatever your beliefs about this level of care, the concept has profoundly affected inpatient care as we have known it. The sincere efforts of the people in the field, managers, and clinicians should be applauded. It is their daily efforts to serve that make any service work.

Ultimately, I'm thankful for the benefit to a specialized spectrum of patients who would not have had access to focused, measured, cost-effective services. And in the end, that's what healthcare services are all about—the people we service. To them, the faces and names I remember and those I don't, and to the individuals I'll never meet, this book is dedicated.

Chapter 2

The Intrinsic Value of Subacute Services

Marshall W. Kelly
President, Rehab Partners, Inc.

Whether or not you philosophically approve of the trend of the development of subacute healthcare (or delivery of this service under the name of transitional, clinically complex, or specialty care), it is being rapidly defined as a new level of care by the marketplace. The speed of the development has been astounding, primarily because of the low barriers to entry, simultaneous timing with healthcare reform initiatives, the focus on cost containment, and the availability of capital to finance expansion. But questions have to be answered: What is the value of this level of service and what is the cost for its development?

If, as a society, we seem to believe that the cost of healthcare service delivery is too high, then we must find ways of reducing the cost. We have choices: We can find a more cost-effective way of delivering the services, or we can limit access to services, or both. Limiting services has both painful and ethical implications that healthcare professionals and legislative contingencies are reluctant to face. Therefore, we need to find the most cost-effective methods available, including prevention, utilizing the lowest-cost settings possible for services, and eliminating overcapacity. All things being equal on service delivery, the most cost-effective site of actual care should be the one utilized.

EVOLUTION OF REIMBURSEMENT

When disease-related groupings, or DRGs, were instituted, they fundamentally changed the nature of services in hospitals and nursing homes. The intent was to put limits on the length of stays in hospitals. The financing source (Medicare) structured a system that did not allow open-ended acute care healthcare costs.

The DRG system in turn has had a significant impact upon the nature of services being delivered in nursing facilities. Hospitals were forced to discharge patients earlier than in the past. Nursing homes were then faced with a long-term care resident population, which was much sicker than previously. By another means, the Medicare system affected nursing homes by defining Medicare distinct units, which allows for aggregate delivery for reimbursement of high-intensity services in a skilled nursing home. This structured a funding stream that offered a financial incentive to provide aggressive services to the Medicare-funded patient. The resource utilization groupings system (RUGS) of reimbursement for nursing home care also has accelerated the trend to accept and treat high-acuity patients.

The explosion of managed care plans provides another source of payment, driving the development for cost-saving programs. Managed care organizations (MCOs) have continually sought methods of containing their medical losses. These organizations have created case management systems to move a patient through a continuum of care, maintaining a philosophy of the least costly, least restrictive environment and focusing on the patient's best outcome. By adopting an aggressive utilization practice, MCOs monitor the patient's course of treatment and outcome at each level of care in the continuum. Since subacute services can offer savings in the range of 50 percent, the subacute service environment has now become an attractive alternative to traditional inpatient hospital care and, for many managed care systems, an integral part of their cost-effective care plans.

One of the characteristics of subacute services is the delivery of care through a programmatic model, and the evolution of these critical pathways has and will continue to create benchmarks by which we will judge the delivery of these services. These critical pathways can be measured and assessed, and included in these indicators will be the referral patterns and timing of services delivered. In some ways, the subjectivity of care delivery is under scrutiny, and will eventually offer a pattern that will create a basis for continued research. Outcome-oriented research will provide the answer for many questions related to the practice patterns and determination of resource utilization. The variances from these patterns will have both clinical and financial implications.

As capitation (also called prepayment or risk sharing) becomes the dominant mode of payment and begins to impact the utilization patterns of the inpatient continuum of care, the trend toward utilization of subacute services will accelerate. This model of payment and service delivery will eventually provide our healthcare system with the most cost-efficient design to date. An emphasis will be placed upon primary and preventive care, and much of the savings to the system will be derived from the reduction and redefining of the need for inpatient care.

As the healthcare industry's financial paradigm shifts from profits that are generated from volumes of procedures, to the delivery of efficient healthcare services, the unnecessary and the profligate will be rung out of our healthcare system.

ISSUE OF CHRONICITY

Our healthcare system has focused on and developed excellent diagnostic and treatment services, prolonging life and curing, until recently, incurable illnesses. Through prevention, miracle drugs, and procedures, we have overcome many diseases that in the past took productive lives.

Much of the remaining challenge to the system has to do with chronic problems. Many of the problems occur because of irreversible lifestyle diseases or catastrophic injuries. The system must cope with the recidivism of conditions, maintenance of well-being, and maximization of the individual's independence.

From an economic viewpoint, the problem is that a small population requires a disproportionate percentage of the healthcare dollars. It is estimated that just 16 percent of the persons receiving care with chronic conditions require 41 percent of the total dollar expenditures.

The question is, Who is best able to handle this patient population? Although I believe that it takes all levels of providers' involvement to craft successful solutions, the underlying issues of independence, supportive services, and conservation of long-term resources may be better handled by the long-term care/home health/community-based spectrum of the continuum of care. We should expect that many solutions will come from these providers.

Subacute services make these chronicity issues logically the domain of the long-term care providers, for they will be dealing with these populations in periodic or extended inpatient stays. Many of the chronic population are currently being treated in subacute settings, including wound care, rehabilitation, ventilator care, AIDS infusion therapy, and so forth. These populations will represent 20 percent of the discharges from acute settings, but they represent a significantly higher proportion of the total acute/subacute patient days, possibly reaching 40 percent.

Access to specialized services is also an issue of our healthcare evolution. Many states have certificate of need requirements or rigorous subjective patient selection processes to access services such as rehabilitative, medical, and psychiatric care. Unlike primary or emergency care, the provision of these specialized services is often reduced by restrictive statutory or extensive regulatory processes.

Under healthcare reform initiatives, rehabilitative care will have heightened emphasis. It is not only in the individual's best interest to achieve his or her highest level of independence and functioning, but it is ultimately cost effective, with proven reduction of resource utilization. The rehabilitative process in the past has been selective, with candidates chosen by patient capacity and attitude, discharge options, payor source, disability type, and other subjective criteria. Where capacity has been limited through regulation, lack of personnel, or lack of innovation, the selective process has been profound. The question for rehabilitative services remains: Should access be limited, or should every individual who can benefit be given the opportunity despite his or her present capacity, limitations, sponsor, or diagnosis? If the service benefits the individual and it is ultimately cost effective, it is rational that the individual should receive the services.

Either a hospital or skilled nursing facility can provide the appropriate site for rehabilitative services. The advantages a skilled nursing setting offers over a hospital include the capacity for the potential extended length of stay and gradual return to the community, which is often reflective of the rehabilitative process, and the flexibility of the bed-usage and service delivery system, which can be designed to meet the individual needs of the patient.

A dramatic example of the benefit of recent innovation in rehabilitation practices is in the weaning process for the ventilator-dependent patient. To date, many hospital-based rehabilitation providers are not yet serving this population. Other providers, like skilled nursing operators and chronic hospitals, are providing access to rehabilitative weaning. These programs are developed to free individuals from dependence upon mechanical ventilation at an enormous long-term financial savings to the sponsor and referral source. Intuitively, we can understand what freedom from a ventilator can mean in terms of the quality of life for an individual. An expectation should be created that the individual who is ventilator-dependent or designated as "chronic ventilator-dependent" should have access to rehabilitative services before a long-term program is provided. There are other similar populations, such as those with AIDS, brain injuries, neuromuscular diseases, and so on, that require similar access to appropriate service issues.

The history of hospitals has been one of increasing specialization. The development of subacute services is a reflection of this trend. The difference lies in that the specialization in hospitals grew out of the medical/surgical units, upstreaming high-acuity patients into more specialized services such as ICUs. This occurred as medical technology and services evolved and a critical mass of patient population could be identified.

Subacute services have developed from specialty patient populations traditionally serviced in the general medical/surgical units, where the lengths of stay were comparatively longer than in other hospital units. Service delivery on medical/surgical units was not, by definition, programmatic. The evolution of subacute has resulted in moving patients downstream from medical/surgical services into these specialized programs. Subacute services started with specific patient populations that respond best to a programmatic service delivery. This evolution is, again, representative of the ever-increasing trend toward specialization in healthcare.

The design of programmatic services versus inclusion in general medical/surgical units illustrates the rationale for the utilization of resources in the development of specialty services. Once a patient population develops a critical mass, services should be delivered in an organized programmatic approach where expertise can be concentrated, critical pathways organized, and staffing, equipment, supplies, and space customized to meet the specific needs of the targeted patient population.

There has been a continued expansion of subacute services from the "outlier population" to an ever-expanding spectrum of care, which includes more generalized services such as postsurgical recovery. This expansion will continue.

NATURE OF THE FACILITY

What levels of intensity and nature of services should be offered in a hospital environment and what in the long-term setting?

Hospitals are geared toward the high-technology interventions. Examples include intensive care units, MRIs, CAT scans, surgical suites, pathology labs, radiology, testing equipment, sophisticated pharmacies, nuclear medicine, and so forth. The nature of the service includes diagnosis and intervention and can be characterized as intense, sophisticated, immediate, and expensive. All the protocols, equipment, and staff focus are oriented toward the sickest patients, and there is a presumption that all patients require and are monitored for this level of intensity of services. Our hospitals provide excellent care and are the envy of the world. Could it be, however, that the longer the patient stay, the less appropriate the hospital becomes as a site for care, thereby lowering the overall quality of care?

If this is true, what is the nature of a nursing home or a chronic hospital? Should a skilled nursing or chronic hospital facility be seen as a resident or a medical service center, or are they both? At what point in a patient's stay should he or she be transferred to a chronic, subacute, and super skilled facility? What is to be considered medical stability criteria in transfer to a nonacute setting? As the capacities of these sites for services increase, so will their ability to handle and define high-acuity and more complicated patients.

The question is, Are skilled nursing facilities homes for residents too incapacitated, or are they sites for services for patients who are medically stable but require acute care?

COSTS ALONG A CONTINUUM OF CARE

Hospitals in the development of integrated service delivery systems will have to look beyond the traditional mind-set of the hospital as *the* cost center to the hospital being *a* cost center. In other words, will the hospital be the center of the service delivery or just another stop along a continuum of care? The executive leadership of an integrated service delivery system (whether it's a hospital, physician group head, or a managed care executive) will need to judge the system by overall cost and the patient outcomes. They should not be protecting an entity along a continuum of care from primary care to chronic care but should look for every efficiency possible. The ultimate measures of an integrated system in the marketplace will be the premiums charged to the financial sponsor, patient satisfaction, and patient outcomes.

Subacute services delivered in freestanding skilled nursing facilities have lower costs associated with the site than a hospital-based program. By having the freestanding subacute center available, there is the potential to create a cost-sensitive platform, stimulating market discipline for that level of service delivery. This market discipline is one of the underpinnings to healthcare reform efforts.

THE COSTS OF THE DEVELOPMENT OF SUBACUTE LEVEL OF SERVICES

It is disingenuous to presume that there will be no cost from the development of subacute services. The primary cost will be the closure of hospital-licensed beds. This will accelerate the current and future overcapacity found in the acute hospital service delivery. Specialty hospitals (rehabilitation and psychiatric) will also be affected.

Traditionally, hospitals have been heavily managed organizations. The ratio of managers to patients (1.2 to 1) in hospitals is extremely high. These traditions of intensity and layers of management will be changing in the near future. In some ways, this is not a bad trend, but it will be a painful one. Efficiency and re-engineering efforts have affected other industries, and healthcare is currently facing the same difficult issues and choices.

Inpatient hospital care faced similar challenges from outpatient surgery centers, outpatient programs, and home healthcare services. Subacute services are not the first to present themselves as an alternative to acute hospital services in the marketplace.

The primary issue will be the quality of care delivery. Will patient care suffer? Will convenience for and reimbursement for physicians be an issue? Patient care should not be compromised. Care should be given that is equal to or better than that offered in other settings, or the subacute service system will have a very short life span. To date, with minimum exception, the care has not been negatively affected.

For physicians, however, continued growth will produce significant changes. Reimbursement for the subacute level of services is lower, and

coverages for physicians will be for a larger patient population than currently. Referrals will be made for reimbursement rationales, in many cases
for cost-efficiency purposes. Also, a lack of convenience to the service
site will lead to deference to the program physician leadership. The question remains, Will these changes in physician patterns, controls, and reimbursement impede the continued expansion of subacute services?

Skilled nursing-based programs have a tradition of being nurse driven,
and subacute services (in comparison to hospital services) have not radically changed this tradition. However, an interdisciplinary approach utilizing the expertise of the whole team should be the primary model of
service delivery for subacute programs.

CONCLUSION

A new level of service delivery has been defined and is in the process of
rapid development. The rationales for the service, whether financial, clinical, or from a program development perspective, are identifiable and relevant to today's healthcare system. The changes are being driven by the
marketplace. Resources in the form of technical knowledge and capital
are readily available. The business cycle will be rapid, irreversible, and
completed within an extraordinarily short period of time. Subacute service development will occur parallel to and be symptomatic of the
healthcare reform initiatives.

Chapter 3

Marketing Subacute Care:
Issues in Developing a Successful Marketing Program

Linda A. Megan
Vice President, Rehab Partners, Inc.

The success of your program depends upon three interdependent areas. First, the clinical services of your specialty care program will have to be of comparable quality and intensity to acute *hospital*-based services. Second, the management of the facility will have to learn the clinical elements of the program, create new management systems (reimbursement), and understand the new market environment in which it's operating. Third, and by no means last, you will have to *market your program professionally, convincingly, and with appropriate resources.*

INTRODUCTION

Facing health care reform, with its drive to treat patients in lower-cost settings and the need for census and profitability enhancement, many types of providers are developing subacute services. Traditionally, providers of subacute services have been for-profit long-term care chains that have developed expertise, programs, and marketing approaches now being widely copied, in name if not in fact. In many areas of the country, the subacute market is saturated with providers. Although the issues no longer relate to the introduction of this level of care to the local market, they are claiming a greater share of the subacute healthcare dollars.

Nationally, the subacute market is the fastest-growing segment of healthcare. The financial community has accepted the concept of subacute as a growth strategy and has pumped over $1.4 billion dollars into publicly traded subacute companies in the last three years. Experts estimate subacute care to be more than a $1 billion dollar business in 1993 and predict the industry could generate as much as $10 billion in revenues by the end of the decade.

The term *subacute* is defined as those services provided for patients who are medically stable and in need of continued health care that traditionally was provided within the medical/surgical beds or comprehensive rehabilitation units of acute hospitals. These patients are no longer in need of the diagnostic, high-technological interventions, intensive care monitoring, or emergency medical interventions provided in acute medical settings. Therefore, it is logical to provide less expensive rehabilitative or nursing care such as that provided by a skilled nursing facility. The higher reimbursement structures for these services, primarily Medicare, exceptional Medicaid rates, indemnity insurance, and managed care, are in turn attractive to the long-term care providers who in the recent past have seen a significant drop in revenues due to a shrinking population able or willing to pay for long-term care.

The long-term healthcare industry has not historically had to pay a great deal of time or attention to sophisticated marketing strategies. Based on the location or exclusivity of the market, most facilities had a fairly predictable market share based on the demographics of the geographic area. However, the evolution of healthcare in the 90s and the proliferation of competitive services in the market have changed traditional attitudes regarding the need for marketing. In the past, geriatric patients have had few alternative choices for placement, which made potential revenues from more aggressive marketing unjustifiable. For specialty services, the potential revenues are substantial and justify the increased allocation for monies and efforts devoted to marketing.

Cost control has been the emphasis in long-term care service delivery because the revenues are fairly predictable, but the strategy changes in the subacute market. If the census and payor mix for a smaller number of patients is stable, then the profitability is significantly higher. Once an operator has seen that profitability can reach hundreds of dollars a day for a single patient, it shifts its focus from cost control to actions that will enhance and develop program census.

The focus of this chapter is the initial marketing process and implementation for the marketing of a specialty program and does not include all of the areas in determining market feasibility, such as other costs related to specialty program development that need to be identified. To determine the total expense of this type of programming, you will need to include the cost for obtaining or developing the clinical protocols, necessary equipment, increased staffing, training, management time, and the marketing budget. The following discussion addresses where to begin, outlines how a start-up facility can develop an initial marketing plan, and provides the steps necessary to position the facility within the local service delivery.

BACK TO THE BASICS

The foundation for any successful marketing is understanding the needs and wants of the marketplace. You must make a thorough inquiry to determine what services are currently being provided in your area and what opportunities exist for specialty programming. To assure the profitability of development and the return on commitment of resources, you first need to investigate current delivery systems and payment or reimbursement sources. We will focus first on ventilator product lines. Currently these services are on the high end of the acuity scale since they are provided in an alternative setting to acute care hospitals.

HOSPITALS

Ventilator Dependency

Contact the local hospitals to determine the number of patients on ventilators and where they are in the hospital. Speak directly to the director of respiratory services and ask the following questions: What is the daily average of both adult and pediatric patients on ventilators? How many of those are chronic ventilator patients versus short term, for example, following surgery or trauma? Do they have a special step-down unit or are they in ICUs? Where are chronic ventilator patients sent within the hospital? (A number of premature babies are placed on ventilators and are weaned off after a short time once they are stable. So, if you are considering caring for pediatric ventilator patients, be aware that newborns may inflate the number of potential candidates but would more than likely not be appropriate for skilled nursing units as they will be on ventilators for only a short period.) Once these questions have been answered, contact the discharge planner in the hospital to determine their needs for placement of patients on ventilators.

OTHER SERVICE LINES

As part of your program development, ask the discharge planners what placement problems they may have and in what way a skilled nursing facility could improve accommodation of difficult-to-place patients.

The administrator should develop a relationship with the hospital. Join or attend (if allowed) the hospital association meetings. Learn its financial structure, political issues, and specialties. Many of these meetings are open to a select public, or ask an associate from the hospital if you may go as a guest. You need to be familiar with the acute care hospital delivery systems. The market is rapidly changing and hospitals are developing skilled nursing facilities and units to protect their market share. For example, in California close to 80 percent of all hospitals have in place or are planning step-down/swing or nursing beds. It is important to learn as much as possible about the hospital's strategic planning.

PHYSICIANS

Identify the influential physicians in your region. Plan to educate them regarding your programming and ask for their input. Ask them where they may see a need for subacute services. Explore the potential for the development of an informal or formal partnership with the physicians.

MANAGED CARE PROVIDERS: HMO/PPOS

Contact the managed care companies in your area and explore their needs for placement of ventilator-dependent patients. Talk to the major insurance companies in your area. Independent case management companies may also provide excellent information. Explain to them that as a skilled nursing facility you are exploring the potential for program development and that you would be able to provide a less costly alternative to the hospital setting. (That should stir their interest.) Be prepared to outline your programs. Ask about competition and try to obtain pricing information. Because many case managers negotiate for lowered rates, they may be reluctant to release specific information but may give you a range for services. Your objective at this point is to gather information from the HMOs rather than seek a specific provider contract. However, depending upon the level of market penetration of subacute services, this is also an excellent source from which to gain competitive information, that is, the HMO may be willing to share names of current contacts and may give you some feedback regarding their level of satisfaction.

MEDICAID

There are many states with progressive Medicaid programs that give enhanced rates to providers of specialty programs. Ventilator rates that reflect custodial care are commonplace. They can take two forms: one is an all-inclusive rate and the other is an enhanced rate with a dual payment to cover ancillaries and supplies. Whatever the rate is, and it varies widely from state to state, it sets the expectations for the long-term ventilator care in the area because Medicaid can be presumed to be the payor for a high percentage of custodial ventilator care.

Check with the state Medicaid officials to see if their program has an exceptional rate or they are interested in establishing one. Use cost-effectiveness justifications to generate their interest in providing this rate. They are well aware of the costs of delivering these services in hospitals. If the state you are operating in does not have or want to set up an exceptional rate, the neighboring states might. Out-of-state referral patterns for specialty populations are commonplace.

A Medicaid ventilator program will be profitable if it is run as a Medicaid unit. There must be a good level of cost control to stay within the Medicaid ceiling. Medicare cost-shifting and a reasonable level of lower care of Medicaid patients will also help to subsidize the program and reduce the cost per day by an averaging effect.

CURRENT AND POTENTIAL SPECIALTY PROGRAMS AND VENTILATOR PROGRAMS

You will also need to identify current providers of specialty services. You may already be aware of specialty facilities through your professional associations; however, a good resource would be the yellow pages, under Rehab or Nursing Homes. If there is a facility offering ventilator or specialty services, do some competitive shopping; for even though a facility may provide ventilator services, the need for your area may exceed its capacity or you may be able to provide superior services, a better price, or a location that offers a distinct advantage within the market. It is extremely helpful to obtain the pricing for the programs and individual services, such as physical therapy, occupational therapy, and specialty programming.

To evaluate the competitive facility and its programming, visit it in person. If the facility management or staff members know you, send someone else. Prior to sending that individual, make sure he or she is prepared to ask the appropriate questions and to observe the physical plant and staff for specific information, such as how many on each shift.

ANALYSIS OF COMPETITIVE INFORMATION

Once you have gathered the information, you need to analyze the risk involved in making a commitment to specialty programming. It is estimated that approximately 15 percent of current skilled nursing facilities are capable of delivering subacute services. Perhaps the best way to begin would be to create a grid of programming currently available in the area.

List the facilities and rank their strengths and weaknesses on the basis of your research. Determine how your facility's services may offer advantages to the market. The specific costs of identifiable improvements to the physical plant, such as separate entrances, signage, staffing, training, and equipment, are not outlined here; rather, the focus is on the development of the marketing message, market position, and operational impact on the organization. To determine total cost, you will need to look at each of these areas as part of the decision process. You will have to develop a program based on cost and anticipated revenues as part of the review.

Other key financial questions you need to address include:

- How much more profit will be generated than your regular business?
- How much do you need to charge?
- What is the census needed to break even?

The following table summarizes possible sources of revenues and expenses.

Revenues	Capital Costs	Operating Expenses
Size of unit and bed/room configuration	Furniture and equipment Construction/renovation/ building improvements	Increased staffing: nursing, administrative, etc.
Diagnosis types and unit mix anticipated	Square footage of subacute areas	Training
Payor types and unit mix anticipated		Recurring costs/higher wage rates for special staff
Daily routine rates by diagnosis and payor type		Additional nonbillable supplies
Fill-up/transition period		Other operating expense increases (marketing)
Projected occupancy percentage once fully operational		
Medicare routine cost limit at facility		
Type of residents to be replaced (or empty beds)		
Additional ancillary activity by payor type		

National companies use the population base as one of the criteria in determining the validity of a start-up operation. For example, for every million people in an area the predicted need would be 100 ventilator beds. However, each catchment area has unique geographic boundaries that you need to consider. The catchment area can be expanded for specialty programming, particularly for ventilator services, as these may not be as readily available in all locations. Postsurgical and high-intensity orthopedic rehab services, because of their dependence on the immediate population base, need to be near an acute care hospital.

CREATING A SUBACUTE ENVIRONMENT WITHIN A SKILLED NURSING FACILITY

A subacute image is substantially different than that of a long-term care facility. In long-term care, you want to provide a comfortable homelike setting that is appealing to the resident and family. Depending on the level of care offered by the facility, the nursing or technical skills required in long-term care may be minimized. Recreational activities, psycho-social services, or appearance (cleanliness of the residents and facility) can become the most important aspects in the decision process.

In subacute care, there is more emphasis on the technical or medical look to the facility. Clean, modern patient rooms with a feeling of efficiency are more appropriate than the popular homey decor. The patient population is younger and may be sensitive to the idea of a nursing home, which may symbolize to them a place where people go to live when they can no longer take care of themselves. Therefore, a facility needs to appear vital, well maintained, and somewhat technical; it must impart an overall feeling of success. If possible, the facility's subacute unit should appear to be separate from the geriatric units. This can be done with architectural barriers and changes in color theme or decor. Creating a separate entrance with marked parking and signage may be the most important first impression to the credibility of the program.

In a recent survey conducted by Rehab Partners, Inc., regarding the development of subacute specialty programming in California, over 100 case managers responsible for directing patients to subacute facilities said that the number one factor in the decision process is location of the facility; number two is how the facility presents its program, that is, is the program well constructed and clinically sound? Number three is the facility's physical appearance to the patient and family. Because many facilities are recent start-up operations within existing geriatric skilled nursing facilities, case managers looked for indicators such as experience with IVs (when looking for high-acuity skilled nursing services) and increased staffing patterns. So even though a facility offers new services, case managers base their decisions on the look of the facility, its staffing, and its program, which to them indicates the degree of the investment that the operators are willing to place in the new service delivery. It also indicates that the operators understand the subacute market and are committed to making the changes necessary to provide these services.

COMMITMENT OF RESOURCES

At this point you have investigated the market for subacute services and developed some assumptions regarding the programs or services that will fit into your local healthcare delivery systems. To assure the success of your new programming, you need to protect your investment by budgeting enough capital for marketing and marketing-related expenses. There are no industry averages or standard formulas based on sales as in some industries, but there are guidelines that should help you in devising your budget.

Many smaller programs develop with great enthusiasm, but fail because of inadequate monies and personnel dedicated to marketing and promotion. National subacute companies spend a great deal of money on elaborate brochures and collaterals because of increased competition and the specification of high-acuity services. Although you may not be able to spend what these national companies do, you must develop an image that leaves the target audience feeling that you have the capability to deliver on what you promise.

HIRING AND MANAGING A DEDICATED MARKETING STAFF

For many skilled nursing facilities, the introduction of subacute services is the first time they will need dedicated personnel whose primary function is to develop census, that is, to attract patients. Traditionally, the marketing in nursing homes has been the shared responsibility of the administrator, social worker, and admissions coordinator. Many of these individuals have no formal marketing or sales training. Hiring the appropriate personnel with a background in healthcare sales or insurance will be a significant factor in the success of the program.

These people should have either a strong clinical background with a marketing personality, or marketing experience and a willingness to learn clinical information quickly. Without a personality that is assertive and outgoing and the ability to handle minor rejections, a marketing person will not be successful. Studies have shown that good marketing personnel are goal oriented and tenacious. In developing expectations and a remuneration package, set goals for the marketing staff linking them to salary and incentives. Incentives should be *at least* 20 percent of the total financial package for the staff.

Managing a salesperson can be significantly different from managing other personnel within a traditional skilled setting. Many marketing personnel are used to working independently on established goals. However, their supervisor should meet weekly with them to make sure that productivity in terms of calls and planned activities is on track and to alert the facility to incoming patients. It is important that feedback to the facility from the marketplace is ongoing in order to shape the direction of the market plan and program development. For example, if the marketer hears that a competitive program is starting up, the facility's management needs sufficient information regarding that program to position the facility positively. Or, if on calls to hospital discharge planners, the marketer hears repeatedly an expressed need for pediatric specialty care or wound care, for example, he or she needs to obtain and maintain this information in a format available for review.

Call reports need to be generated daily and updated weekly. Good sales/ marketing personnel are highly sought after and as in most competitive industries salespeople do move around frequently. To protect your facility's investment in the sales effort, good record keeping is essential. Developing and maintaining accurate referral/account contact records can be invaluable during transitions between sales staffs; therefore periodic reviews of actual contact records must be taken by management to assure that record keeping is consistent.

Many sales/marketing people dislike paperwork, viewing it as unproductive; however, the rule that a weekly report with a summary of call activity should be submitted every Friday must be consistently enforced. The key to managing salespeople includes:

• Clearly defined responsibilities, goals, and levels of activities based on timelines.

- Clearly defined census goals.
- Established format for reporting of activities and information.
- Established format for communication with management.
- Recognition and praise for outstanding accomplishment.
- Ongoing support for problem solving, and a team spirit among all players in the program.

A sample of a weekly marketing report is found on the next two pages. You may also wish to ask for a prospective call planner on a weekly basis to monitor upcoming calls.

THE MARKETING BUDGET

Travel and Entertainment Expenses

Marketing positions require local travel, and therefore compensation for the expenses should be part of the remuneration package. Anticipated travel may also include attending national conferences. Most organizations usually reimburse for car mileage at the current IRS approved rate. Purchasing donuts or lunch, for example, is also helpful when visiting discharge planners or insurance case managers. Most office space for discharge planners is usually fairly small and shared among several staff people, which causes much distraction; therefore, sometimes it is easier to conduct a meeting elsewhere. If you do not have company-issued expense forms, you can purchase standard forms from an office supply house. One way of controlling costs for lunches would be to require approval prior to the expenditure; however, some spending should be left to the discretion of the marketer.

Conference Attendance and Continuing Education

Networking is extremely important in the healthcare delivery business. Many professional groups host conferences and seminars that allow facilities and suppliers to market themselves through promotional booths; these provide opportunities to present information either at annual meet-

CENTER
WEEKLY MARKETING REPORT

Staff _____ Title _____ Week Ending Date_____

Monday_____

_____

_____

_____

Tuesday_____

_____

_____

_____

Wednesday_____

_____

_____

_____

Thursday_____

_____

_____

_____

Friday_____

_____

_____

_____

Sat/Sun_____

_____

_____

_____

SUMMARY

Telemarketing _____   Conferences _____

Direct Calls _____   % Time Spent on Reports _____

Inquiries _____

Schedule Appts. for Next Week _____

Attendance Prof. Mtgs. _____

Tours _____

Mtgs./Internal Amount of Time Spent (list separately) _____

_____

_____

_____

Issues/Competitive Information _____

_____

_____

_____

_____

_____

_____

_____

_____

_____

_____

_____

_____

Planning/Other _____

_____

_____

_____

_____

_____

_____

ings or individual events. Many of these organizations are national, state-wide, or within the local community. Examples include the state respiratory therapist associations, critical care associations, state pulmonary physician associations, discharge planner or social workers' associations, case management associations, and insurance claims associations. You may also want to invite associations to hold meetings at your facility, which will present an excellent opportunity to market your programs. Depending upon the conference, a team consisting of a marketer and a clinician may provide the best coverage and appear to be the most credible.

Booths and displays come in a range of styles and costs. A threefold tabletop, with felt-like material (using Velcro tape to attach signage or photos) and some type of attached lighting should offer flexibility in presentation and is not as expensive as many other full-standing models. Keep in mind that although there is an initial cost, the booth can be used for many other purposes, such as job recruitment fairs, open houses, and special events. Many facilities will use them year-round in their lobbies or other public areas to educate or publicize information.

Staff development requires attention regarding continuing education opportunities. Attracting and retaining quality staff is difficult because of national and regional shortages. As part of a recruitment and retention plan, be sure to offer opportunities for continued education to marketing personnel. Sales, marketing, communication, and even motivational seminars can often enhance productivity. Although it is difficult to schedule key staff away from the unit, providing opportunities to expose staff to new ideas and develop new contacts and skills can lead to increased referrals and greater job satisfaction.

Advertising Newsletters, Trade Magazines, Yellow Pages, Special Community Publications

Print advertising can be expensive, particularly national trade magazines, and the return is sometimes difficult to measure. However, an advertisement placed in the appropriate vehicle, for example, a newsletter, targeted at the respiratory care industry, may be a worthwhile expense, particularly for a new program. Again, unless you track the responses from telephone inquiries or referrals, it is extremely difficult to judge the impact.

Newsletters, Dear Doctor Letters, Fact Sheets, Patient Profiles, and Other Collaterals

Newsletters are an excellent vehicle for ongoing communication to consumers. There are several ways to develop the format and the production of a newsletter. The least expensive method is to develop a staff committee to create a format (there are many software packages available to assist in the process); if your budget allows, contract with an advertising or communications company to design, write, print, and distribute your newsletter. Regardless which method you use, the staff will have to be responsible to supply story or article information.

Since most facilities cannot afford to produce a newsletter for a narrowly targeted audience, it must contain a mixture of clinical and general information that would appeal not only to medical personnel but have information of interest to patients, their families, and managed care/insurance readers. One way to accomplish this balance is to establish ongoing columns dedicated to specific audiences. Patient case histories and profiles are of interest (if not in highly technical language) to all consumers and providers. Below is a sample of a story list:

Special events—coverage of open house or educational event.
Highlight a clinical or staff person.
Highlights from published and appropriate clinical articles.
Success stories of patients or outcome data.
New staff additions/staff changes.
New programming or services.
Impact of recent or ongoing legislation.
Regional/local or facility related support groups, resources, and events.
New accreditation.
New clinical information.
Reimbursement information.

Make sure that you obtain releases from any patients, staff, or family who appear in photos to be printed for newsletters, trade promotions, clinical publications, or advertising.

"Dear Doctor" letters are used frequently by the pharmaceutical industry to draw attention to new products or product changes within the industry. Doctor letters need to be extremely concise (not longer than one page) and should include a contact name and phone number for additional information.

Fact sheets (simple one-page pieces) are used throughout the medical industry in marketing programs because they are inexpensive and direct salient points to a specific audience. An example appears on page 32. You may wish to develop one fact sheet to outline all of the subacute services or develop separate sheets for each product/service line.

Patient profiles are an excellent way of clarifying the type of patient you treat as well as the resulting course of treatment and outcome. Mature facilities use patient success stories to describe the capabilities of their staff and resources.

Other promotional collaterals can include highlights from outcome studies; pricing information sheets; local, regional, state, and national resources; guides used in selection of facilities (usually published by third-party sources, such as *The National Brain Injury Guide to Rehabilitation Facilities*); frequently asked questions and answers; facility staff rosters and phone numbers; additional admission information; families or professional references or contacts regarding patient care (with previous consent); family handbooks; and appropriate newsletters from support organizations.

Special Events and Public Relations

A grand opening is probably one of the most logical special events for a new subacute unit. National companies often spend much money on elaborate displays, refreshments, promotional giveaways, and so forth at their openings, as they know that this is one opportunity to announce new services, build relationships, and provide a vehicle for referring representatives to visit the facility. General costs may include invitations, flowers, refreshments, and entertainment.

Other special events can be worked into facility activities; these include talks by educational speakers, reunions of patients and their families, special success publications, and accreditation announcements. Although many facilities plan events quarterly, regional success of these events is often predicated on local preferences for attendance to these types of events. Smaller markets often have much better attendance than those in larger urban settings.

(Your Letterhead)

FACT SHEET

Brookfield Extended Care proudly announces the opening of one of the first skilled nursing-based, discrete ventilator-dependent units in the New York metropolitan area. Brookfield's program is directed toward rehabilitating patients, or weaning ventilator patients from their reliance on mechanical respiration. Our ultimate goal is to discharge the patient to the most appropriate and cost-effective environment.

The ventilator-dependent unit has an intensive staffing pattern, including specially trained nurses; respiratory, physical, occupational, and recreational therapists; and pulmonologists and other healthcare professionals who are lead by a highly experienced administrative team.

Program Description

The ventilator rehabilitation program provides a comprehensive team approach lead by the clinical care coordinator providing 24-hour supervision. The treatment team includes:

Medical Director	Occupational Therapist
Pulmonologist	Pastor
Primary Care Physician	Speech/Language Pathologist
Respiratory Therapist	Recreational Therapist
Physical Therapist	Dietitian
Specialized Nursing	Social Services

Comprehensive consultants are utilized as needed by the patient.

Admission Criteria

- Ventilator dependent
- Medically stable
- Age 16 and older
- Demonstrates the potential to benefit from an aggressive weaning rehabilitation program

Program Cost $945.27

The program is charged on a per diem basis (description of baseline services and any additional ancillary charges are available upon request). Consultant charges (i.e., cardiologist, neurologist) are not included.

Anticipated Length of Stay

Discharge plans are initiated at the time of admission. This program is not designed as a long-term placement, but rather the next step in the recovery of an individual who is newly ventilator-dependent. We anticipate the average length of stay to be 90 days.

Admission Procedure

For more information please call the Linda Megan, case manager for the Ventilator Rehab Unit, at (212) 421-1234. An onsite patient assessment and admission committee review will determine appropriate placement. All referrals will be handled through a streamlined process for rapid admission.

Brookfield is an accredited facility through the Joint Commission of Accreditation of Health Care Facilities, and has been providing quality healthcare services for over 25 years. Executive Director—Marshall W. Kelly.

Press kits should be mailed to community newspapers, hospitals, and radio and television stations a minimum of three weeks prior to the event, with personal follow-up calls made to the contacts. The extent of a public relations campaign is often based upon the experience of the marketing staff or administration. Many long-term care facilities have well-established contacts within the media. You may wish to consider having a proposal developed by a local public relations or advertising firm.

Mailing Cost for Direct Mail—Updates, Seasonal Holiday Cards, Thank-Yous for Referrals

Other costs are often overlooked in a marketing budget. These include postage, which may be substantial for special events, newsletters, or direct mail. Promotional items, such as pens, mugs, and key tags, are often used to develop name recognition. One facility sends a basket of fruit to all new referring physicians.

DEVELOPING COLLATERALS

Brochures are used to communicate the benefits and features of your program and can be the first exposure one will have to your facility. Take the time and effort to carefully think out what will go into the copy and how you want the brochure to look. There are several ways in which you can get brochures produced. The most expensive would be to contact a design or advertising company to assist you in the writing, photos, graphics, and production. If there is someone on your staff with some writing background who will work with your clinical staff and then utilize a printing company to help with the layout, you can generally develop something adequate. When you do market research, gather samples of program brochures for ideas particular to your market. The brochure should include a minimum of the following:

Program description with listing of services.

Facility background.

Admission criteria and process.

Credentials of the facility.

Highlights of key staff.

Accepted funding sources.

Phone numbers and addresses of contact people.

Map and written directions to the facility.

Picture of facility or staff.

You may already have many of these items from previous brochures. Carefully proofread the copy before you go to print. Have three people look over the copy for errors. Mistakes are costly, and a misspelling or misused word can negate all of your efforts.

When thinking about the copy, you need to identify your strengths and weaknesses in order to develop a marketing message. When considering your strengths, think of how they would benefit the consumer. For example, if your facility has a long-standing, excellent reputation for quality care, you might want to point out that the same administration that has managed geriatric long-term care is ultimately responsible for the new programming as well. Clinical expertise is an extremely important feature to highlight. If you have contracted with a local pulmonology group, it would be advantageous to highlight it in the brochure. The important issue here is that you anticipate the selling points and the objections that you may encounter in the marketing process and develop a strategy to overcome the barriers.

TARGETING THE MARKETING EFFORTS

First, identify and understand the potential referral sources for the sub-acute or specialty services.

Hospital Administration

Administrators should know that hospitals lose a significant amount of money on chronic ventilator-dependent patients, particularly those funded by Medicare. But some administrators might be unaware of the amount of money lost, due to the lack of analysis of these particular patients.

Many hospitals keep these patients in their intensive care units (ICUs) even after they are medically stable. The alternative placement within a hospital is a medical/surgical bed on a general patient service. If a hospital's ICU is full of ventilator-dependent and other patients, its emergency room has to be closed. Therefore, having ICU beds available is important for the hospital's census. Protecting that availability is an important function of hospital staffs. Having a placement option for difficult-to-place ventilator patients is one way of protecting a hospital's incoming flow of patients.

In skilled nursing ventilator units, history of operation has shown that over 60 percent of patients will be placed directly from an ICU. Having a unit available for placement provides a vital continuum of care. A study done by the Gallup poll for the American Society of Respiratory Care documents the losses associated with ventilator-dependent patients and identifies the issues with placement of them. According to the study, each patient generates a loss of around $25,000 for the hospital. According to the study by Temple University, the figure is even higher.

Potential hospital arrangements that need to be discussed include (*a*) access to technical knowledge, (*b*) utilization of ancillary services (lab and X-ray), (*c*) contracting with the hospital's respiratory department for respiratory therapists, (*d*) utilization of on-staff pulmonologists, (*e*) a turnaround agreement, and (*f*) exclusive referral arrangements. A possible joint venture discussion might be fruitful, if start-up capital is necessary.

  a. You can access technical knowledge from several sources, such as a respiratory contract therapy program. Hiring an appropriate staff and consulting service is another method. Do not overlook the hospital as a referral source. Unfortunately, they will probably not have the information immediately available and it will not be focused on the services and licensure you would like to develop.

  b. The acuity of your patients will require higher utilization of ancillary services. If the hospital is convenient, this is a mechanism of returning revenue to the hospital. These services are not something you would like to replicate on site.

  c. Under Medicare guidelines, you *must* contract for your respiratory therapists from a hospital. The cost is based upon a salary equivalency, so the charges are limited to the cost of the therapists within a profit margin. You can in turn make up your overhead and pass the bill to Medicare. For your insurance patients, hospital fees are not that exorbitant. The cost of having a therapist on staff is probably lower; however, to access the Medicare payment stream you must contract out. The cost is not prohibitive, and the therapists will generate revenue for the hospital.

d. Another way to utilize the hospital is to use their pulmonology group to supply medical direction and coverage for the unit. You can approach this group directly or through the hospital administration. Generally this is of no direct financial benefit to the hospital but could be construed as a courtesy and a credibility enhancer. It would be courteous to inform the hospital beforehand that you would like to talk to their pulmonology group.

e. If in your locale Medicaid does not reimburse for a specialty service for ventilator patients, then the hospital needs to be informed. This will limit your funding streams to Medicare and insurance patients who have limitations on their coverages. Under Medicare guidelines, you will have 100 days of coverage for your ventilator program. Under insurance coverages policies will limit by dollar amount or by inpatient days. If a patient is still on the ventilator and exceeds Medicare and insurance coverages, and the Medicaid reimbursement is totally inadequate, you must consider alternative placement.

   The key to avoiding this situation is to work with the referral source beforehand. The referral source for these patients has a financial interest in the initial placement. The two options you should work out beforehand are either a binding turnaround agreement that states that the referral source will take back the patient, or a payment schedule by the institution to pay for the placement. For Medicare patients, the hospital can save money during the 100 days, and a high percentage of patients (generally over 60 percent) will either be weaned from the ventilator or will have died during this period. Hospitals have been willing to go either of these routes in the past to gain placement for these patients.

f. Whenever possible you should work toward exclusive geographical agreements. This should be with either hospitals or managed care operators. The referral source will be reluctant to negotiate this agreement. Their concern about exclusivity is the limits on their choice; for you it can mean a barrier to your competition. Point out the start-up risks and capital required, and state that exclusivity is needed to justify the risk. Exclusivity is one of the ways to predict a volume of patients. Remember, everything is a negotiation. Geographical exclusivity is determined in terms of miles from the facility or borders, like county lines.

The important administrative people to meet are the hospital CEO (or executive director for an academic institution), the chief financial officer (CFO), or vice presidents of nursing or operations. Generally, all of these people are sensitive to the financial concerns of the institutions, but they have different perspectives on the issue.

If you would like to make a strong financial case, focus on the CFO. His or her biases and viewpoints are determined by the financial situation of the hospital. In this time of financial constraints, the CFO has an increasingly powerful voice within the hospital's hierarchy.

Social Workers and Discharge Planners

Social workers and discharge planners are the professionals who make discharge placements along with other clinical professionals for the hospitals. Their focus is the placement of difficult-to-place patients, which includes ventilator-dependent patients. Since these individuals are often under pressure to find rapid placement, your admission criteria, clinical assessment, and admission procedures need to be efficient and responsive to their needs. They also look for facilities that have a high degree of acceptance by families. Image and reputation are two of the most important criteria they consider when making referrals. Particularly for patients that hospitals are losing money on, these individuals will be the primary placement officials along with physicians. They do not have the clout or inclination, though, to place privately funded patients as ardently as those funded by Medicare or Medicaid programs. Privately funded patients will be primarily placed by insurance case managers or physicians.

These professionals and their roles are well understood by the long-term care industry. They have traditionally been the main contact for placement into skilled nursing facilities. Knowing how to market to and work with them are necessary skills in the long-term care industry. Some of these relationships are political, so it is sometimes necessary to go around them and market to other decision makers in the team. Each region has a different emphasis on the ability of these professionals to control the referral flow.

Facilities willing to take the more difficult cases, for example, patients with infections, will gain credibility within the market. The broader your admission and clinical capabilities, the more apt the discharge planner will be to make higher-acuity referrals.

Some discharge planners are interested in the final dispositions of patients. They are concerned with how the patients fare once they return home. Where there is expressed interest, make a point to relate patient outcome back to the discharge planners.

Nurses within the Acute Hospital

Nurses, particularly those within the ICU setting, have close contact with the family, physicians, and sometimes the insurance case managers, who are probably nurses themselves. Remember, all healthcare professionals see the care of the patient through the perspective of their particular discipline. Nurses are very sensitive to appropriate training on the unit, experience with the patient population, and having enough trained nursing coverage. Nurses on ICUs and pulmonary units should be aware of your services and have confidence in your ability to deliver the care that approximates that provided in a hospital setting. As a professional courtesy, you should provide feedback regarding the outcome of a patient referred to you. Some of the nurses working in your unit will presumably be colleagues of the nurses in the ICU or pulmonary unit, and your staff should be encouraged to network, share program information, and invite their associates to tour the facility.

Physicians

For the ventilator unit, the first choice for the medical director should be a pulmonologist, with an internist or family practitioner being the alternates. Since pulmonologists are specialists, manage or consult on ventilator patients in the hospital, and generally are in a group of similar physicians who can provide coverage, they have the technical expertise, credibility, and appropriate political connections for your unit.

The pulmonologist should be willing to provide clinical education, training, and guidance, assistance in referral development, and coverage of the unit at all times. Discuss these expectations before contracting with the pulmonologist. If the unit becomes very successful, the physician's allegiance should remain with it, thereby preventing the transfer of technology or credibility to another player. State this clearly in the contract.

Presently, subacute units in the industry have a payor mix of approximately 50 percent Medicare, 40 percent insurance, and 10 percent HMO, so physicians who have a high percentage of Medicare patients should be targeted. Gerontologists, internists, orthopedic surgeons, general surgeons, and pulmonologists should receive primary attention. Historically, most physicians are skeptical about the care given in skilled nursing facilities. Again, consistent education is the key, and recognition when a new physician refers a patient should be included in the marketing program. Direct mail, dear doctor letters, brochures, newsletters, and direct calls to community doctors must be an integral part of the marketing efforts.

Case managers and the clinical care coordinators should accompany the marketing representative on calls to physicians. Target the state and local physician association meetings and specialty groups whenever possible for marketing opportunities.

Physiatrist (Physical Medicine and Rehabilitation Physicians)

Physiatry is the specialty of physical medicine and rehabilitation (PM&R), whose primary populations are rehabilitative and orthopedic patients, stroke victims, and those who have sustained spinal cord or brain injuries. The national study centers have physiatrist consultants on staffs of their ventilator units, primarily because they understand how to use therapy in the rehabilitative process. When marketing to physiatrists, you want to emphasize the rehab element of your program. Having a physiatrist as a consultant might not have a direct referral benefit, but it would enhance credibility for an aggressive weaning program. In a competitive area with a lot of rehabilitation beds, the major competitive player could be a freestanding rehabilitation hospital. Physiatrists have a strong presence at these hospitals. Having a representative of this discipline would be a desirable element in working with these hospitals as a referral source.

Therapists

Among the clinical personnel who come in contact with patients in the hospital setting are speech pathologists, physical and occupational therapists, and psychologists. These clinicians have contact with patients' families and the ability to influence the referral process by their opinion of the services you offer. Again, you want to emphasize the team-rehab approach to your program. In your marketing, do not overlook your therapy staffs. In addition, your therapy staff should understand that you expect them to do their own networking.

Case Managers

Case management has become one of the hottest medical professions of the 90s. Monitoring, and sometimes directing, the patient's course of treatment and the quality of services has become an obvious way to control cost for medical services. Some insurance companies have historically used case management on the more expensive, complex, and catastrophic cases such as cancer, transplant, or major stroke, sometimes termed *large case management*.

However, since the growth of managed care companies, HMOs, PPOs, and so forth, traditional insurance companies have begun to duplicate some of the methods these companies utilize to contain resources and control costs. For example, in Michigan and New Jersey, auto no-fault laws have led to a strong case management practice group—with a relatively small number of professionals handling a large percentage of the cases. In these states, the direction of the cases is not dependent on the actual language of the policies because they fall in a separate category.

The individual with the title "case manager" can have a variety of experience, education, and credentials, depending on the organization. Some hospitals are now using the title for social workers who coordinate discharge services. County and state social welfare agencies use the title for their counselors. Rehabilitation providers in facilities with both inpatient and outpatient units are using the title for individuals responsible for coordinating services. In the past five years we have seen the development and growth of several national-level organizations that respond to the industry need for credentials, definitions, and education particular to this profession: For example, the Independent Case Management Association and another more recently created group called the Case Management Society are dedicated to legislative issues regarding healthcare. Both of these organizations are forming statewide and local chapters.

Insurance companies may have internal departments that assign catastrophically injured or ill patients to specific case managers. Generally, these case managers are RNs who have some rehab background or are certified rehab nurses. Some companies assign the patient's case based on specific diagnosis, because it makes sense to have certain nurses specialize within specific disciplines, such as head or spinal cord injuries. Some companies will assign cases based solely on case load, and many nurses may have a general acute background.

There are leaders in the insurance industry that often set the trend that others will follow. Once leaders such as Liberty Mutual or Aetna use your services, other insurance providers will note your credibility. If your facility has success with these respected companies, do not hesitate to ask the case managers for either a letter of reference or permission to have other insurance companies contact them regarding their experience with your facility. Depending on the size of the company and the type of insurance lines it sells and to which markets, nurses may have only sporadic incidents with ventilator-dependent patients. This means that you may deal with someone who is extremely knowledgeable regarding the treatment and current pricing, or someone who has very little experience within the field. It is important to discern the level of experience since most case managers expect to negotiate on the price.

Insurance Carriers

There are two levels of cost savings for insurance companies with ventilator-dependent patients. The high cost of these patients is of chief concern to carriers since, if not managed well, they will deplete the maximum on their policy limits. The justifications for cost savings are the following:

   a. The first cost savings is the movement from a high-cost to a lower-cost location. Insurance companies know the costs of hospital-based locations, particularly ICUs. These costs can range from $1,000 to $3,000 a day, depending upon the individual state's acute care reimbursement structure. Transferring this high-cost setting to a skilled nursing facility ventilator program saves money immediately. This means that the patient's coverage will go on for a longer period of time.

b. The second is the weaning from ventilator dependence, resulting in an enormous potential financial savings for the carrier. Since most patients continuously on a ventilator will go through their benefits, weaning the patient off the ventilator will cap the financial expenditures and limit the exposure with a potential savings of hundreds of thousands of dollars to an insurance company.

Each patient will have a different financial scenario, depending upon the money or time spent on the respirator, the previous history of medical care expenditures, and the limits of the policy. Also, the probability of weaning can only come from outcome statistics. Given this information, the potential cost savings can be estimated for each individual patient. These eventual outcomes should be compiled by the case manager for each successful discharge and sent to the insurance company. Case studies with names removed can be used for marketing purposes.

Cost savings can be demonstrated in the same manner for subacute services as well. The cost of home infusion therapy is extremely high, and a skilled facility can often offer inpatient care at a reduced rate from home nursing and rehab care. In addition, moving a patient out of the hospital as soon as he or she is medically stable substantially reduces the chances of secondary infections. Most patients are more relaxed in the less intense environment of a skilled nursing facility and receive better overall care than in an acute hospital.

Managed Care Companies: HMOs/PPOs

Managed care companies have become a significant force driving the success of the subacute industry in many areas of the country. Obtaining and maintaining a profitable contract can provide a predictable number of patients, and many subacute providers are moving toward the ultimate goal of capitation.

In mature managed care markets, HMOs are driving hard to reduce the cost for subacute care through careful negotiations. Each market is unique as to the acceptance and utilization of HMOs. Many hospitals have controlling interest in the local managed care industries and may perceive the subacute providers as a threat to their medical/surgical beds. In some markets, HMOs are concerned about reduced care in the subacute level of services, fearing that hospitals will react by raising acute/surgical and diagnostic care pricing. In addition, with the advent of subacute care, some facilities have begun by quoting hospital rates that are much higher than the lower rates the HMO has negotiated. From their perspective, many of the original subacute providers came into the market at a premium.

In newly emerging managed care markets, knowledge of the managed care companies is the number one priority, as many marketplaces do not have a comprehensive understanding of the capabilities of subacute providers. Managed care providers are interested in cost savings and control of the patient, which includes diagnostic tests, length of stay, and outcome. HMOs may perceive that the skilled nursing facilities provide Medicare-level of services and charge higher rates. What they have to be convinced of is to move the patient as soon as they are medically stable to the lower-cost structure.

Patients and Families

Marketing should attempt to assure the families and patients that the facility can provide the level of expertise and care that they expect based upon their experience in the hospital. In the general population, the perception is that skilled nursing homes are for elderly patients who are living out the last days of their lives. Your marketing should compare the expertise, training, equipment, and technical know-how your program to that of the hospital. These patients are moving from an intensely technical setting, to what they may perceive as a less technically supportive environment within the skilled nursing facility. That they will have feelings of apprehension is entirely understandable.

Encourage prospective families to tour your facility, and make sure that they sit down and meet the staff. If possible, provide the staff with some background information regarding the patient prior to the meeting so that they can gear their discussion to that specific case.

Some acute hospitals experience the family's reluctance to move the patient from within the hospital system, for example, to a step-down unit or a hospital-owned freestanding skilled facility. In these environments, the hospital has a distinct advantage to market the family. It will try to make the family feel that the only choice is the hospital program. It has established rapport with the family, and the physicians may prefer that the patient stay within the hospital so that he or she can follow the patient. In these cases, the important catalyst is the insurance company or managed care company, which can encourage the family to look at other options; or if you have developed a preferred provider relationship, they can direct the patient out of the hospital and into your program. But the important aspect here is that you work diligently to establish a relationship with the family and present your program as a credible alternative to the hospital.

MOBILIZING THE TROOPS

Especially during the start-up phases it is important for personnel to present the program to the multiple new referral sources. Remember, administrative and clinical personnel will be busy with financial, education, training, hiring, and other processes and will not have significant portions of time to spend marketing the program. Having a dedicated person, or persons, is essential in the development of the program's census on a prescribed timeline.

The job descriptions of the administrator, assistant administrator, director of nursing, assistant director of nursing, and unit managers should include some performance criteria for marketing of specialty programs as the workload required in the development process will decline. Make the time commitments and goals of the performance specific and measurable, and link the performance to their financial incentives.

For subacute programming to be effective, all staff on the unit and in support areas, such as accounting, pharmacy, housekeeping, and so forth, must recognize that in the delivering of these types of services timing is essential. The facility personnel should develop the attitude of "Get 'em in and get 'em out." This attitude is radically different than long-term care, where the emphasis is on making the patient feel "at home" and the pace is generally more relaxed.

If patients remain in the facility too long, the business office will see an increased volume of bills, insurance contacts, charge processing, and follow up. You may need an additional billing position, enhancement of computer hardware to add terminals, and increased internal reporting requirements. The dietary staff will see an increased number of meals served in the patient rooms.

Service areas must work efficiently as a team. Starting with admissions, the initial documentation systems need to be in place to rapidly assess, approve funding, and admit. This means taking patients late on Friday or the weekends. For example, the facility may only have an approved two-week length of stay, and in that time all disciplines need to evaluate and assess the patient in order to immediately begin treatment. Higher-intensity models of rehab may have to provide care for longer periods during the day and weekends. Most subacute facilities provide therapy on a six-day-per-week basis. Recreational therapy programs also need to extend programming into evenings and weekends.

Recruitment of qualified staff becomes a central goal in establishing a new subacute center. One of the major features that will offer an advantage in attracting staff is the opportunity to be on the ground floor of a newly emerging clinical delivery system.

Clinical development and marketing are the driving forces equally contributing to the success of the program. In the initial establishment of the unit, both components require successful and highly motivated individuals to provide the leadership necessary to drive the project forward. Acquiring staff who have either experience directly in the subacute arena or closely related service delivery systems can be an invaluable asset and worth the investment in terms of compensation.

If administrative or clinical personnel have special skills, such as public speaking, support and incentives should be provided to encourage these activities. Learning new skills and technical information will be part of the reorientation process for existing employees and part of the training of new personnel.

If in your facility the admissions personnel are the ones who conduct tours for prospective families, make sure that they know the program. Features of the facility that may be appropriate for a general geriatric tour may not be key for subacute care. The following are program highlights that should be communicated during the tour:

- Physician involvement, with weekly review.
- Nursing ratio similar to an acute care pulmonary unit.
- Case management and rehabilitation team approach.
- Distinct and specialized staff from the rest of the facility.
- Special training of the staff.

All staff on the unit, including nurses and aides, need to understand and be prepared to answer questions regarding the program. Build a marketing team environment. Everyone in the facility needs to know the kind of patients you are looking for and understand how to make a referral to the program.

A successful word-of-mouth campaign is one of the ways in which you can build census. The key is to make sure that everyone understands that they have a role in marketing the program and that there is an advantage to creating a responsive environment that is attractive to patients and families. Too often, jobs are compartmentalized in a skilled nursing facility, making it difficult for individual staff to see the whole picture. It is the manager's job to assure that staff not only do their jobs well, but also that they feel they have a stake in the larger success of the facility. This is accomplished through communication and goal setting.

Goal setting with staff includes discussing not only the census goals for the unit—for example, we need 10 patients in the first three months—but also the steps needed to see that goal to reality. Discuss referrals with the staff. The marketer should report feedback regarding the unit to the staff in regular formal meetings. Make marketing activities part of the job for the therapy team. Give them specific activities, such as calling an associate at least once per month to invite them for a tour of the facility or making a presentation at their local physical therapy association. Give a marketing or customer service champion award once a month, or reward staff with plaques or movie tickets (use some imagination).

CREATING YOUR MARKETING PLAN

When developing the marketing plan there are some elements you need to keep in mind. Define clearly goals that are realistic and quantifiable. An example would be to generate 150 referrals in six months through facility and representative marketing efforts. You may also want to organize the plan according to the referral source. For example, develop three managed care plans within six months through the joint efforts of marketing and administration.

Whatever you determine the goals to be, make sure that they are reasonable. Make sure that you identify who is responsible for accomplishing the activity and that there is an established system developed to measure whether the outcome has been met. An example may be that the marketing representative will meet with the discharge planners of the hospital a minimum of once per month. A monthly or quarterly review must take place to assure that the activity is taking place and results are monitored. Reasonable timelines and target dates need to be set.

Commit this plan to paper and have the administrative and marketing managers sign the document. Make sure that the budget reflects the activities, tools, and resources necessary to achieve your goals.

SUMMARY

The saying from the movie *Field of Dreams*, "If I build it they will come," no longer holds true for marketing healthcare. Even after you have completed a thorough feasibility assessment, determined to move forward, defined the clinical program, developed a highly qualified treatment team, and built an appropriate physical environment, you are still not guaranteed an endless flow of patients. It takes time and consistent marketing efforts to create a referral pattern to sustain a program. Ongoing systematic evaluation has to take place with your marketing efforts to assess new opportunities for program development, new partners, and strategies to gain a greater market share. Managed care contracts can be lucrative and in some markets guarantee a predictable flow of patients. Depending upon one source of referrals, however, can be dangerous; therefore, a more comprehensive approach offers long-term stability and growth. Solid planning and attracting the talent to develop relationships with the referral sources may seem expensive at first, but this investment is the best way to ensure success for the effort and capital required in developing a subacute program.

Chapter 4

Evolution of Subacute Marketing within a Maturing Market

Marshall W. Kelly
President, Rehab Partners, Inc.

Linda A. Megan
Vice President, Rehab Partners, Inc.

As the subacute marketplace evolves, you can anticipate continuing changes in the marketing practices of your business. You must actively listen to the marketplace through various communication channels and respond accordingly.

A dilemma can arise as the marketplace matures and your business places greater emphasis on managed care contracts and capitation. Although this can result in the security of a predictive flow of referrals, it threatens the job security of your marketing staff; they are the greatest source of information regarding the evolution of the marketplace and the most likely to be affected by the mature market. Managers must be aware that there is a potential conflict of agendas; and although they must be sensitive to the security needs of the personnel, they must heed the signals from the marketplace that indicate the need for an assessment of the continued value of a sales force.

Your marketing efforts should be shaped to understand the forces in the marketplace as the field becomes more complex through the consolidation or diversification of providers, networks, and funding sources. Classically, marketing is defined in terms of how the "product"—or in healthcare delivery, the "service"—is aligned in relationship to its purchasers or consumers.

EVOLUTION OF THE MARKETPLACE

There will be significant changes in the healthcare environment that will affect subacute services. The development of subacute services has paralleled the high growth of marketplace-based healthcare reform initiatives. Changes include the movement of referrals on an individual case basis to more predictive referral patterns based on contracts and risk. There will be an increase in prepayment for services, which in turn will force the need for efficiencies and the move to more predictive utilization. Census will be built on established referral sources; in other words it will be repeat business. Major payment sources, including Medicaid and Medicare, will have significant percentages of recipients in managed care organizations.

TERTIARY MARKETING PRACTICES

The current marketing practices were conceived by the rehabilitation and psychiatric fields. Providers in these industries relied on tertiary referrals to transfer patients from one institution into their facilities, and such referrals could be difficult to obtain. These providers not only had to convince the clinical community, such as discharge planners and physicians, of the advantages their facilities offered; equally important, they had to positively influence the family in the decision-making process. The most effective way to assure that referrals were going to be secured was to utilize full-time marketing personnel.

So, psychiatric and rehabilitation providers devoted considerable resources to hire full-time personnel with "sales" profiles, sometimes with very little clinical background. Many of these individuals were highly motivated through incentive plans to build or maintain census levels. These people were directed to educate and quickly establish rapport with referral sources, or families, through personal contact and education, and to differentiate their facility from the other competitive providers. Many of the companies that followed these models were extremely successful.

Unfortunately, some of the companies in both industries exceeded the lines of propriety and engaged in overly aggressive persuasion practices with referral sources and families. This included paying bounties, using high-pressure closing techniques, and in some cases lying outright and using unethical practices. Regulatory agencies responded appropriately to these excesses. These lessons should be valuable for the setting of limits required in the marketing practices as associated with sales and admission practices.

FIELD SALES PERSONNEL

In the initial phases of start-up, a key goal will be to establish the identity and referral patterns for your programs. The most predictable way to accomplish this is to hire, train, and motivate personnel dedicated to marketing your program. These individuals should not have responsibilities in other operations of your business; they should focus on the targeted census/profitability/contact goals.

One of the key ways to use and view these individuals' roles is as door openers, that is, the people who establish contact with the target audiences for your marketing effort. Essentially, the field force will operate with a sales mind-set. The individuals involved should be focused to work outside the facility and not become involved with internal politics. These personnel should be self-directed, tenacious, impervious to rejection, and capable of directly asking for the business.

The target audiences would include managed care case managers, hospital social workers and discharge planners, physicians, provider relations personnel, consumers, and so forth. The audiences are varied and diverse, and their language, justifications, thinking, and levels of sophistication are very different. Therefore, your personnel should be sensitive to the needs of different target audiences and have the ability to educate and communicate with professionals and nonprofessionals. The requisite skill, persistence, self-motivation, and, perhaps most importantly, the ability to handle rejection are all elements of the right profile for field salespeople.

Once relationships are established, ongoing contact should become the responsibility of the program case manager, clinical coordinator, or facility manager. The nature of this relationship is collegial and should focus on problem solving. The external marketing personnel shouldn't lose all contact, but the main interaction point is internal. Thus, there is an evolution from introduction to ongoing connection, from outside contact to internal contact, from "sales" orientation to "problem-solving relationship," from initial skepticism to ongoing trust, and from in-person to phone contact.

One of the main requirements in hiring the initial management and marketing staff is likability. As we all know, successful leadership and sales often depend on personality. A good personal response has always been a key to sales, networking, and leadership. The very basis for the time-honored good-old-boy network has been friendship and familiarity.

The many individuals who rely upon such personal relationships believe that friendship and familiarity are all-important. And all things being equal, they are key factors in most cases. But in business, decisions are made on hard facts and figures, no matter how popular and close the individuals involved are with each other.

The cultures of managed care organizations are *actuarial driven* and *risk adverse*. This means that the predictive numbers of incidence, cost-effective use of services, customer satisfaction, and cash flow dominate the thinking and culture of such organizations. If a new company presents a better case for its cost-containment services and high-quality outcomes than a current provider, the managed care organization (MCO) will accept the new offer. The movement toward capitation is the ultimate example of this type of rationale.

Capitation as a form of payment is basically pushing risk onto the provider of care. As a managed care marketplace gets more competitive, as evidenced by premium competition for payors, the managed care organization has greater incentive to include providers in risk sharing. This is primarily because managed care organizations cannot contain the spiraling cost of services. Surveys of the buyers of managed care—for example, employers and state governments—indicate that low cost and access to care are most important to them. Quality of care is rarely identified as the important variable. Therefore, to ensure the maintenance of their market share and the profitability of their company, managers pass as much risk as possible onto providers. In the extreme, an integrated service delivery is a prepaid health system, with the HMOs viewed as the marketing arm of the organization.

The logical extension of the growth of managed care will be more competition between entities. Therefore capitation as a method of payment will gain wider acceptance and utilization as market penetration increases.

Relying upon personal relationships in the face of hard, objective numbers is perilous. Individual managers tend to rely upon historical formulas for success, which may not be best for the future. Managers who cling to the belief that relationships drive the enduring success of programs will be unprepared for the new alignments and approaches used in the future.

COMPETITION FOR MARKET SHARE
INTENSIFIES IN A MATURE MARKET

It is inevitable that financial margins will become compressed as the sub-acute field evolves. Since in most areas there is an overcapacity for inpatient services in the healthcare delivery system, we can expect that competition will escalate. Even for organizations that dominate a marketplace, the changes can be subtle yet deliver quite a blow to those caught unprepared. Marketing should be an organized function of your operation in which you plan, gain market information, and monitor how your services are being perceived by the marketplace. Obviously, the ultimate goal is the provision of service, that is, delivering the expected patient outcome for the lowest resource utilization. Yet many providers are still looking to provide quality at a too-high price rather than innovating to reduce costs.

The principle in times of evolution is to expand the vision outward to the macro level. The fundamental reason for the fervor about cost containment in our healthcare delivery system is that current costs built into our services and products are outrageously high. The best course of action is to prepare and plan for the inevitable. However, predictive changes will be a threat for many providers that have become lulled into a false sense of security. Not many of us are willing to test the assumptions that have made us successful to date. Many providers will be surprised by the rapid maturation of this market, and many successful programs will lose their market position to other providers that have designed services better aligned to the changes in the marketplace. After all, subacute services are not a completely new level of care; they are a new lower-cost solution to a higher-cost structure of services.

In an earlier chapter, we discussed how an initial marketing operation can quickly develop a program census for a new subacute facility. What is of particular importance during the early stages of establishing a program is developing its credibility and educating the marketplace for acceptance of its services.

The primary issue for a new facility is, Can it deliver the service? In a hospital-based program, the credibility issue relates mainly to the ability to deliver the service in a cost-sensitive manner and be competitive with lower-cost settings.

The key changes in the evolution of marketing practices will be centered on market penetration and sophistication of managed care organizations. These changes will be important even if you have a monopolistic position. As in other businesses, the key will be to offer and deliver a high-quality product for the lowest price. Not only have businesses learned this lesson, so have nations.

INVOLVEMENT OF HIGH-LEVEL MANAGEMENT

One of the early predictors of success in subacute programs to date is the active involvement of the leadership/administration in the marketing effort. This is primarily because the leadership's involvement in the process enhances the credibility of the message. Many of the important target audiences of marketing efforts—top hospital administrations, managed care officials, and physicians—want to deal with what they perceive as their peers. They want to know that the individuals they are dealing with have the authority to make commitments on behalf of the organization and will carry through on agreements.

Managers will have to become comfortable with this process and with the language, attitudes, and concerns of their new audiences. Most long-term care personnel are not familiar with the world of acute care. Leadership must keep abreast of the financial, clinical, and other realities in the marketplace to deal effectively with the referral sources.

The activities that managers (including administrators, nursing management, and therapy leadership) can be expected to participate in include presentations to clinical and managerial audiences, business meetings with hospitals and managed care representatives, contract negotiations with managed care organizations, supervision of marketing leadership, assessment of marketing data, advocacy of facilities, clinical development leadership, and organizational development and redesign. These activities consume a considerable amount of time and energy, sometimes up to 50 percent of the executive managers' time. Obviously, the functions that these managers fulfilled prior to the development of new services must be delegated to others, which creates the need for additional positions.

The difficulty of staying abreast of the proliferation of information has created a new level of career position, unique to subacute provider organizations. Because of time, knowledge, and skills requirements, facilities that have a critical volume of subacute services (at least 30 beds) must hire a new executive, generally over the licensed administrator. This individual handles the executive functions, particularly the exterior relationships. The background of a person in this position should include acute hospital experience or knowledge of the industry.

CHANGES IN SALES BUDGETS

During the start-up phase of a subacute program, the marketing budget commands a higher percentage of the overall budget than in mature and higher penetration stages. Therefore, monitoring costs and changing budget requirements is very important.

In the beginning stages of development, it is advisable to budget a minimum of $100,000 for a subacute program. If you are part of a hospital or partnership continuum, this level of expense may be unnecessary. Among dedicated personnel, brochures, announcements, events, public relations, expenses, conferences, and so forth, the budget at this level can be very tight. The marketing resources reflect the payor mix, fill-up expectations, desire for assurance of success, alliances within the continuum of care, and the level of understanding of the importance of the marketing effort.

If management personnel have the time to commit to the marketing effort, the budget for dedicated personnel can be lowered. The major challenge in establishing commitment to the marketing effort will be convincing personnel of its importance and the required level of intensity or focus. Skilled nursing facilities have placed a relatively low priority on marketing as they have been able to rely on demand greater than the capacity to serve. In the past, a skilled nursing facility would think a $30,000 marketing budget was high. Hospitals, in contrast, routinely spend enormous amounts of money in soft marketing costs such as public relations campaigns.

The percentage of the budget for the marketing effort in the initial stages will be higher than in the mature stage. Excluding the issue of cash flow, marketing expenses can reach up to 25 percent of the initial cost of starting a program. As the program becomes more successful, a dedicated staff will focus on continuing the effort to open new relationships, while the internal marketing effort by case managers, staff, and managers will emphasize the maintenance of existing referral sources and relationships.

The budget for the marketing program can be reduced once census levels reach saturation, referral sources are consistent, and the marketplace begins to demonstrate signs of reaching maturity. This is particularly true if the customer service function is being facilitated by the internal personnel and the marketing staff is perceived as the external "sales" staff or door openers. As a cautionary note, prior to making reductions in outside marketing staff, you should assess the status of the total market, that is, analyze the census in competitive facilities or new competitive entities entering the market and determine provider market share. If the market remains fluid or if you are planning to introduce new product lines, then you should maintain the marketing staff to remind referral sources of your presence.

NATIONAL COMPETITORS

The three areas in which national competitors will generally excel over smaller, local operators include marketing, program development, and clinical management information systems. National or large regional operators search for a success formula that can be replicated in the majority of environments and include a sizable, focused, sophisticated marketing effort to ensure a high probability of success.

These companies have learned the unhappy lessons of underfunding the marketing effort and the importance of giving sufficient lead time to create a credible image prior to the opening of a new unit. In addition, they have the resources to deliver excellent training, leadership, and experience from which the local personnel can benefit. Also, these companies can bring additional credibility in the form of connections to political bodies, examples of contracts with managed care companies in other locales, potential for national contracts (related to geographic spread), and impressive credentials.

Moreover, these national companies have resources to spend on centralized program development efforts and facility-initiated experiments in test markets. They can then refine and implement the programs in other markets. Models of care for increasingly sophisticated segments of the marketplace are created, establishing a knowledge base from which to expand into additional niches much faster than smaller providers can. In many situations, the new programs are introduced and entrenched in the marketplace before other competitors can react. You can expect that the larger companies, with some exceptions, will be the innovators in this industry if the experience of the psychiatric and rehabilitation fields holds true.

The larger companies, both proprietary and nonprofit, will have the resources and foresight to develop the information systems that can provide hard data concerning clinical outcomes, clinical pathways, and their variations. Most important of all are the actuarial data about incidence of disease and illness patterns that will assist in predicting the volume of patients.

MANAGEMENT INFORMATION SYSTEMS

Management information systems will be a key element of the marketing effort for subacute providers. Financial sponsors for new patients will require outcome information on those previously treated at the facility. Outcome evaluation as an act of justification to financial sponsors is therefore an essential part of the marketing effort. The data will focus on mortality, functional capacity, recidivism, and cost. Comparison between providers will become commonplace, and the provider that can demonstrate outcome-to-cost efficiencies will be in a position to compete in this new information-driven environment.

For subacute care providers trying to establish credibility, commitment to this process is essential. Many managed care organizations will be familiar with outcomes from other locales or competitive providers. National or large regional subacute care providers, in response to this information, will be able to demonstrate their outcomes from other established locations. Many national or regional managed care companies will access this information as an example of the potential outcomes that can be delivered.

THE CHANGING INFLUENCE OF CASE MANAGERS ON PRIMARY CARE PHYSICIANS

Currently, one of the key target audiences for marketing efforts are insurance case managers, who manage the continuity of care for indemnity and managed care organizations. As described in an earlier chapter, case managers can work for managed care companies or for integrated service companies, or they can be independent contractors or physicians in capitated groups.

As capitated physician groups and systems are developed, the patient's doctor will increasingly become involved with placement of patients beyond their current level of interest. Therefore, the emphasis on marketing to the insurance/case manager switches to the physician as physicians evolve from "providers" into "care managers." Physicians' control of the patients' treatment settings will increase, particularly if they are at financial risk for the care delivery.

Conceptually, the key issue for utilization review is whether it is an external or internal process. Many case managers for managed care organizations are specially trained nurses charged with the responsibility to move patients through a continuum of care. Most of their contact with patients is through documentation and telephone communication. This is the description of an external utilization review process. Within the industry, however, many physicians who are part of managed care plans resent their decisions being second-guessed by nurses, in some cases with little intimate knowledge of the patient.

Under a global capitation scenario, where the primary physician functions as the gatekeeper or care manager, the physician is geared toward efficient and cost-effective care. Decisions will be under concurrent and retroactive review by fellow physicians. This peer review can significantly change physician behavior and consequently can result not only in financial savings but have clinical implications in routine and exceptional treatment practices. The review protocols are established by the physicians within the group, and they operate not only as a resource for current decision making but offer potential analysis for clinical baseline understanding in judgment of the physician practice patterns. This type of system makes the utilization review process an internalized effort.

Initial data on California HMO inpatient utilization patterns have shown that, compared to external case managers, capitated primary physician groups can dramatically reduce costly inpatient days. An approximate 30 percent reduction has occurred for both Medicare and commercially insured populations. The initial conclusion therefore is that an internal review delivers the desired outcome at a lower cost. This change in inpatient patterns is one of the reasons capitated physician groups have become a major focus of the healthcare industry, gaining credibility and acceptance as well as garnering a tremendous interest on Wall Street.

INDIVIDUAL CASE TO POPULATION CAPITATION

The current postacute referral system is based upon individual episodic cases. This parallels the healthcare system as a whole. Reimbursement, referrals, and the design of care are linked to specific cases. Under the capitated reimbursement paradigm and organizational structures, the focus of the payment, referral pattern, and measurement of care will move toward a segregated population base.

The enrollment in a managed care plan will become the capitated population base for an integrated service delivery system. In an integrated system, illnesses and injuries will be treated at specified, appropriate sites, and service will be delivered along a rational, clinical pathway. Providers will assume the risk for the delivery, and incidence will be reimbursed as a percentage of the overall medical loss of the managed care premium. Therefore, the referral patterns will change in volume and nature. As the capitated reimbursement system grows there will be a reduction of referrals made on a case-by-case basis; rather, the system will become more integrated and use automatic treatment pathways. Obviously, the power of the discharge planner for control over placement will change. Patients will be informed of the predetermined plan, and choices and options will be discussed at a much earlier point in the patient education process. Discretionary choices by the referring party as well as the individual will be limited through these established pathways.

To summarize, referrals are based on each individual case in the current system. The referring institution, case manager, or physician often refer the patient to the next level of care or services on the basis of personal biases, established relationships, and so forth. The actual clinical decision to discharge a patient varies greatly from institution to institution or physician to physician. Admission patterns are not systematic but random in many cases. This will change as systems are developed that define the patient threshold for standardized treatment and level of services required for an anticipated outcome. The systemization of clinical service places the emphasis on program development and the establishment of clinical pathways. As we move to prepayment or capitation, the marketing and admissions functions will increasingly mirror the clinical delivery side by focusing less on individual cases and more on programs.

IMPORTANCE OF COST STRUCTURE OVER PHYSICAL PLANT

When the referral process involves choices for families, marketing has a much different objective than under a fully integrated continuum of care. Unsophisticated purchasers of healthcare depend upon the tangible aspects of a program, such as the appearance of the facility or credentials of the staff, in developing opinions regarding quality of care that provide the basis for comparison between competitive offerings.

An old marketing adage used by Theodore Levitt is that you use intangibles to sell a tangible product (like saying a car is sexy) and you use tangibles to market an intangible product like a service (hang diplomas in a nice office, for example). For an intangible service like healthcare, providers have learned this lesson well and developed or renovated facilities to provide pleasingly aesthetic physical plants to connote a high level of care to market their programs. With the absence of hard clinical data to validate outcome, families and even payor sources are left to make assumptions based on what they can see. And certainly, as subacute care has only recently been codified in the marketplace, many consumers grapple with how to make an intelligent decision in light of the lack of agreed-upon industry standards of care.

Many existing inpatient facilities have completed costly alterations and enhancements to prepare them as subacute settings, as much for marketing purposes as for efficient service delivery. This includes adding the space or technology required. In the evolving environment, the physical plant will have less impact than currently because consumers' judgment will be biased toward the most efficient, high-quality, low-cost, outcome-oriented provider, not the facility with the newest wallpaper.

REGIONAL SERVICE AREA TO LOCALIZED BASE

As subacute services broaden and delivery matures, the catchment area of the referral patterns will become smaller. Convenience is an important factor for transportation, visitation, and continuity of physician involvement. As more providers enter the contracting arena, the referrals will depend more on ease of access to the local facility than follow a tertiary pattern. As the industry matures and if barriers to entry remain low, the availability of the technical knowledge and pool of experienced personnel will make convenience of location the compelling issue. It is important that facilities plan for this eventuality of localized referral patterns. Many facilities initially have a wide geographic referral pattern, possibly including out-of-state referral bases.

Even though contracts with managed care organizations will have a relatively wide catchment area, the pattern for subacute services will most likely mirror the availability of acute care service, not the MCO's geographic area. For providers with wide and deep distribution of service sites, the issue of broad local access will be a positive differentiating point. For most of the larger subacute companies, this strategy of heavy concentration is the cornerstone of their effort to dominate in a local market. By providing services in a wide distribution pattern, the providers can be a one-stop shopping area for contractual referral sources, and the size of their presence means that they cannot be ignored.

WHO HAS THE CRYSTAL BALL?

Predicting the future in this changing environment would certainly be easy if we could peer into a crystal ball and envision what the healthcare system will look like in the next 5 or 10 years, even next year. However, none of us has access to such magical powers. Although it is not simple, in the absence of absolutes, savvy providers will extrapolate what the reality of creating low-cost, efficient, outcome-oriented, and integrated health systems can mean to the subacute industry. Positioning for change requires the ability to react quickly to the fluidity of the marketplace and prepare for the eventuality of maturing market forces. Nationally, there is great diversity in the evolution of subacute services, from unstructured to the final stage. Ultimately, this final stage will see the development of networks with true partnerships and payor systems that effectively manage patient populations. The difficulty is learning how to gauge where your local market is in the evolution process and position your facility through innovative marketing practices. This challenge can be met with the development of management and information systems that will allow you to continue to compete by maintaining or gaining market share.

Invaluable during start-up, the sales personnel who focus on obtaining individual referrals may become unnecessary as the referral patterns become static through contracts with managed care organizations and physician care managers. Market forces will constrict to the confines of the local hospital-based catchment area, and profits will be squeezed by the ever-increasing competition and propensity for managed care to lower costs. The development of programs versus levels of care will enable the provider to enter into the arena of capitation, which will become the dominant method of payment. And the ultimate winners will be providers that have gained the ability to access data, determine cost to outcome, and promote their programs and services as part of an integrated network.

Chapter 5

Subacute Nursing Services

Jane E. McGeough Danzl, RN, BSN, NHA, CCRN
Director of Nursing, Integrated Health Services

A critical factor for success in subacute care is a well-developed nursing service. Having the right quantity of properly trained nurses performing to the expectations of the subacute patient differentiates the well-regarded facility from one with a more dubious reputation.

Subacute nursing care is the answer to many nurses' frustrations. The anxiety produced from not really knowing your patients because of rapid patient turnover, not being assigned the same group of patients for several days in a row, and not having the time to enact a plan of care is driving nurses from acute inpatient care to the subacute environment.

For acute care nurses, especially critical care nurses, subacute care offers the opportunity to utilize the advanced assessment skills they have developed in their nursing practice. It also allows them the autonomy that they have become accustomed to in the intensive care unit (ICU), and most of all gives them time with their patients to develop strong nurse/patient relationships.

For traditional long-term care nurses, subacute care allows them to develop new skills and still maintain the "high-touch" component of nursing care that lead them to choose the long-term care specialty.

TEAM NURSING CARE

By definition, the typical subacute patient has had an acute event as a result of an illness, injury, or exacerbation of a disease process, has a determined course of treatment, and does not require intensive diagnostic or invasive procedures.

Nursing care is provided to subacute patients in an organized fashion. Team nursing assignments are distributed among the registered nurses (RNs), licensed practical nurses (LPNs), and certified nursing assistants (CNAs) throughout the unit according to patient acuity and staff efficiency. Interdisciplinary team meetings (ITM), inservice education, and unit conferences are scheduled at times when patient care will not be disrupted.

ADMISSION PROCESS

An extensive pre-admission evaluation is required to determine if a patient's needs can be met in the subacute environment. For most subacute patients, this requires a nurse to perform a full assessment of the patient at the acute care hospital prior to accepting the admission. Preliminary goals are developed and a discharge plan must also be made prior to admission. The family should be encouraged to tour the unit and meet the nursing staff.

On admission, a full patient assessment is conducted and repeated at least every eight hours at the beginning of each new shift. The assessment documentation is not easily accomplished using traditional long-term care nursing forms. Additionally, ICU chart forms are too detailed. The best format for the nursing record appears to be a flow chart similar to those used on acute care medical step-down units. A folding four-page flow chart can accommodate four to five days of assessments and utilizes a checklist format. The checklist has three advantages: (1) it organizes the documentation, (2) it easily notes condition changes from shift to shift, and (3) it reduces the amount of narrative charting.

MEDICATION ADMINISTRATION AND CHARTING

Medication administration records (MARs) using the traditional nursing home format are not suitable for the variety of drugs given in subacute care, nor for changes in drug, dosage, or timing that frequently occur. Pharmacy consultants providing the required weekly and biweekly MARs have won high praises from the nursing staff.

A separate intravenous administration record (IVAR) is necessary in subacute care in order to safely record and maintain IV solutions, IV riders, and the volume of additional fluid intake. All IV fluids must be on a rate regulation device.

Because of the frequent entries made in the medical records by nursing and service staff, a clipboard at the point of care facilitates efficient charting. The nurses' notes, intake and output sheet, care plan, treatment sheet, and respiratory therapy notes, combined on a clipboard and maintained in a chart holder outside the patient's room, prevents documentation errors and omissions.

CARE PLANNING

The home-like atmosphere of a subacute unit and liberal visiting regulations allow the patient's family the opportunity to participate in the care. The patient and family are included in the development of the care plan. The family is encouraged to attend rehabilitation therapy sessions with the patient. Nurses use the opportunity of family visits to teach both patient and family about medications, dressing changes, hygiene, and a myriad of other healthcare topics. Family members having difficulty dealing with their loved one's illness are referred to a family support group that is facilitated by an RN and a social worker.

The length of stay in a subacute unit is usually longer than the acute care phase; therefore, a nurse is able to develop meaningful nurse/patient and family relationships. One of the most important functions of the staff nurse in subacute care is participation in the interdisciplinary team meeting (ITM). Team members (see Figure 5–1) convene once every two weeks, or more frequently if necessary, to discuss the patient's current status and progress toward goals. Necessary changes to the patient's care plan are discussed during this meeting, and approved and noted in the patient's medical records.

Patients and families are encouraged to attend the ITM. However, except for the initial ITM and predischarge ITM, many families and patients are confused by the medical jargon and prefer an individual update from a team member after the conference, or a family conference at a different time. Insurance case managers and the patient's financial planner may also attend periodically.

FIGURE 5–1

Interdisciplinary Team Meeting Participants

- Clinical coordinator (chairperson)
- Physician
- RN case manager
- Staff nurse
- Physical therapist
- Occupational therapist
- Speech and language pathologist
- Therapeutic recreation therapist
- Dietitian
- Respiratory therapist (if indicated)
- Social worker
- LPN
- CNA
- Patient (optional)
- Family (optional)

ITM conferences are regularly scheduled at a fixed time to facilitate attendance. If the physician cannot attend, the RN clinical coordinator of the unit is responsible for conveying the recommendations to the physician.

Acute care nurses describe the ITM approach as one of the biggest advantages in subacute nursing. The input and joint decision making with their professional colleagues in other specialties during the development of an individual, meaningful plan of care is personally and professionally satisfying.

QUALITY

Continuous quality improvement (CQI) is necessary facilitywide and in the subacute unit. Safe, cost-effective, competent, and quality care is an expectation of all of our customers. In subacute care, the customer is the patient, family, visitors, physicians, referral sources, other departments, and in some cases, corporate headquarters.

The CQI process enables staff to look at the process, analyze it, and take steps to improve the system. The nursing staff is very receptive to CQI and enthusiastic in participating in activities that improve services.

Nursing is also represented on the ethics committee by both the director of nursing and a staff nurse.

ORGANIZATIONAL STRUCTURE

Director of Nursing

The facility's director of nursing (DON) should be knowledgeable about the types of patients admitted to the subacute program in order to determine the levels of staffing required to properly care for them. In addition to staffing, the DON must consider capital equipment needs, infection control and safety requirements, regulatory requirements, and human resource practices for the subacute unit. The policies and procedures for the subacute unit must parallel existing policies regarding housekeeping, dietary, and other support services in the facility.

Clinical Coordinator

The RN nurse manager for the subacute unit is the leader of the entire interdisciplinary team. He or she gathers information from all of the ITM members and coordinates the plan of care. The clinical coordinator should have recent acute care experience in the specialty area of the subacute unit. This person should also be credentialed in the respective specialty, for example, certified critical care registered nurse (CCRN), certified rehabilitation registered nurse (CRRN), or oncology certified nurse (OCN).

After the selection of the clinical coordinator is made, orientation should include the regulations specific to long-term care, because they differ so greatly from acute care regulations.

The Clinical Coordinator's primary duties include:

• Preadmission evaluation of patients referred to the subacute unit.
• Selection in hiring and evaluation of staff.
• Maintaining staffing patterns.
• Frequent communication with the unit medical director.
• Coordinating the interdisciplinary plan of care for each patient.

• Maintaining standards of care.
• Ensuring quality of care.

Case Manager

The RN case manager works as a liaison between the facility and the payor and monitors patient progress to assure proper utilization of resources. The case manager should have a background in acute care or acute rehab as well as knowledge of managed care, Medicare, Medicaid, and other third-party reimbursement procedures.

Nursing Staff

The nurse staffing patterns are dependent on the type of subacute unit developed. While a subacute unit specializing in orthopedic rehabilitation may require five to six hours per patient day (PPD) of nursing care, a high-tech or cardiac unit may require seven to nine hours PPD. The determination of hours per patient day must be based on patient acuity. While few acuity systems are in place that relate to the subacute model, a creative blending of the acute care systems and existing long-term care methods are used as a starting point.

Subacute units offer the opportunity to provide a mix of registered nurses, licensed practical nurses, and certified nurse assistants that ensures quality patient care in a cost-effective manner.

The staff mix is adjusted according to the subacute unit. The higher-acuity units require the mix to be adjusted toward a more professional staff. Figures 5–2 through 5–4 demonstrate the different RN:LPN:CNA mixes and hours-PPD needs on varying types of subacute units.

Nursing care must be directed 24 hours per day by a professional registered nurse, with team nursing the most common model used in subacute care. The RN uses the nursing process of assessment, planning, implementation, and evaluation in the care of patients. Individual aspects of the nursing process can be delegated to nonprofessional staff and supervised using the team nursing approach.

FIGURE 5–2

Subacute Orthopedic Rehabilitation Unit Nursing Staff Mix

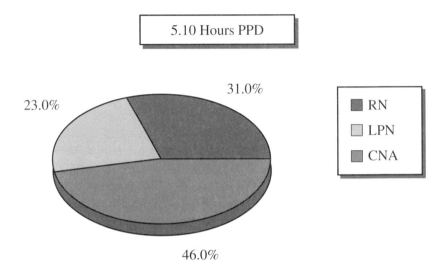

FIGURE 5–3

Subacute Medically Complex Unit Nursing Staff Mix

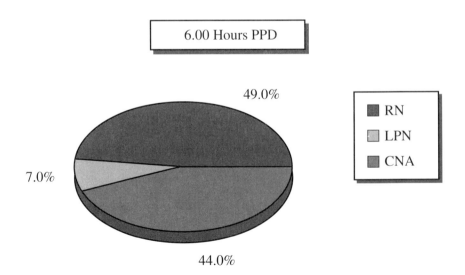

FIGURE 5–4

Subacute Respiratory/Ventilator Unit Nursing Staff Mix

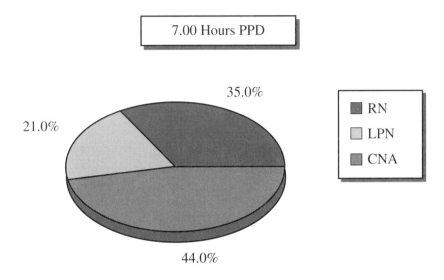

7.00 Hours PPD

35.0%

21.0%

■	RN
☐	LPN
■	CNA

44.0%

Registered Nurses

The registered nurse (RN) needs to have recent acute care, rehab, or other background applicable to the subacute unit. The rapid changes in healthcare delivery, procedures, diagnostics and drugs dictate that the RN have knowledge of current treatment modalities and the confidence to appropriately apply the necessary intervention.

Subacute care can be an extremely difficult environment for new nursing graduates without acute care background. The facility does not have 24-hour coverage of other professionals, such as physicians, pharmacists, phlebotomists, or EKG technicians. Consequently, the registered nurse requires expertise, experience, knowledge, and excellent assessment skills. He or she must be able to make appropriate judgments regarding changes in the patient's condition, communicate the information to the physician and other members of the interdisciplinary team, and then implement any changes in the plan of care. The RN must be able to evaluate the results of the interventions and modify the plan of care as necessary. The physician relies upon the RN to communicate observations and assessments to get a clear picture of the patient's status.

Recruitment

Opening a new subacute program means selecting the right people for staff positions. A long-term care facility opening a new subacute unit will probably find recruiting qualified RNs challenging. It may be necessary to match or pay salaries higher than those paid to RNs at local hospitals in order to attract the ideal candidates. While the seasoned nurse may be frustrated with present work conditions at the hospital, he or she may be reluctant to take the risk of losing current benefits (sometimes several weeks of vacation, flextime, and investment in a pension plan) for a program that is new and not proven. The facility's human resources manager and clinical coordinator must work closely with administration to determine fair and equitable salaries. Human resources expense is the largest cost in the subacute program, but hiring capable, competent, and knowledgeable staff is the key to providing quality care and achieving favorable patient outcomes.

Now that subacute care is better known in the healthcare community, advertising in newspapers and professional journals may be successful. Recruiting an experienced RN for an existing subacute unit may not be as difficult because nurses in area hospitals hear about the good patient outcomes and facility reputation through various informal networks. A recruitment booth at local nursing job fairs is also a good vehicle for exposing the subacute unit. The booth needs to be manned by nursing personnel who can thoroughly explain subacute nursing to interested RNs. The marketing department can provide banners, brochures, and other materials for distribution.

It is necessary to continuously monitor RN salaries at area hospitals. To attract and retain professional nurses, the salary differentials for shift, charge, and weekend, as well as the benefit package, must be competitive with acute care hospitals in the region.

The clinical coordinator and staff nurses should belong to the specialty nursing organization for their program. For instance, the manager and staff in a respiratory/ventilator program should belong to organizations such as the American Association of Critical-Care Nurses (AACN) and participate in local chapter activities. The facility or subacute unit could sponsor a meeting or education program to further promote subacute care.

Local chapters usually have a newsletter, which is an excellent source for advertising the subacute program and open staff positions.

Nursing units benefit from having a mix of full- and part-time staff. The mix allows flexibility when scheduling weekend coverage, staffing for peak periods, and allowing for requested time off. Twelve-hour shifts are also an option to consider when scheduling. Hourly employees working 12 hours should sign a 40-hour work agreement to reduce overtime expense rather than the traditional 8/80 policy.

Another option for recruitment, as well as scheduling, is an in-house registry (or per diem staff). Acute care nurses who are reluctant to sever ties with the hospital may choose the registry option as an opportunity to see if the subacute model is the type of nursing they can commit to permanently. When using an in-house registry, the employee needs to sign an agreement detailing the responsibilities and obligations. In-house registry staff must attend the general orientation and an abbreviated specific nursing orientation (usually for three days).

Orientation and Training

Orientation to the subacute unit for an experienced acute care nurse includes general facility orientation such as fire, safety, infection control, personnel policy, and OSHA. Nursing orientation includes unit policy, procedures, equipment, and unit routine. The experienced RN does not require orientation to learn how to nurse but rather how nursing is practiced on the unit. Total orientation must follow an established protocol including a full checklist of topics. After the "classroom" session is completed (two–three days), the new nurse should be assigned a preceptor on the unit to accomplish the "hands on" orientation (seven–eight days).

Particular attention to compliance with long-term regulations needs to be addressed in orientation. Until a separate subacute license is in place, subacute units in long-term care facilities operate under nursing home regulations. Although acute care nurses will argue that the minimum data set, triggers, RAPS, and level-of-care forms are tedious and have little or no effect on patient care, the fact remains that they must be completed. Nursing home regulations regarding patients' rights, privacy, and use of restraints also differ from acute care and must be included in orientation.

LPNs

LPNs need to be assured that they have a defined and vital role in sub-acute care. All LPNs in the facility must have the opportunity to request a transfer to the subacute unit and be interviewed for any open positions. Although some LPN staff may prefer to continue to work in long-term care, those who are challenged by higher-acuity patients should be allowed the opportunity to transfer.

It is necessary to provide additional education and training for the LPN in a subacute unit. A formal program to include pathophysiology, physical assessment, and pharmacology, followed by a clinical component with an RN preceptor, is a minimum standard and can usually be accomplished in five to seven days. A skills checklist is helpful during the clinical component to ensure all required experiences are completed.

CNAs

Certified nursing assistants (CNAs) are usually in place when a long-term care facility opens a subacute unit. Like with LPNs, nursing administration needs to meet with the CNAs to explain the program, job roles for each level of staff, performance expectations, and the vision for subacute care in the building.

All CNAs must have the opportunity to request a transfer and be interviewed for the subacute unit. After selection of staff, the CNA requires orientation specific to the types of patients on the unit. Formal classroom orientation can be accomplished in a one- to two-day program. Clinical orientation with an RN preceptor and a skills checklist can usually be completed in three days. Experience has shown that CNAs take pride in learning additional skills and working with more technical equipment. As a vital member of the patient care team, the CNA demonstrates enthusiasm toward new challenges, while exhibiting their expertise in direct care activities.

Staff Development

A regular schedule of inservice programs must be maintained for all levels of staff on the subacute unit, as well as support departments and other members of the interdisciplinary team.

A minimum of two formal inservice presentations per month should be offered and made accessible to all three shifts. These should be used to communicate information about new products, pharmacology, changes in policy or procedure, disease processes and treatment modalities, quality improvement findings, and plans.

Cardiopulmonary resuscitation (CPR) drills should be conducted monthly on different shifts in different locations. In addition, each nurse should have a monitored medication pass at least annually to document compliance with policy and procedure. This should be coordinated with the consulting pharmacist.

A popular method for ensuring annual compliance with accreditation and licensing standards is the "skills day" method. Each employee is scheduled to attend a full day of classroom assignment off the nursing unit during his or her anniversary month. All required annual inservices are presented. This includes CPR renewal, fire and safety refresher, infection control, restraint usage, new policy and procedure, CQI updates, health screening, and TB testing.

Each employee maintains their personal education record. CNAs are federally required to have 10 hours of inservice per year to maintain certification. RNs and LPNs must also maintain an educational standard. In addition to the mandatory inservices mentioned in the previous paragraph, nurses in most states must provide evidence of attending at least eight hours of continuing education per year. This may be accomplished by attending in-house inservice classes, or an outside lecture, or a seminar. Facility policy differs on allowing compensation for inservice attendance, but is usually restricted to mandatory inservice.

STAFFING PATTERNS

Long-term care regulations typically identify quantity of nursing staff in hours PPD. A percentage of these hours must be by licensed staff. State regulations may also mandate the percentage of staff distributed over 24 hours. The formula for calculating hours per patient day is: Number of staff on duty for 24 hours $\times$ hours in the shift divided by census. Example: A unit has 7 RNs and 5 LPNs working 8-hour shifts. There are 11 CNAs working 7.5 hour shifts. The unit census is 35.

Staff	Number × Hours
RN	7 × 8 = 56
LPN	5 × 8 = 40
CNA	11 × 7.5 = 82.5
	Total 178.5 hours PPD $\frac{178.5}{35}$ = 5.10 hours

For a 39-bed subacute rehabilitation unit with an average daily census of 35 patients requiring a 5.1 PPD, Table 5–1 notes an example 24-hour staffing plan with the corresponding full-time equivalent (FTE) for each level of staff. The FTEs can be calculated by taking the number of staff on a shift and multiplying it by a 1.5 factor. The additional 0.5 component allows for the two scheduled days off per week, vacation, and holiday time. Tables 5–2 and 5–3 illustrate staffing patterns for higher acuity patient units, such as a complex medical and a respiratory/ventilator unit, requiring 6.0 and 7.0 hours of nursing care PPD, respectively.

TABLE 5–1

*Staffing Pattern and FTEs for Sample Subacute Rehab Unit Requiring
5.1 Hours PPD*

Subacute Rehab Unit	Staff/Day	FTE Required
Average census	35	
Day Shift Staffing		
# RNs	3	4.5
# LPNs	2	3.0
# CNAs	4	6.0
Total day	9	13.5
Evening Shift Staffing		
# RNs	2	3.0
# LPNs	2	3.0
# CNAs	4	6.0
Total evening	8	12.0
Nocturnal Shift Staffing		
# RNs	2	3.0
# LPNs	1	1.5
# CNAs	3	4.5
Total nocturnal	6	9.0
Total Staffing		
# RNs	7	10.5
# LPNs	5	7.5
# CNAs	11	16.5
Total all	23	34.5
Total Nursing Hours		
RN hours per day (7×8)		56
LPN hours per day (5×8)		40
CNA hours per day (11×7.5)		82.5
Total hours per day		$178.5 \div 35 =$
Nursing hours PPD		**5.10**

TABLE 5–2

Staffing Patterns and FTEs for Sample Subacute Units Requiring 6.0 Hours PPD

Subacute Medically Complex Unit	Staff/Day	FTE Required
Average census	17	
Day Shift Staffing		
# RNs	3	4.5
# LPNs	0	0.0
# CNAs	2	3.0
Total day	5	7.5
Evening Shift Staffing		
# RNs	2	3.0
# LPNs	0	0.0
# CNAs	2	3.0
Total evening	4	6.0
Nocturnal Shift Staffing		
# RNs	1	1.5
# LPNs	1	1.5
# CNAs	2	3.0
Total nocturnal	4	6.0
Total Staffing		
# RNs	6	10.5
# LPNs	1	7.5
# CNAs	6	16.5
Total all	13	34.5
Total Nursing Hours		
RN hours per day (6 × 8)		48
LPN hours per day (1 × 8)		8
CNA hours per day (6 × 7.5)		45
Total hours per day		101 ÷ 17 =
Nursing hours PPD		**5.94**

TABLE 5–3

Staffing Patterns and FTEs for Sample Subacute Units Requiring 7.0 Hours PPD

Subacute Respiratory/ Vent Unit	Staff/Day	FTE Required
Average census	20	
Day Shift Staffing		
# RNs	3	4.5
# LPNs	1	1.5
# CNAs	3	4.5
Total day	7	10.5
Evening Shift Staffing		
# RNs	2	3.0
# LPNs	1	1.5
# CNAs	3	4.5
Total evening	6	9.0
Nocturnal Shift Staffing		
# RNs	2	3.0
# LPNs	1	1.5
# CNAs	2	3.0
Total nocturnal	5	7.5
Total Staffing		
# RNs	7	10.5
# LPNs	3	4.5
# CNAs	8	12.0
Total all	18	27.0
Total Nursing Hours		
RN hours per day		56
LPN hours per day		24
CNA hours per day		60
Total hours per day		140 ÷ 20 =
Nursing Hours PPD		**7.00**

SUMMARY

Many nurses have been frustrated working in the acute care setting for several years. Some of the reasons for this include:

- Declining census caused hospitals to cut back on staff, both on nursing units and support services.
- Patients are admitted to the hospital on the day of major surgery, allowing little time for preoperative teaching.
- Patients are discharged within hours or few days after major surgery.
- Frequently the patient lives alone or the other family members are at work for a large part of the day.
- The patient is too acutely ill at discharge to be receptive to discharge teaching.
- The patients are admitted and discharged so rapidly, the nurse is not able to develop a nurse/patient relationship.

Home healthcare has compensated for early hospital discharges in several situations, but subacute care has become a viable alternative for patients who are still acutely ill and need inpatient care.

Nurses working in subacute care describe the environment as professionally challenging because they are offered the opportunity to deliver nursing care by using a defined plan shared with other services to optimize the patient's potential. There is the opportunity to involve the family and the patient in the plan of care and achieve the best possible outcome. That is the primary reason they chose the nursing profession as a career, and now with subacute care, they can achieve their goals.

Chapter 6

Subacute Care in the Medicaid Program

Stephen H. Press, JD
Vice President, Acquisitions, Meditrust

s a former director of the Medicaid program for the State of Connecticut, I am often asked for comments about reimbursement under the national Medicaid program. I believe that there is no such program. There are instead as many programs as there are states. Each program is shaped by the plan options the state has agreed to participate in, the budgetary resources the state is willing to invest in the program, and the philosophy that state has toward the provision of medical care for the poor and elderly.

Anyone who has glanced at a comparison of Medicaid nursing rates for the states of New York and Texas would recognize that their programs must be significantly different. Imagine skilled nursing care under the Medicaid program for $450.00 per day in New York City or $56.00 per day in San Antonio, Texas. Similarly operators throughout the country could cite hundreds of other differences that would differentiate their own state programs. With all these differences, how have these Medicaid programs reacted to the significant change occurring currently in the healthcare arena? Clearly the state programs are not in the vanguard of change being driven by managed care. So far they have been bringing up the rear.

To understand the rapid change of the present, one must look at the past for its rationale. Medicaid is a federal-state medical assistance program that provides coverage for certain low-income individuals and families. The program was established under Title XIX of the Social Security Act, under which federal matching grants are made to the states. All states currently participate in the program to some extent. Essentially the states enter into an agreement with the federal government to provide certain mandatory services (long-term care is one) and certain optional services (dental services and eyeglasses, for example). In return, the federal government agrees to pay 50 percent or more of the Medicaid bill, depending on the percentage of the state's population that lives in poverty. The Medicaid program is often the largest program in any particular state's budget, and long-term care the largest budgetary segment of the program.

The fact that nursing home rates can differ so drastically is evidence of the flexibility states have in setting payment rates and conditions for nursing homes. In the early years of the program, some states set flat payment rates. Others moved into cost-related systems either prospectively or retrospectively. Rates paid, as noted in the comparison above, were significantly lower in some states than in others. A number of states also attempted to limit the number of homes or beds that could be available to the Medicaid program. They did this by restricting the number of beds that could be built through a certificate-of-need process. An example of this exists today in Connecticut, where the construction of any new nursing homes has been frozen since the spring of 1993. Other states restrict the number of Medicaid beds they will contract for to treat Medicaid patients.

The problem for states in restricting reimbursement for nursing home care was that they could cause a large number of patients to remain in their communities without care or remain backed up in hospitals. In many states both of these situations occurred. While some states, because of their philosophy, were not unhappy about keeping patients in need at home, few wanted to cause longer and more expensive stays in hospitals because of the lack of available nursing home beds. Clearly, state and federal budgetary pressure militated against such hospital back-ups.

In the 1980s changes began to occur at the hospital level that made it even more imperative that states solve their problems at the nursing home level. One change was the adoption of the disease-related group (DRG) payment system, which provided incentives to hospitals to discharge patients as early as possible to the community or to nursing homes. Other changes occurred in the treatment milieu, where new methodologies and equipment increasingly brought about the saving of life and stabilization of stroke and accident victims in hospital ICUs. These patients would previously have died early in the process. Rehab and long-term hospital companies arose to care for and rehabilitate these patients at less cost than acute care hospitals. The major effort of these facilities was aimed at insurance and Medicare patients. The Medicaid patient was avoided by these new care providers, as well as by ordinary nursing homes, which lacked the capability as well as the reimbursement to treat these new heavier-care patients. This was a difficult problem area for state Medicaid directors trying to avoid backing up patients in more expensive hospitals. Most state rate-setting systems did not have the flexibility to pay for the higher costs of long-term ventilator patients, for example, or coma or traumatic brain injury patients. Many states, like Connecticut, began to contract, at rates above that provided by their rate-setting systems, with out-of-state nursing homes for this higher-level service. They did this because federal rules did not allow states to pay higher rates for heavier-care patients in their own states but left the door open for such payments elsewhere. Companies like the Greenery and New Medico, which dealt with traumatic brain injury and coma management, grew rapidly by treating patients in their nursing homes from out-of-state Medicaid programs. For example, New Medico's Massachusetts facilities would take patients from Connecticut Medicaid, but their Connecticut facilities would not. Many state Medicaid programs to this day still send these specialized patients out of state to avoid restrictive state rate-setting plans. Connecticut actually passed legislation in 1985 allowing its Medicaid program to establish higher rates for traumatic brain injury and AIDS patients, but the Medicaid program never put the law into practice. Other states changed their systems to pay higher rates for heavier-care patients or adopted case-mix or DRG-like systems to pay nursing home rates that are tied to a patient's condition. Illinois and Maryland were leaders in this movement.

All of these changes preceded the movement in the 90s for the provision of subacute care and postacute care in skilled nursing facilities. Market forces, driven by managed care, were bringing about the early discharge of sicker patients from hospitals to a number of alternative sites. The goal was the overall reduction of cost, and if the patient could be rehabilitated and sent home or to a lower-cost alternative (such as a nursing home), the savings would be even greater. Managed care was not looking at price alone but outcomes as well. Meanwhile, some state Medicaid programs had altered their reimbursement systems to allow for the higher payment for heavier-care patients. States such as California, New York, New Jersey, North Carolina, and Michigan did establish higher rates for the treatment of what they perceived to be subacute patients, for example, ventilator and traumatic brain injury patients. However, their rates were for long-term care of these patients and did not in most cases provide for the necessary active therapy that would allow them to be rehabilitated. California actually called its program a subacute program. However, at $250 per day or less for care of a ventilator patient in a nursing home, few patients were removed from the ventilator and most (nearly 850 by 1994) remained in their long-term care beds for life. Michigan and North Carolina had similar programs and similar rates for nursing homes, but Michigan paid a much higher rate for like treatment in a hospital.

As the 90s began, managed care was striving harder to find alternative placements for acute care hospital patients. Companies like Vencor were organized to treat subacute patients in long-term hospitals. A variety of alternative care placements was initiated, from recovery hotels to cancer treatment centers. Nursing home operators like Integrated Health Services (IHS), sensing that they could provide subacute services competitive to those offered in rehab and long-term hospitals, jumped into the fray. They offered subacute services for private pay and Medicare patients only. They avoided Medicaid at first, because of the lack of adequate reimbursement and the fear that accepting that reimbursement would force them to lower their care standards. Meanwhile rehab and long-term hospitals began treating these Medicaid patients because they were reimbursed at higher rates because of their hospital licenses.

IHS avoided Medicaid by operating in either private pay facilities or in states that allowed their Medicaid patients to be treated in distinct parts (Missouri, for example), separate from their subacute units. In other states they tried to reach agreement that the state would not try to place their Medicaid patients in the subacute unit if it could not pay the higher rate. Of course that approach works well when you have only a few selected facilities offering subacute care and your competition is limited. It is much more difficult when you try to expand rapidly into many different markets. It is also difficult when you start to face competition from the many other companies and individual facilities beginning to provide subacute care. When an acute care hospital is told one company is only accepting private pay and Medicare subacute patients, and a competitor is willing to take Medicaid patients as well, the competitor may be given the edge on all of the subacute patients. Today there are a number of companies providing subacute care in selected urban areas. Obviously the growth of competition was one incentive to take Medicaid patients. Another was the growing competition with assisted-living facilities and their ability to take private patients who previously would have gone to nursing homes. For some facilities subacute patients were necessary to replace patients re-cruited by assisted-living facilities. On the other hand, some nursing home operators, such as Horizon, tried to avoid the Medicaid reimbursement problem by converting part or all of their facilities to a long-term hospital licensure where they receive higher rates.

In the midst of all this turmoil on subacute care came the push for healthcare reform. First of all, many states began to look at how they dealt with subacute care. States such as Indiana and Pennsylvania began to al-low additional payment for subacute care, particularly for therapy, where the treatment provided had the potential of discharging a patient to a lesser level of care. Illinois passed legislation that would allow the licensing of all or part of a nursing home as a subacute unit. This would allow for significantly higher reimbursement. California developed regulations for a higher level of payment for rehabilitative subacute care. A whole host of states began to discuss the potential of subacute care to save money by discharging patients to lower levels of care. Much of these discussions arose after nursing home operators began negotiating with states for higher reimbursement for subacute care. The discussions with IHS involved their outcome studies on non-Medicaid patients and how much money could have been achieved by individual states if similar outcomes could be achieved on their subacute patients. Many of the states essentially began to allow negotiated rates for exceptional cases.

On the other hand, spurred by managed care and healthcare reform a good number of state Medicaid programs are trying to move large num-bers of their recipients to managed care programs. If that really occurs it will also improve the potential for successful treatment of subacute pa-tients at the nursing home level. That is because managed care, unlike Medicaid, has clearly been willing to pay higher short-term rates in nurs-ing homes to achieve early discharges of subacute patients to lesser levels of care.

Still, what we see today in relation to subacute care are as many Med-icaid remedies as we have states. The issue is an active one. The federal and state governments are moving positively toward a recognition that subacute care can be provided in nursing homes with a resultant savings to government. Nursing home operators have taken advantage of this by treating more and more Medicaid subacute patients, separating them into rehabilitative and long-term components. With all the activity in this area by national associations and operators, one would hope that future progress will continue to be made.

Chapter 7

Financing for Subacute Facilities

Stephen H. Press, JD
Vice President, Acquisitions, Meditrust

There are major capital implications for nursing home operators exploring the provisions of subacute care in their facilities. For one thing, conversion costs for beds may range in the area of $5,000–$10,000 per bed, but there are other capital implications as well. First, there are working capital requirements that may far exceed those for ordinary nursing home beds. Some of this will be caused by slower reimbursement for both insurance- and Medicare-covered patients. This will be exacerbated if the nursing home Medicare costs exceed the Medicare regional cost limitations and the provider is forced to seek an exception to those limitations in order to be fully reimbursed. For example, Integrated Health Services' average exception request was for over $280,000 per year, per facility. Second, there will certainly will be extensive start-up marketing costs that might come close to equaling the initial costs of renovating a unit for subacute patients of perhaps $5,000 per bed. For operators seeking to expand by acquiring additional facilities there will be additional growth and capitalization needs as well.

SOURCES OF FINANCING

There are a variety of ways to finance nursing home acquisitions or renovation/expansions. The main ways are bank loans or conventional financing, loans or leases from real estate investment trusts (REITs), and FHA-insured mortgages. In addition, tax-exempt bonds are a principle choice for nonprofit facilities. Venture capitalists and joint ventures may be helpful in the financing process as well. Newer lenders have entered the field, particularly the Wall Street firms that are developing conduit programs that pool groups of mortgages for long-term care facilities and sell them. Lending is much more limited for new construction and start-ups.

Conventional Financing

Banks are the main source of conventional financing, although there may be financing available from insurance and credit companies. Much of this has not been available in recent years, but more of these lenders have returned to the market in 1994 and 1995.

Loans will be in the form of mortgages, construction loans, and lines of credit. The terms of loans will vary greatly by lenders, but loans will principally be available for five to seven years, with amortization from 10 to 25 years. Banks will generally be comfortable with loans at 60–70 percent loan-to-value ratios. The biggest banks are more comfortable lending to providers with multiple facilities, while community banks might be more willing to lend on a single facility in their community. Interest rates might vary from prime plus one or more on short-term loans, to 200 to 300 basis points over the treasury note for the corresponding period of the loan offered (for example, 10-year loan–10-year treasury note).

Advantages for bank loans include an easier application process, lower rates, and perhaps faster approval or disapproval. In addition, banks may provide working capital loans or acquisition lines. Disadvantages may include lack of familiarity with the business, limits on the size of the loans, loans where banks participate strongly in earnings, construction loans without take-outs, shorter loan maturities, and tighter financial covenants.

FHA Loans

The current FHA 232 co-insurance program provides up to 90 percent loan-to-value financing for new construction or substantial rehabilitation of an existing nursing home. It is nonrecourse financing, provided for a 40-year term. Under this program the federal government is able to insure the payment of principle and interest on qualifying loans. These loans are usually made by lenders in the public debt market through Ginnie Maes and tax exempt bonds. As part of their process, FHA reviews the demand for nursing home beds, site suitability, facility pro forma, management capabilities, and so forth. Requirements include that the borrower contribute at least 10 percent equity toward the cost of the project and provide certain letters of credit. In addition, fees include 1.3 percent of the loan at closing, an annual service fee, and an annual insurance premium. With that, the cost of the program is relatively low even though on the whole the loan-to-value provided is closer to 80 percent. The biggest problem is the amount of time consumed by the application process, which is frequently much more than a year. A new program is to begin in 1995 that allows FHA 232 loans to be provided for the refinancing or purchase of existing nursing homes, without the previous requirement for substantial rehabilitation. While it is said this process will be substantially shorter and less cumbersome, that remains to be seen.

Advantages of the FHA program are its high loan-to-value, longer-term loans and nonrecourse debt. Disadvantages are the overly long and cumbersome application process and the fact that borrowers may not take any equity out of loans for themselves or to underwrite future acquisitions.

REIT Financing

REIT financing is a growing source, and through the last recession, sometimes the only source of financing for the industry. There are three basic types of REITs: mortgage, equity, and hybrid. Mortgage REITs are similar to the banks or mortgage institutions, in that they provide secured financing for properties without assuming title to these properties. An equity REIT purchases the real estate and enters into a long-term lease with an operator. Hybrid REITs will participate in both mortgages and equity transactions. For example, Nationwide REIT is essentially an equity REIT seeking to purchase properties and lease them back. LTC Properties is mainly a mortgage REIT. Meditrust is a hybrid REIT doing either sale/leasebacks or mortgages. In addition, Meditrust will finance up to 100 percent of the construction cost on a new facility and provide permanent financing when it is ready for occupancy. Some REITs like Nationwide and LTC will not finance new development. Many REITs will finance working capital requirements if the project has the necessary strength. They will also provide acquisition lines.

REITs obtain their capital by selling stock or debt to the public. Some securitize the mortgages they hold by selling them to the public. In general, one of REITs' greatest strengths is their ability to readily raise money. That strength means that they are almost always capable of lending that money. Meditrust is the largest of the healthcare REITs with assets at the beginning of 1995 approaching 1.6 billion dollars. That one REIT did approximately 300 million dollars in new transactions in 1994. HRPT, which is the second-largest healthcare REIT, did over $300 million in transactions in 1994 as well.

Loans from REITs will mainly be available for 7- to 10-year terms with amortizations from 20 to 30 years. Loans will be granted at 75 to 80 percent and higher loan-to-value ratios. This is a major advantage over banks. Some REITs specialize in smaller, more risky companies; others seek larger growing companies with which they can provide more financing. Interest rates vary with the cost of money to the particular REIT. The larger, more established REITs raise their money at lower cost and therefore charge less. Rates may range from 300 to 400 basis points over the related treasury bill, with one to two points up front. One of the key features of REIT loans is a requirement to pay a portion of the project's growth in revenues in addition to the on-going interest payments. This is sometimes mitigated by various approaches, including the capping of this additional interest. This money is used to increase the dividends paid to REIT shareholders in order to keep their share offerings attractive to buyers.

Advantages for REIT loans include the lender's knowledge of industry, longer-term loans, higher loan-to-value ratios, and unlimited cash. Disadvantages include costs, preclusion of smaller projects, and participation requirements.

Tax Exempt Bonds

Nonprofits do have a significant advantage when it comes to raising capital because of their ability to access the tax exempt bond market. Tax exempt bonds are issued by municipal and state authorities. The costs range from two to three percent for rated borrowers and four to six percent for unrated ones. The bonds provide nonrecourse debt with 30-year fixed interest rates ranging from 6 $\frac{1}{2}$ to 9 $\frac{1}{2}$ percent depending upon the sponsor's credit quality.

Advantages for tax exempt bonds include lower cost, nonuse of appraisals, and access to a different source of capital. The key disadvantage is the complexity and time necessary to carry out an offering.

Joint Ventures

The individual nursing home operators may find all the preceding approaches very difficult or costly to undertake. They also may be faced with the need to move more rapidly into subacute care than any of the previous alternatives would allow them to do. An operator's answer might be to affiliate with a joint venture partner that would be willing to provide all or part of the capital necessary to convert part of the facility to subacute care. That joint venture partner, for example, might be a therapy provider that deals in a single form of subacute care, such as ventilator or wound care. Or, the partner might be a therapy provider that handles the whole gamut of subacute care, or a subacute nursing home company that might be interested in providing the necessary capital and expertise in exchange for managing the unit. Other possibilities might be the hospital in your community, a physician's group practice, or HMOs. Any of these groups might be willing to participate in the conversion of your facility and contribute to its success if they can share in the resulting project.

Accounts Receivable Financing

It has been stressed that new subacute providers may face large cash flow problems. They will be dealing with a much greater array of insurance payors and likely receiving a higher percentage of Medicare patients than they had in the past. In regard to Medicare, they may have to request an exception to the Medicare regional cost limitations and be forced to wait up to three years for exceptional reimbursement. When facing these kinds of problems, operators do have a major resource available: their accounts receivable.

There are an increasing number of third-party groups or factors that are willing to purchase or lend against medical accounts receivable. They are willing to do this with small or large providers. Under these programs providers will receive an immediate cash payment from 50 to 80 percent of their eligible accounts receivable. These payments can be made as often as weekly and on either current or backlogged receivables. The transactions can be either on a recourse or a nonrecourse basis, with interest charges applied against actual monthly usage. When it is on a recourse basis, uncollected receivables can be submitted back to the provider for payment, or subtracted from the payment due the provider on current receivables. When the cash collected on a batch of receivables exceeds the original payment to the provider, the factor will make additional payments to it. Consider the following example.

On May 1, provider submits batch A of 100,000 in receivables to factor.

On May 8, factor pays provider $70,000 (program is 70 percent).

By May 30, factor collects $90,000 of batch A.

On June 6, factor pays provider another $20,000 from batch A.

Periodic payments to the provider will continue until the receivables are fully discharged. Some factors simply lend against the receivables and the providers actually carry out the collection process. Others assume full responsibility for collection of the receivables and interaction with third-party payors.

One of the quirky areas in regard to government (Medicare and Medicaid) accounts receivable is that they must be paid directly to the provider that delivered the care. Even so, providers may still assign Medicare or Medicaid receivables. To do this, the Health Care Financing Agency (HCFA) must send payment to a bank account in the provider's name. This account can then be accessed by the factor/purchaser, which in turn will deposit the funds in its own account.

LOAN PACKAGE PRESENTATION

Many borrowers put together inadequate loan packages, thus failing to make the best case for their loan request. Most lenders review a large number of packages for every one they finance. A poorly packaged loan request is more likely to be rejected. The following is a list of information that should be included in the initial request:

1. Property name(s) and location(s).
2. Price/loan amount.
3. Detailed sources and uses of funds.
4. Property.
    a. Number of beds.
    b. Age.
    c. Acreage.
    d. Photographs.
    e. Description of recent renovations and additions.
5. Operational experience of the borrower—including information on any similar projects done. If your reported expertise is turning around projects, the lender will look at other projects to see if this is true.
6. General discussion of the project—including any changes you are planning in the physical structure or program. If you are purchasing a nursing home and adding a subacute unit, this should be explained.
7. Financial statements for the past three years and any interim financial statements (for existing facilities).
8. Occupancy rates and patient mix history—the percentage of patients by payor type.
9. Detailed projections for the facility(s) for the next three years— for facilities to be built or those to be renovated. You should show the impact of any beds taken out of business for renovation and the increased income from these when converted to subacute care.
10. Financial information on the borrower or any guarantors.
11. Demographic data and information regarding competitors.

Other information that may be requested during the review process of the loan may include most recent Medicaid cost reports and the most recent health department surveys. In addition to that information, most lenders will also require that the borrowers will provide Member Appraisal Institute (MAI) appraisals and environmental reports prior to the loan closing.

LOAN CRITERIA

1. Strength of management team—One of the keys to gaining successful financing. What is their past experience with projects of the same type and their knowledge of reimbursement systems?

2. Financial strength of the project—Does the project make financial sense? Is it currently adequate in covering its debt payments and if it is not, how will the borrowers change it to bring about success in the future?

3. Debt service coverage ratio requirements—Lenders impose minimum requirements for how much the projected cash flow of the facility will exceed the debt service payments due the lender from the borrower. For example, at a debt service coverage ratio of two or one and an annual debt service payment of one million dollars, the borrower would need a projected annual cash flow of $2 million.

4. Equity requirements—This represents the part of the transaction that would either have to be paid out by the borrower as part of the transaction or be available to guarantee payment of the debt.

5. Maturity—This is the term of the loan. For example 5-, 7- or 10-year maturities.

6. Amortization—Sets the amount of the payment of the loans as if it will be paid over the number of years amortized. Payments will be smaller as the number of years the loan is amortized for is increased.

7. Variable versus fixed interest rates—Variable rates relate to the sort of index used, possibly the rate of a particular treasury bill or note, and may rise annually or otherwise in accordance with the related index. Fixed interest rates lock in a particular rate for the length of the loan.

8. Commitment fees—These are fees, sometimes called *points*, due at the transaction closing, which are sometimes funded in the transaction in addition to the requested loan.

9. Security—Lenders require various levels of security, ranging from a promise to repay the loan, to a first mortgage on the financed assets, to additional security in the form of letters of credit, payments in advance, deposits, or use of any other form of the borrower's assets.

10. Contractor and architect requirements—On new construction, renovation, and expansion projects, a lender may impose its own requirements for contract bonds and contractor experience. Government lending programs may require that the borrower use a contractor with union employees.

11. Covenant—These are minimum continuing standards that lenders set during the loan period that borrowers must meet in order not to go into technical default. Examples of such standards are maintaining debt service ratios, net worth requirements to the borrower, minimum working capital requirements, and current ratios. Many lenders use these standards as benchmarks to determine whether the borrower is beginning to have problems.

Chapter 8

Pediatric Subacute Care: An Introduction

Burton Grebin, MD
President and CEO, St. Mary's Hospital for Children

Stuart C. Kaplan, MBA
Executive Vice President, St. Mary's Hospital for Children

The term *subacute care*—which at its most general refers to a level of care that is more intensive than traditional nursing facility care, but less intensive than acute care—is on its way to becoming a permanent part of our nation's healthcare lexicon. The chapters in this book will help to speed that process along, as will the scores of articles yet to be written on this still-evolving level of care. Nevertheless, as our understanding of subacute care increases, we face a challenging question that confronts us whenever healthcare in this country is discussed. That question, simply stated, is this: Is the model of care before us designed to meet the needs of adults or does it also take into account the needs of children? If one looks at contemporary subacute care policy and practice, the answer seems clear: Subacute care, like our healthcare system generally, is designed primarily to meet the needs of adult patients.

That fact is regrettable, although far from surprising. Adults, after all, are by far the largest consumers of healthcare services in this country and account for the largest portion of total healthcare expenditures, including total subacute care expenditures. That many skilled nursing facilities and other major providers of subacute care target this market would appear to make good economic sense. But, while children as a whole use fewer healthcare resources than adults do, the cost of caring for very young children and children with chronic and congenital conditions is higher, according to the National Association of Children's Hospitals and Related

Institutions (NACHRI). A study conducted for NACHRI by the Center for Health Policy Studies found that, per day of inpatient care, "nurse staffing costs were 39 percent higher for children under age two and 24 percent higher for children between two and five than for the average patient." [1] The study turned up similar per unit cost differences for "respiratory therapy, physical and recreational therapies, certain ancillary services . . . , and social services."[2]

One way of controlling such costs, as more and more providers are discovering, is to offer a similar array of services in a lower-cost, subacute care setting. SNFs, for example, have begun to "broaden beyond geriatric clientele to include younger patients," as a recent front-page story in the *New York Times* indicated.[3] Still, only a relative handful of these SNFs *specialize* in children, and those that do tend to focus on caring for children with long-term chronic illness.

This leaves a range of children beyond those who are chronically ill who could be appropriately and cost-effectively cared for within a subacute setting. These children offer the most persuasive argument yet for broadening our perspective on subacute care beyond the adult model. In this chapter, we will draw upon our own experience as administrators of pediatric subacute care facilities, St. Mary's Hospital for Children, Bayside, NY, and Friedman Rehabilitation Institute for Children, Ossining, NY[4] to:

1. Identify specific treatment programs for such children.
2. Discuss how the typical adult-centered subacute care model needs to be modified to meet the needs of the children.
3. Offer what we believe are necessary amendments to the current adult-centered definitions of subacute care.

PEDIATRIC SUBACUTE CARE TREATMENT PROGRAMS

Alternate Settings

With some exceptions, current definitions are overly restrictive when they come to discussing *where* subacute care can be delivered. But just as hospice care has come to be accepted as services delivered to terminally ill patients in a combination of inpatient and community-based settings, subacute care ought to be viewed less as a place or site of care than as a *level* of care. When we view it in this way, we quickly realize that subacute care can be delivered in a variety of settings, an especially important consideration when treating children. At St. Mary's Hospital and Friedman Institute, for example, we provide a subacute level of care to children in a number of alternate settings. Our total inpatient program consists of 139 beds—95 at St. Mary's and 44 at Friedman; in our Home Care Program, we currently serve over 800 children daily in the greater New York City metropolitan area. At St. Mary's, additionally, we provide a subacute level of care within our Medical Day Care Program, which offers children with special health needs—ages 2 to 16—early childhood, afterschool, weekend, and summer comprehensive medical and treatment services.

The following treatment programs are delivered in the settings identified above:

Premature infants. A comprehensive subacute inpatient treatment program tailored to the medical and developmental needs of premature infants. Treatment of premature or small-for-date infants fits into two categories:

1. Low birth-weight babies with complications.
2. Babies with respiratory problems such as bronchopulmonary dysplasia and other related complications.

Infants (full-term with complications). A comprehensive subacute inpatient treatment program tailored to the medical and developmental needs of full-term infants with:

1. Intrauterine contracted infections.
2. Other postnatally acquired infections.
3. Developmental complications.
4. Genetic or congenital abnormalities.

Asthma. A comprehensive inpatient and home care program for the treatment of children with refractory asthma. This program consists of the following components:

1. Controlling severe asthma symptoms.
2. Training parents and children in the management of the disease.
3. Re-engineering the home environment.
4. Periodic monitoring of medication compliance in the home environment.

Diabetes. A comprehensive treatment program for brittle diabetics using the inpatient and home care settings. The program has three components:

1. Controlling severe diabetic symptoms.
2. Educating the patient and family in the management of the disease.
3. Periodic monitoring of medication compliance in the home environment.

Neurologic rehabilitation. Inpatient multidisciplinary rehabilitation for traumatic brain injury and postoperative brain and spinal surgery patients. Most patients require extensive medical support and monitoring as well as intensive rehabilitation therapy.

Orthopedic rehabilitation. Postoperative inpatient specialized rehabilitation for children requiring intensive therapy following multiple fractures and corrective orthopedic surgery.

High-tech services. High-tech services for children dependent upon technology and requiring continual supervision and clinical intervention. These services include: (1) ventilator care, (2) oxygen dependency, (3) CPAP (continuous positive airway pressure), (4) TPN (total parenteral nutrition), (5) cardiorespiratory monitoring, (6) pulse oximetry, (7) ostomy feeding, (8) pain management, (9) suctioning, and (10) tracheostomy care.

Burn rehabilitation. Intensive inpatient rehabilitation therapy for burn patients who require a subacute level of care.

Genetics. Expert case management services for complex genetic cases.

Programs such as those outlined above serve a population of children that can effectively benefit from pediatric subacute care, if properly delivered. That last phase—"properly delivered"—raises a whole range of issues that need to be addressed if we are ever to escape the unproductive notion that pediatric subacute care is simply a level of care delivered to patients who are not adults. The truth is, children have *special* needs, particularly in a subacute context, and any program model that does not take that fact into account will simply not serve children adequately.

PEDIATRIC SUBACUTE CARE: A PROGRAMMATIC MODEL

Essential Features: Family-Centered and Age-Appropriate Care

One essential feature of the subacute model we pioneered at St. Mary's/ Friedman is a comprehensive, program wide emphasis on family-centered care. We offer a more detailed discussion below of how this kind of care can be incorporated into a subacute program for children, but here we might simply say that, if, as we believe, the goal of pediatric subacute care should be to return a child home as soon as possible, families must be actively involved from the very first in the overall care plan. Clearly, the focus on family involvement and training is less critical in adult-centered subacute programs. But for a successful pediatric subacute care program, it is essential. For this reason, we have represented our commitment to family-centered care in our hospital's logo (two children whose outstretched arms point skyward to form the apex of a house) and more crucially, in the long-range and day-to-day decisions we make on how best to deliver a subacute level of care to our children, whether in an inpatient, home, or medical day care setting.

A second essential feature of the St. Mary's/Friedman model is its ability to tailor a subacute program to whatever pediatric subdivision is focused on. Thus, a subacute program for infants will need to include well-child care—including immunizations and check-ups—as well as infant stimulation. Of course, a facility treating children of different ages must make extra efforts to ensure that both its programs and physical environment can accommodate a range of needs.

Both these essential elements of the St. Mary's/Friedman model are woven through the following discussion, which focuses on the issues of staffing, facility/space design, family involvement, and reimbursement.

KEY MODIFICATIONS

Staffing

A skilled nursing facility that has decided to "broaden beyond geriatric clientele to include younger patients" in its subacute program might be tempted to utilize existing staff. That, in our opinion, would be a mistake. Whatever the setting, a pediatric subacute program should recruit and hire a specialized staff—one that will meet the medical, psychological, social, and educational needs of children.

Besides pediatricians, the medical staff should include pediatric nurses, preferably ones who come from such acute care settings as neonatal or pediatric intensive care units or recovery units. Nurses who have this kind of experience will not only be more familiar with common infant, child, and adolescent diagnoses, they will also be able to provide the "high-touch" nursing so important to a child's growth and development, especially during infancy. There is also an economic incentive for an SNF or another subacute provider to recruit and hire nurses who come from an acute care pediatric background. Such staffing practices eliminate the necessity of redundant staffing—hiring one nurse to supplement the lack of pediatric experience and knowledge of another.

Nurses who provide a subacute level of care within the home will need the same experience and training as their inpatient counterparts, plus the resourcefulness to deal with the variety of situations that arise in the field. For some nurses, that challenge, along with the flexibility and greater independence of home care, is precisely what they are looking for in their practice; for others, the more predictable routine of an inpatient setting is preferable. In either case, nurses hired to provide a subacute level of care to children should be able, along with other key staff members, to help model appropriate behaviors for children and to deal comfortably and well with family members who need to be an intimate part of the care plan.

Therapists of various kinds should also be recruited and hired with an eye to how well they can work with a pediatric population. A therapist, for example, who may be quite good at helping adults relearn a skill they once had (*rehabilitation*) may be at a decided disadvantage when it comes to helping a child learn a completely new skill (*habilitation*).

To meet the emotional and psychological needs of children, child psychologists and pediatric psychiatrists should be incorporated into the program. In our adolescent healthcare program, for example, we understand that the normal stresses of adolescence are complicated by special health problems. In such cases, therefore, we develop a comprehensive plan of care—one that responds to both an adolescent's specific medical condition, and to the psychological and developmental issues that may be jeopardizing his or her return to good health.

Given the key role that families play in a child's treatment and successful return home, the appropriate staffing decisions need to be made when it comes to hiring social workers, including directors and supervisors. Social workers need to have a background that enables them to understand and effectively deal with issues that children and their families inevitably face in the course of an extended plan of care. The social worker or, in the larger picture, the social work department, is the liaison between families and the program, whether it be inpatient or home care. Initially, families need to be introduced to the program and to the vital importance of family involvement in the care plan (see below, "Family Involvement"). As the course of treatment moves forward, social workers will assume a variety of roles, including family counselor, family ombudsman, problem-solver, and referral source. Social workers are also instrumental in hastening a child's return home by developing plans, preferably at the time of admission, to link children and families to concrete services upon returning to the community.

Finally, inpatient pediatric subacute care programs need to make staffing or related decisions in response to the inevitable developmental and educational challenges that arise in caring for children of varying ages for a time period of anywhere from several weeks to several months. Unmediated, that length of stay will almost certainly prove disruptive. At St. Mary's/Friedman, among the specialists involved in meeting the developmental needs of children and adolescents are infant stimulation specialists, early interventionists, and early education teachers and assistants. At St. Mary's, school-age children receive instruction on site from licensed teachers from the New York City Board of Education. We have also hired recreational therapists and assistants to provide children and adolescents with a range of afterschool and therapeutic activities.

Facility/Space Design

In a subacute program geared to a pediatric population, the *physical* environment in which care is delivered must also be tailored to meet the needs of children of all ages. One obvious design element that needs to be kept child-focused is the element of *scale*—of both physical space and equipment. Facilities and programs that ignore such a design consideration place children in a threateningly oversized world—a world much like the one Jonathan Swift's Gulliver found himself in when he visited the land of the giant Brobdingnagians. The fact is, space that comfortably accommodates the adult patient may be totally unsuitable for even older children. Similarly, adult-sized therapeutic equipment may have little application when working to improve the gross and fine motor skills of young children.

At St. Mary's, we have worked hard to design a facility that meets these challenges. In our units, for example, light switches, displays, and other architectural elements are placed at levels appropriate to children six years of age and up. Our infant and toddler units, on the other hand, have been designed to accommodate the needs of children who experience the world at a much lower height level and who need ample floor space to explore their environment.

We have also designed our units to be not only safe but happy places for children. Colorful posters and paintings hang in the units, while crafts produced by children fill display boxes along the hospital's main corridor. We have also constructed a Children's Activity Center, where children go for arts and crafts and to listen to music and see movies. A lounge on the older children's units permits them to watch TV and to play a variety of games, including pocket billiards. Visiting family members can be accommodated for either overnight stays or for extended stays at bedside.

Outdoor spaces at St. Mary's have also been designed with an eye to accommodating a diverse pediatric population. The hospital has designed and constructed a therapeutic playground, which combines child-safe surfaces with such whimsical attractions as a water-spewing dragon and a double-decker pirate's ship. Also on the grounds is a full-size basketball court, an olympic-size pool, and a covered picnic/barbecue area.

Of course, not every subacute program geared to children can or should, follow *all* these design guidelines. A subacute program that cares for infants exclusively, for instance, clearly can do without the equipment and other elements designed to accommodate older children. For this reason, in making design choices, administrators of a new or existing inpatient pediatric subacute program need to keep in mind one rather simple overriding goal: How can we create an environment that meets the medical and rehabilitative needs of children while being as safe, happy, and nurturing as possible?

A similar question is relevant to the delivery of subacute care to children in a home setting, although the degree to which any particular home environment can be modified to accommodate a child's needs is more limited. Nevertheless, it remains crucial for home care professionals to advise families about how they can make their home as safe, happy, and nurturing as possible. In the case of the severely asthmatic child, for example, "re-engineering" the home environment to eliminate dust, synthetic fibers, and other identifiable bronchial irritants may very well be necessary for an effective course of treatment. Similarly, a home environment may need to be altered to accommodate equipment used in therapy. A nurse or other home care professional might also encourage families to brighten a younger child's room with posters of favorite cartoon characters or with decorations. Where a family's living arrangements actually place a child's well-being or continuing medical progress in jeopardy, social workers will cooperate with public housing authorities to locate and secure alternative living arrangements.

Family Involvement: The Key to Early Release of a Child

Although offering children with special needs a "stepped down" level of care is proving to be a medically sound, cost-effective alternative to other, more expensive treatment options, subacute care for children delivered in an inpatient setting can only remain attractive to patients and payor sources as long as children can be returned home as soon as possible. Otherwise, we have simply made up in average lengths of stay what we have saved in per diem costs. And what is the key to returning children home as soon as possible? It is, as we noted above, a programmatic emphasis on making family members a vital part of the care plan from the very first.

Making the right staffing decisions, along with designing child/family-friendly units, will help this process. Families must also be given training, education, and support, as well as a range of opportunities to be a vital and consistent part of the day-to-day care and rehabilitation of their child, from participation with the interdisciplinary care team, to helping in therapy sessions, to feeding and holding, to simply doing laundry. The more this happens, the more likely it is that children will be cared for optimally once they return home, which, in turn, makes quicker discharges possible. At both St. Mary's and Friedman, we interview parents prior to a child's admission, assessing strengths and determining the nature and scope of training and education necessary to involve family members as part of the care plan.

We also do a number of small things, which, cumulatively, have an impact on family involvement. For example, in our Infants Program, our education assistants put together a "baby book" for each infant they work with, and then present the book to parents at discharge. In this way, parents can relive those precious "firsts" that they may have missed while they were away from their child. We have also established a policy of flexible visiting hours, which encourages family members to spend time with their child whenever they find it convenient. We also involve families in discharge planning, which takes place at the time of admission and may involve any number of discharge options, including referral to a child's physician, school placement, and medical monitoring. Depending upon the circumstances of a particular case, children and their families may also be linked to certain services in the community. This kind of community referral is especially important to technology-dependent children, a growing segment of the total pediatric subacute population.

For children requiring ongoing medical monitoring, discharge planning may also include admission to our Home Care Program, which provides comprehensive home-based services to children and families in the greater New York City area. In general, home-based subacute care for children, whether at St. Mary's/Friedman or elsewhere, and whether involving new admittees or longer-term cases, clearly places an extra burden of care on families. In this setting, family involvement is assumed. The only real question is how effective that involvement will be in the course of a child's treatment. To help ensure an optimum level of involvement, medical and other home care staff should train and support families to assume, depending on the specific case, a variety of responsibilities, including the accurate and timely administration of medications, the changing of bandages, or the active participation in any number of designated therapeutic or rehabilitation activities and exercises. Staff members should also look upon the family as a primary source of day-to-day information about the child's medical, developmental, and psychological well-being. In our Home Care Program, our nurse coordinators utilize an electronic information and messaging system, developed in cooperation with Novell/WordPerfect Corporation, to collect and share patient data gathered during a home visit.

Reimbursement

Traditional long-term care, that is, care delivered primarily to adults within a skilled nursing facility or similar setting, is initially covered under Medicare, and then picked up under Medicaid, which is subject to state-by-state conditions and restrictions. In most cases, children requiring long-term care are not eligible for Medicare. That fact presents a major challenge to many prospective providers who wish to establish a pediatric subacute care program, leaving them dependent upon private payor sources, which frequently base reimbursement rates on the *site* of care rather than on treatment needs. For instance, the same HMO that might pay up to $2,000 per day for services delivered in an acute care setting might be unaware that such services delivered to children in a subacute care facility or program would cost considerably less. How much less? Adult model studies suggest that when similar services are compared, inpatient subacute care is typically *one-third* the cost of acute care, while subacute care delivered in a home setting is up to *one-tenth* the cost of acute care.

At St. Mary's, we have initiated a major campaign to persuade insurance companies and the managed care industry that pediatric subacute care is an available and cost-effective alternative to paying for specialized services and rehabilitation delivered in an acute care setting. At the same time, we have been fortunate in New York State to have the majority of the expenses we incur, in the course of providing specialized care and rehabilitation to children, reimbursed through the state-sponsored Medicaid program. Because of this program, and because of funding available to children under the age of five through the federal Individuals with Disabilities Education Act (IDEA), we at St. Mary's and Friedman are currently able to serve over 1,500 children annually in our three clinical program settings—inpatient, Home Care, and Medical Day Care. In addition to a significant population of children whose families could not otherwise afford such care, we also serve families with private funding sources— families whose children are covered under Medicaid once private funding has expired. Referrals come to us from a network of over 60 hospitals in the greater New York City metropolitan area.

Clearly, both in New York State and in states where Medicaid funding for long-term care for children is more limited, the future of pediatric subacute care will depend to a great degree on: (1) the continuing appeal of subacute care to private payor sources, and (2) the movement of these sources to adopt more needs-based reimbursement policies.

TOWARD A BROADER DEFINITION OF SUBACUTE CARE

At this point, we have discussed not only specific subacute treatment programs for children but ways in which we believe the typical adult-centered model of subacute care should be modified to serve children with special health needs. With this discussion behind us, we are now in a better position to offer certain amendments to the current adult-centered definitions of subacute care. Representative of these definitions is one recently adopted by the American Health Care Association (AHCA) and the Joint Commission on Accreditation of Healthcare Organizations (JCAHO), which we reprint here. For the purposes of our discussion, we have both numbered and italicized those parts of the definition that, in our opinion, are insufficiently broad or do not inadequately reflect the needs of children requiring a subacute level of care:

> Subacute care is comprehensive **[1]** *inpatient care* designed for someone who has an **[2]** *acute illness, injury, or exacerbation of a disease process.* It is goal-oriented treatment rendered immediately after, or instead of, acute hospitalization to treat one or more specific complex medical conditions or to administer one or more technically complex treatments, in the context of a person's underlying long-term conditions and overall situation.
>
> Generally, the individual's condition is such that the care **[3]** *does not depend on high-technology monitoring* or complex diagnostic procedures. Subacute care requires the coordinated services of **[4]** *an interdisciplinary team, including physicians, nurses, and other relevant professional disciplines, who are trained and knowledgeable to assess and manage these specific conditions and perform the necessary procedures.* Subacute care is given as part of a specifically defined program, regardless of the site.
>
> Subacute care is generally more intensive than traditional nursing facility care and less than acute care. It requires frequent (daily to weekly) patient assessment, and review of the clinical course and treatment plan

for a limited (several days to several months) time period, until the condition is stabilized or a predetermined treatment course is completed.[5]

This, then, is the AHCA/JCAHO definition of subacute care, which could apply to children except, we believe, in those places we have indicated:

1. "Subacute care is comprehensive *inpatient care.*" As we have said—and as the AHCA/JCAHO definition itself seems to indicate at a later point—subacute care is a level of care that can be delivered in a variety of settings. The variety of settings in which we treat children at St. Mary's/Friedman—inpatient, Home Care, and Medical Day Care—by no means exhausts the number of possible sites in which subacute care can be delivered, whether to children or adults. Other sites include acute hospitals, specialty hospitals, rehabilitation facilities, freestanding skilled nursing facilities, outpatient ambulatory centers, assisted living facilities, and educational settings. What is important to keep in mind, however, especially when serving children, is that the specific site of care should not be decisive in determining whether or not subacute services will be delivered. Indeed, many of our sickest children are treated at home, rather than in our inpatient program. And that trend is not simply the result of a cost-consciousness managed care industry pushing for shorter inpatient stays; it also reflects our deeply held belief that home is where children thrive best, and the more we can offer our services in that setting the better it will be for all concerned. For this reason, any definition of subacute care that does not include the idea of "alternate settings" fails to meet the needs of not only children but the adult patient as well.

2. "Subacute care is . . . designed for someone who has an *acute illness, injury, or exacerbation of a disease process.*" This part of the definition is limiting, in that it unnecessarily and inefficiently precludes, for example, newborns who have either a genetic or congenital abnormality. Treating such children in the typical acute care setting will not only be costly but may very well deprive them of the educational services they need to remain developmentally on a par with children their age.

3. "Generally, the individual's condition is such that the care *does not depend heavily on high-technology monitoring.*" In fact, as children come to us "quicker and sicker" from, for example, neonatal ICUs, we have a growing population of children who are technology dependent. Recently, for example, "the California Department of Health Services issued regulations and reimbursement rates for pediatric subacute care provided to

technology-dependent Medi-Cal (Medicaid) patients under 21 years of age," as a news story that ran in *The National Report on Subacute Care* pointed out.[5] Among the patients qualifying for the new program are those dependent on some combination of medical technologies, including tracheostomy care, mechanical ventilation, suctioning, room air mist or oxygen, continuous intravenous therapy, peritoneal dialysis, tube feeding, naso-gastro or gastrostomy tube, or parenteral nutrition or other intravenous nutritional support. The story went on to say that, "by providing subacute care to Medi-Cal pediatric patients in skilled nursing facilities (SNFs) rather than in acute care hospitals, the California health department estimates it will save the state and federal governments more than $11 million annually."[6] For these reasons, we believe that any definition of subacute care that does not take into account the technology-dependent patient once again fails to address the needs of a significant pediatric population.

4. "Subacute care requires the services of *an interdisciplinary team.*" As we emphasized repeatedly in our discussion of staffing above, it is not enough to recruit an interdisciplinary team when planning to provide a subacute level of care to children; it is also necessary to recruit a team whose members have the pediatric training and experience to enable them to deliver optimal care to children with a broad range of special health needs. And, just as important, that specialized interdisciplinary team should also include—and make part of the decision-making process—family members.

In summary, we believe that the AHCA/JCAHO definition of subacute care, or any similar definitions, should be modified or expanded to include references to (1) alternate sites, (2) genetic or congenital abnormalities, (3) technology-dependent pediatric patients, and (4) a specialized interdisciplinary team for the care of children. Such a broadening of the prevailing definitions of subacute care will help us to escape the unproductive notion that *pediatric* subacute care is simply a level of care delivered to patients who are not adults.

CONCLUSION

In this chapter, we have not only championed the pediatric perspective in the current subacute care debate, we have also drawn on our experience to set out what we view as a workable and generally replicable pediatric subacute care model. That said, we realize that no one model, however well thought-out, can set the standards for an entire subacute industry, especially one as fluid and diverse as today's. In heavily rural states for instance, a *regional* subacute care model, to which a network of acute care hospitals referred children, might be the best and most cost-effective alternative to a series of expensive-to-run smaller programs. In other, more densely populated areas, it might make sense for providers interested in establishing a freestanding or hospital-affiliated program to limit their program either by the population served or the service offered, or both. Thus, a program might be developed that cared only for full-term infants with certain complications, such as intrauterine infections or congenital abnormalities. And in still other areas, it might make sense for a pediatric program to be started that treated a range of conditions in children of varying ages, much like the St. Mary's/Friedman model we've offered here.

Whatever the case, we believe strongly that more efforts are needed at every level to define what subacute care for children is, to set high standards for its delivery, and ultimately, to develop guidelines for licensure and certification that reflect those standards. When this happens, we will have taken a giant step toward ensuring the best healthcare possible for our children.

Notes

[1] National Association of Children's Hospitals and Related Institutions (NACHRI), synopsis of study conducted by Center for Health Policy Studies, March 1993.

[2] Ibid.

[3] Esther Fein, "As Competition Expands, Nursing Homes Diversify," *New York Times*, April 4, 1994, p. 26.

[4] Unless otherwise indicated, subsequent references will be to "St. Mary's/ Friedman" or to "St. Mary's and Friedman."

[5] "California Issues Regulations on Pediatric Subacute Care," *The National Report on Subacute Care* 2, no. 16, p. 3.

[6] Ibid., p. 4.

Chapter 9

Hospital Perspective on Subacute Care

Marshall W. Kelly
President, Rehab Partners, Inc.

I s the development of subacute services negative or positive from the hospital perspective, and to what degree? It's a question best answered by looking at the state of the marketplace evolution, reimbursement streams, and the subacute options as they impact the hospital.

The healthcare marketplace is undergoing an evolution from fee for service to a globally budgeted, integrated service delivery system. In many environments where fee-for-service reimbursement is still dominant, subacute services may not appear to be attractive options. Where the evolution of the market is strong and capitated systems are the dominant financial paradigm, subacute care is another method for a lower-cost service delivery.

Once the prospective payment system (PPS) was inaugurated by Medicare, the development of subacute services was inevitable. The PPS bases payment on the disease-related grouping of the patient and is linked to acute hospital licensure and increased utilization of outpatient services and specialty services such as rehabilitation and psychiatric services. Referral to a subacute setting also capitates the costs associated with the acute stay of the patient and moves the reimbursement to a cost-based system. But for insured patients, discharge from an acute setting into a subacute setting represents a loss of revenue to the hospital. If the reimbursement system is fee for service or an all-inclusive per diem, then early aggressive discharge means a financial loss. Under a capitated system the financial incentive is to move a patient aggressively through a continuum of care, to save on the total cost of care.

Depending upon the reimbursement environment, the availability of subacute services is either a win/win or win/lose situation between the acute hospital and the subacute site. In capitation situations, which use future payment systems, and in Medicare situations, there is a strong incentive for the development of a subacute reimbursement environment. In situations involving commercially insured patients, uncontrolled indemnity fees are relatively scarce, with some form of managed care being the financial sponsor. MCOs will use case management to actively drive a patient through a system of care. So in the final analysis, if the clinical community controls the referral pattern and sources of payment, then subacute care offers a strong financial incentive.

Many hospitals have excess bed capacity that they could easily convert to subacute services, or they have or own an existing skilled nursing facility or unit. For these hospitals it is desirous to investigate the development of subacute services. Hospitals that do not have a skilled nursing unit or facility or that are in states with a strong barrier to entry in the form of a certificate-of-need process can view subacute services as a threat of a loss of revenue, control, or both. Subacute care from this perspective has negative connotations.

One critical factor is the stage of evolution of subacute services in the marketplace. If subacute services are being developed or exist at a competitive site—either a hospital-based or a freestanding skilled nursing facility, a chronic or long-term hospital, or a hospital within a hospital—in the geographic catchment area, then the hospital planning must acknowledge that the market influence favors the initial providers. In reality those initial providers often maintain a long-term advantage, as they have opportunities to gain the managed care contracts before a competitive situation arises. The freestanding skilled facility will have the advantage of setting the pricing structure for managed care contracts as they often have lower costs associated in their financial structure. In addition, the learning curve for clinicians and managers have given them a lead in the evolutionary stages of the subacute development.

WHICH SITE FOR SUBACUTE SERVICE?

Although there are several options for sites, including long-term chronic hospitals or hospitals within hospitals, most subacute sites will be in either a hospital-based, distinct skilled nursing unit, or a freestanding skilled nursing facility. Which site is appropriate? Which site delivers the desired clinical outcome? Which is the most cost efficient?

The question of whether hospitals should develop subacute services in formally licensed acute beds is one of the essential and central issues. Service delivery being equal, is control over the referral process or cost of the service more important? If it is control of the process, then hospital-owned units will be successful; but if cost structure is paramount, then hospitals will have a hard time competing with the pricing of a freestanding skilled nursing facility. Managed care (service delivery being equal) is primarily concerned with the cost of the service. Medicare does not presently have the mechanisms (except in Medicare at-risk managed care programs) to take advantage of cost savings of market forces.

Currently being debated is the role of Medicare as a payor versus other reimbursement sources. Many legislators at the national level are expressing concern regarding Medicare becoming the highest payor for certain services. In some cost-sensitive markets, like California, Medicare cost-based reimbursement for hospital-based subacute services is significantly higher than freestanding SNF managed care rates.

Legislative initiatives on the horizon could shape the ultimate setting and reimbursement standards for the subacute industry. Possibilities that could have significant impact include a mandate to move Medicare recipients into managed care, limits on the acceptable levels of general and administrative costs in relation to clinical costs, a prospective payment system for subacute services, and the elimination of the three-day admission rule into hospitals. If any or all of these would occur, the lowest-cost structure delivering the desired outcome will have a distinct advantage.

HOSPITAL SUBACUTE PROGRAMS

The following elements can negatively influence the choice of whether to establish a subacute unit:

• Associated cost structure
• Timing of initiative
• Governance
• Experience with regulatory overview
• Experience with revenue streams
• Shorter lengths of stay
• Medical surgical services by another name
• Inappropriate physical plants
• Defensive strategy

As we have stated elsewhere, the cost structure associated with hospital-based units is higher primarily because of the general and administrative overhead. This cost structure is not a significant issue at this time for Medicare, but it is for managed care companies. By the time many hospitals are ready to make the decision to develop subacute services there are alternative sites in existence that have established cost structures and contractual relationships with managed care organizations.

The positives can include:

• Convenience for clinical staff
• Control of referral flow
• Resources available
• Necessity for survival
• Vision and experience of management

Although the list of negatives may be relatively lengthy, the positives outweigh them. Hospital-based programs can gain distinct advantages through convenience, control, and available resources; and necessity for survival may be reason enough to establish one. So even though hospitals might not be proactive about subacute services, often accepting a defensive strategy, they can still maintain a position with inherent advantages. These advantages include resources, both monetary and managerial. By definition, hospitals provide entry to the healthcare continuum through emergency rooms, diagnostic services, and procedural/treatment intervention along the continuum of care. With a long allegiance of clinicians and payors, they are well positioned to be the center of an integrated health services network. In other words, subacute services are theirs to lose. If the hospital determines to move forward, even a modest execution should give them a high probability of success.

The biggest barriers to success are mind-set, a sense of timing, and regulatory pressures. Denial on the part of the hospital administration that subacute units are serious providers of services can create a false sense of complacency. Often the hesitancy is based in protectionism: not wanting to sacrifice an established service line with a higher reimbursement under a medical/surgical licensure than under the subacute licensure. However, by not being proactive hospitals allow the service to be developed by other providers, who then have the advantage of developing contracts with payor sources prior to their creating a competitive service line.

The cost of this success:

- Decreased acute care capacity
- Contradictory financial-success formulas between Medicare and managed care
- Decrease in medical/surgical capacity
- Diluted focus from acute care
- Reduced revenues (although increased profitability)

For hospitals that would enter into the subacute field, the options are to convert completely to chronic long-term care licensure, develop a relationship with a hospital-within-a-hospital company, convert some hospital beds to long-term care licensure, or create a subacute unit in a skilled nursing facility that they own, manage, or lease.

Many hospitals have established skilled nursing units within the hospital walls, or they own or lease skilled nursing facilities. The past reasons for having a skilled facility or unit were primarily to control placement of difficult-to-place patients or to place high-acuity Medicare patients in order to shorten length of stay under the acute hospital licensure. For those facilities that have developed these units for these reasons, the coming of subacute care is a positive trend, as the new level of care legitimizes the concept and will facilitate higher and better payment for the services.

As assessment of the regulatory environment would quickly tell you whether a conversion of acute hospital beds is an immediate option. Some states are eager to convert excess hospital capacity to long-term care licensure. Other states view more long-term care beds as increasing the size of the long-term care Medicaid budget. The best strategy for convincing state officials that this is a reasonable request and will not influence their budget is to present the case that the majority of the patients would be funded by the Medicare program. Another path a hospital can take to enter this market is by purchasing the license of a small, skilled nursing facility and moving the beds into the hospital.

Strategically, subacute services can operate as a component in establishing a tertiary referral pattern in a hub-and-spoke system. Many hospitals have looked to establish affiliations between tertiary and community hospitals from networks or integrated service delivery systems. As an alternative or a substitute, the tertiary hospital can develop a subacute operation by owning, affiliating, joint venturing, or supplying ancillary services with a skilled nursing facility. This is a solution if the tertiary center sees the draw for patients as coming directly from the satellite community and being referred back to the local subacute setting for rehabilitation or recovery.

CRITICAL PLANNING ISSUES

One of the first critical planning decisions is to define the patient populations to be served in the new unit. Probably the easiest division to make is between rehabilitation-focused and medically focused services. The current proportional division between the two service areas is 30 to 40 percent rehabilitative services and 60 to 70 percent medically based services. For mainly political reasons, the decisions in many circumstances have been made too narrowly.

Many programs have taken a focus on the patient population to be served that reflects the internal dynamics of the organization rather than the opportunities or needs of the marketplace. This is generally seen in the favoring of either rehabilitation or medically based programs. If one service has taken on the development responsibility and has a distinctive bias or orientation toward a particular service or services, then the new program will reflect that imbalance. Generally, the integration of rehabilitation and medically based services is difficult, primarily because of the staffing orientation, space utilization, location, physician leadership, open or closed physician staffing, or leadership's focus.

After deciding which patient population to serve, the next important decision to be made is the location and size of the subacute unit. Some of the critical considerations in the location choice are the long-term code requirements for the state, proximity to therapy space or discretionary space that can be renovated into therapy space, and other physical plant considerations.

Another issue to address is how to design the internal organization systems to facilitate the continuum of care that the subacute unit provides in alignment with other levels of care. These basic levels include:

1. Intensive care units
2. Medical/surgical units
3. Subacute units
4. Rehabilitation or psychiatric units (PPS-exempt units)
5. Outpatient services
6. Home healthcare services
7. Skilled nursing units

The key issue is the definition of the units or services and the movement between the service levels. This includes defining both the entry and the exit criteria to the service. Expect that these definitions have some fluidity as the services evolve and mature. As the subacute unit matures, the capacity to service patients earlier will expand and the lengths of stay in the unit will shorten. The trends will affect the entry/exit criteria.

There is an evolution of the function of social work and discharge planning into case management services. Case managers should be monitoring patient flow through the different levels of care. They will work with the appropriate physicians to facilitate their programmatic options, communication with family members, the timing, and the placement. Development of this function can lead to the success of a continuum of care that will benefit patients and meet the organizational goals of the system.

Adapting the current system of case management is one of the critical planning efforts in the inclusion of subacute services in a continuum. Getting the approval of the case managers is essential, and defining the service delivery will be important in decreasing the potential internal competition from other units, predominantly PPS-exempt rehabilitation units and medical/surgical units.

INFORMATION SYSTEMS

Critical information systems involve cost accounting, resource monitoring, and measuring outcome.

One of the more difficult knowledge bases for a hospital to learn is in the area of reimbursement streams. Hospitals understand fee for service, DRGs, Medicaid, and managed care and are starting to learn the capitation financial paradigm. For the most part, they do not have any experience with long-term reimbursement, particularly in the atypical Medicare reimbursement exception process. They will need to access this information through professional consultants or via contracting management. In fact, this is generally the main reason subacute units are contracted out to other companies.

Other than the accounting, billing, and collections functions, the main areas of need in information systems are outcome data and other management information data. Hospitals have on a wide basis instituted total quality improvement initiatives that will work with subacute operations as well as any other level of care.

PHYSICIANS

A hospital's medical staff and referring physicians will have critical impact on the success of the subacute unit. Since it can be argued that physicians can influence or control 85 percent of all referrals in the healthcare industry, to ignore their concerns is to imperil the utilization of the unit. Their issues include reimbursement (levels and revenue streams), convenience, habits, control, and governance.

Physicians will have to be taught how to bill under new systems. Medicare exception guidelines limit billing by the primary physician to three visits a week, with one specialist consultation a day. This does not compare favorably with allowable billing under acute hospital licensure. Some subacute units might not be as convenient as the current medical/surgical facilities.

The issue of whether to have either an open or closed staff can be complicated. For rehabilitative services (approximately 30 to 40 percent of subacute services), having a closed staff (where there is a physician on staff who handles the case) is generally not an issue. Hospital-licensed rehabilitation units generally have a physician with specialized training in a leadership position. In medically based programs there is a greater propensity to have an open medical staff. Referring physicians can follow their patients into the unit. The more specialized services like wound care, pulmonary, oncology, and HIV will more likely have attending physicians for the program.

There are physicians who will be champions for the development of subacute services. These include the surgeons who do not receive additional reimbursement after the one-time surgical fee and are therefore eager to switch the licensure under which the patient is served. Other physicians are interested in developing specialty programs in which they can become medical directors. Physiatrists, pulmonologists, and plastic surgeons are examples of those who develop physician/service relationships.

Of course, as changes occur in reimbursement through disease carveouts and primary physician groups assume global risk capitation, physician relationships and controls are going to change. Primary care physicians or representatives from the groups in the medical coverage of the subacute unit will become politically important.

FINANCIAL ANALYSIS

Most hospitals have the internal capacity to financially analyze the feasibility of whether they would find the subacute service line to their advantage. The main financial benefits to the hospital are in spreading the overhead cost of its general and administration expenses, lowering the costs associated with a PPS, and protecting against the final loss of revenue from a decrease in medical/surgical beds.

Currently, the payment for skilled nursing based services is based upon costs. A licensed skilled nursing unit offers the opportunity for downloading much of the general and administrative cost of the hospital. In many cost centers this can be as much as 25 to 40 percent, a significant amount of the hospital overhead. One of the primary reasons a hospital-based subacute unit has a higher cost structure than a freestanding skilled nursing unit is the inclusion of the high level of general and administrative costs.

For Medicare-funded patients, the PPS system uses a single payment schedule, regardless of costs of lengths of stay associated with the care delivery. Therefore, the hospital has a financial incentive to be as efficient as possible in the service delivery. For many hospitals, inclusion of a subacute unit along a continuum of care not only makes for an easier transition from an acute unit to home, it also provides an opportunity to discharge earlier, thus lowering the cost associated with a particular DRG payment. As we have seen, case management systems and financial incentives reduce the lengths of stay in hospitals, and the inclusion of subacute services offers the possibility of further reductions through faster discharges. For hospitals, the discharge options of subacute services to on-site, wholly owned, or freestanding units give the acute provider a strong financial incentive for placement.

Since the implementation of the prospective payment system, hospitals have used skilled nursing beds to avoid costs. They view the nursing bed as a placement option for patients who require long lengths of stay, an option that is more financially beneficial than a hospital inpatient stay. As subacute services grow, the total patient volume days in medical/surgical beds decreases.

SUBACUTE MANAGED CARE REIMBURSEMENT AND BILLING

Freestanding skilled nursing facilities have established the patterns and cost structure for subacute services that hospitals will have to adopt with managed care companies. Since freestanding facilities do not have the complement of accounting support staff such as the hospitals, they have developed new billing procedures that are simpler than those of the typical hospital.

Freestanding skilled nursing subacute units have developed all-inclusive per diems based upon nursing acuity scales (generally four to six levels). A skilled nursing center does off-site evaluation of the patient's needs and then negotiates an all-inclusive per diem rate according to how those needs fit a profile of acuity levels. This procedure simplifies billing.

The next step in the evolving reimbursement world of subacute care is to move to an all-inclusive per case billing. Managed care favors this approach because it puts a cap on the cost of the care and incentives for more aggressive inpatient lengths of stays than under a negotiated per diem basis. It will take an experienced operation to make this type of prediction of the per case costs and charges. Some cases are more predictable than others, and in one facility you might find a mix of per diem and per case reimbursement.

Finally, payment will be prospective under a capitation schema. The movement in this reimbursement approach is toward outcome measurement and efficiency. This evolution should also parallel the competence of the staff as they gain experience with the service delivery, measurement mind-set, and reimbursement.

The more complicated issue will be the presentation of the number of cases over the cost per case. By the time of assumption of capitation, a facility should have the ability to understand the costs of a service. But the actuarial presentation of the number of cases is of greater importance for the predictive assumption of risk of a population base.

HOSPITAL-BASED SUBACUTE CARE UNDER CAPITATION

Most of today's healthcare providers believe that capitation or prepayment will become an increasingly important and probably the dominant form of payment for healthcare services. An alignment to the capitation reimbursement scenario changes the hospital-based subacute strategy. The goal of this financial alignment is to become the lowest-cost, most efficient provider delivering the best possible outcome to the patient.

Providers will become purchasers of healthcare, forcing them to rethink services and payment for these services. In other words, there is an emphasis on *controlling costs* rather than *enhancing reimbursement*. From a values perspective, in an era of budgetary constraints, it is important not to have excess expense in any area of the service delivery, because another area of the total service delivery will have to make up the difference. Interestingly, in environments where there is maturity regarding capitation, subacute services are a much stronger and visible part of the continuum of care.

Also interesting, when providers operate under a global budget, they become more efficient providers. The financial gaming of any reimbursement system will come to end when it is clear that the total overall financial incentives drive a capitated global budget for a patient population, whether it is a broad-based community care or a specialty disease carve-out. The party assuming risk, whether insurer or provider, or both, will have clarity of the task and its limits.

For a hospital-based subacute unit under a predominantly capitation paradigm, the focus will be the low-cost alternative in inpatient care. The cost structure of the unit will be kept low, the clinical service will assume that the patient is in a relatively stable condition, management overhead will be significantly reduced, administrative decision making will be streamlined, discharging of patient will be facilitated as early as possible, and discretionary capital costs will be limited.

BUILDING A CONTINUUM OF CARE

Under capitation, the development of a streamlined integrated continuum of care will be paramount. For the subacute component of the continuum, with its central force being cost reduction over the current medical/surgical cost structure, definition of its service delivery, realignment of its operating principles from the current practice, and execution of new service design models will be the challenge.

Critical pathways, clinical protocols, and other methods of creating benchmarks, guidelines, and "cookbooks" are in the process of being developed and implemented. Part of the focus will be determining utilization patterns of differing parts of the service delivery. Not only will entry criteria be important, but an increasing emphasis on exit criteria will be stressed.

One critical question will be what percentage of the current subacute patient population could be treated in even lower cost settings like home health care, hospice, and outpatient service settings. Cost containment will both benefit and challenge subacute service sites.

NEW REGULATORY EXPERIENCE

One of the new experiences for hospital executives and clinical personnel will be living under the regulatory experience of long-term care licensure. In many ways, long-term care is regulated much more heavily than the acute hospital situation. The process orientation of oversight is heavier under skilled nursing licensure.

Many states require that a nursing home administrator (NHA) be the licensed operator of any skilled nursing unit, no matter the location. This means that an NHA must be hired, or an administrator in a hospital must become one. This could mean preparation for the licensure test, a possible preceptorship, and other time commitments.

CULTURAL DIFFERENCES BETWEEN HOSPITAL AND LONG-TERM CARE BACKGROUNDS

Even if you are developing subacute services in a hospital setting, you will have to understand the operations and mind-set of a freestanding skilled nursing subacute operation, if only from a competitive viewpoint. There are major cultural differences that come from some of the basic biases of the respective industries.

Long-term care is a relatively predictive business. Census is extremely high, revenues and expenses are fairly predictive. The mind-set for a financially viable long-term care facility is delivering quality services in a cost-effective manner. This requires an accounting focus, particularly on controlling costs. Hospitals on the other hand are willing to spend for the technology, quality personnel, and reputation. Census, expenses, and revenues are less predictive than in long-term care; therefore, the focus is more on utilization since fluctuations are greater. The mind-set for hospitals is a marketing focus; costs are less a concern than developing revenue sources.

Additionally, hospitals have a high level of involvement with physicians. For skilled nursing facilities, physician presence is minimal except for the development of a subacute unit. Nursing staffs have more autonomy in long-term care and have to get reoriented to physician-directed subacute units.

DEVELOPMENT ISSUES

Experience has shown there are several areas that have proven problematic for hospital-based subacute decision makers. These include financial planning, a too narrow or biased focus on the patient populations, the pricing strategy, internal competitiveness with existing medical/surgical units, underestimating the adjustment internally, and a lack of definition of the services along a continuum of care. Through careful preparation and research, hospitals can prevent these from becoming major problems.

As we have outlined, the financial planning for a subacute unit needs to include the impact on the hospital census and patterns. Primarily, the budget projections need to include the net effects on the hospital financial performance. Many institutions are seeing the most dramatic improvement on the hospital side of the financial benefit. This is primarily from the improved financial performance from the costs associated with DRG payments for Medicare patients.

A major strategic issue is with pricing. The focus on process and cost-based reimbursement for Medicare funding puts the emphasis on downloading a high percentage of costs associated with the service. Managed care organizations are driven by a desire for efficiency and outcome. These can be contradictory in nature. Also, Medicare regulations specifically state that it will pay the lower of costs or charges, that is, if charges to an MCO are lower than the cost-based system, Medicare will reimburse the lower rate.

The pricing strategy, therefore, will have to include the expectation of the mix of payor source for patients and the cost structure that a managed care organization would be willing to reimburse. The cost structure of a hospital is significantly higher than that for a freestanding skilled nursing facility. Many managed care organizations will be establishing the pricing levels for subacute services at the level of a freestanding facility. It will be difficult for a hospital organization to compete with this pricing within its physical plant. The differences in cost structure between sites is mainly in managerial overhead, capital costs, cost shifting among services, and payor sources. The similar costs between sites are staffing patterns and supplies, with the freestanding sites in many instances having higher marketing costs.

Establishing demarcation lines between medical/surgical units and subacute units eliminates internal competitive forces. Decisions as to the most appropriate site can be determined by the lengths of stay, clinical appropriateness, reimbursement issues, outcomes, licensure, space, and medical leadership. In many cases there will be a continuum of care between medical/surgical and subacute units; in others, an intensive care unit will refer to the subacute unit.

Another method of identifying the differences and appropriate utilization between services is to clearly establish both the entry criteria and the discharge criteria, which are generally overlooked. This establishes the clinical estimation of the pathway of clinical service delivery. The exit critera of one stage should ideally be the entry criteria of the new stage of the continuum of care.

Other problems associated with a continuum of care are issues like self-interest of the unit. If there is census softness, a unit might be interested in expanding the criteria to maintain census. If a reduction in census means a reduction in staff, these census issues can become contentious. Since we are currently dealing with overcapacity, this situation is almost inevitable. When capitation becomes the dominant mode of payment these criteria take on greater importance. Capitation gives incentives for aggressive utilization along a continuum of care.

HOSPITAL SUBACUTE DEVELOPMENT OPTIONS

There are a limited number of options in developing a subacute unit under the control of the hospital. But the options are complicated depending upon regulatory issues, strategy, capital, and ability to develop a cost-effective structure. They are as follows:

1. Conversion of an existing hospital-based skilled nursing unit into a subacute unit.
2. Development of a subacute unit within the walls of a hospital.
3. Purchase, lease, management, or ancillary provision of a free-standing skilled nursing facility.
4. Purchase of a licensure of a skilled nursing facility; movement of the licensed beds into the hospital building.
5. Utilization of the underutilized section of a PPS distinct unit (either rehabilitation or psychiatric care) for subacute patients.
6. Development or purchase of an acute hospital and conversion of the acute licensure into a long-term care hospital licensure.

A significant percentage of hospitals have the option of developing skilled nursing units within the hospital walls. In states where there is no certificate-of-need process (18), laws are issued with the conversion of hospital overcapacity to skilled nursing beds. In states where there is a certificate-of-need process, this becomes a regulatory barrier. If there is skilled nursing bed availability, then the hospital can apply for the beds. Some states are so eager to reduce hospital overcapacity that they will allow the conversion. Once a hospital has the unit designated as a skilled nursing unit there is no barrier to providing subacute services.

Many hospitals have an existing skilled nursing unit within its walls. In the past, many hospitals made the decision to create a unit because they were having problems placing patients into local facilities. These units were already providing services to a higher level of acuity and staffing than comparative freestanding facilities. Most of these facilities have concentrated their efforts on short-term lengths of stay with a focus on Medicare reimbursement.

Conversion of these units to a subacute unit is a relatively easy process. There is generally a high turnover in beds, allowing for easy bed transition. Staffing can be easily increased to meet subacute staffing patterns. The primary difficulty will be if the unit has been in existence for three years with a routine cost limit already established. This would create a cash flow problem because of the Medicare exception process.

Under the current HCFA regulations, hospitals cannot own a hospital within a hospital. There must be a separate administration and governance. This has generally meant that a hospital will have to contract with an outside company. The benefit to the hospital will come primarily from the early discharge for Medicare patients.

Many hospitals will choose to have their subacute operations in a freestanding facility. This option has the least impact on a hospital from an operational perspective and gives multiple options for programs. Convenience for physician involvement (over an in-hospital unit) could be an issue, depending upon the location of the facility. The usual issues of space, cultural change, cash flow, and training apply.

The facility can either be on or near the hospital campus, depending upon what strategic role the subacute unit is going to play. For a major tertiary hospital, a potential strategy is to use the subacute sites as part of a hub-and-spoke system. Many hospitals are setting up this strategy using local community hospitals. Developing a network of subacute centers in lieu of the hospital, in conjunction with developing groups of primary physician groups, could be a lower-cost or substitutional strategy.

The main financial difference between hospital-based and freestanding situations is the general and administrative download onto the subacute unit in the former. A hospital-based unit has the ability to justify a higher percentage of general and administrative downloading.

If the lease, purchase, or management of a site are not an options, a hospital can provide ancillary services to a facility that some other entity owns or operates. The services can include contract therapy, pharmacy services, and other professional services like accounting or maintenance.

If conversion of acute hospital beds to skilled nursing subacute beds is not allowed, then the options are very limited. One of the last options is to purchase an older, smaller, marginally profitable skilled nursing facility and move the licensed beds into the hospital site. This satisfies the requirements for skilled nursing licensed beds and, from the regulatory perspective, reduces the number of marginally profitable, older facilities.

Hospitals that have PPS distinct units, as opposed to rehabilitation and psychiatric units, have the option to use any underutilized beds for subacute patients. These units must maintain a 75 percent occupancy to meet the TEFRA financial requirements for the specialty PCPs/DRG exempt units.

Lastly, many hospitals have organized themselves into systems or networks of multiple hospital locations. If one of the hospitals, in rationalizing the services available, does not have any viability as an acute hospital, there is the possibility of relicensing it into a long-term care licensure and using the site as your subacute platform. This licensure requires a minimum length of stay of 25 days for at least six months. This can create a significant cash flow issue, which is the major barrier to entry through this delivery site.

POTENTIAL REIMBURSEMENT CHANGES

Recent market-based cost containment forces have decreased or leveled the inflation of healthcare benefit premium costs. At the same time, the government programs have not broken the inflation cycle. This fact has not been lost on regulators or politicians, who are eager to reduce spending or at least inflationary levels.

The reasons for the decrease in healthcare costs, other than the attention being paid to the issue, is primarily the conversion of fee-for-service payment into managed care systems, the increasing competitiveness between managed care plans, and the increased utilization of the purchasing power of healthcare buying cooperatives and other purchasers of benefits.

A key challenge for Medicare cost reduction is to localize a national program to smaller market efficiencies, cost structure, and controls. This is primarily accomplished by use of the Medicare "at risk" managed care programs, which enroll Medicare recipients into managed care organizations. This enrollment to date has been voluntarily filled as a result of increased benefits offered by the HMOs. These benefits include low or no co-payments and coverage of pharmaceutical costs; in return, those who enroll must utilize the organization's physicians and practices.

Another option for Medicare is the development of a prospective system for subacute services, or a cap on general and administrative payments for Medicare exempt units. The prospective payment system for subacute services must take into account the regional variances in the service delivery and must overcome lack of history in the field. Just which specific programs a PPS for subacute services would be limited to would have to be decided upon. Given the lack of history of the types of services, and the lack of knowledge about the eventual breath of services for the subacute setting, this would be problematic.

Given the variances between reimbursement for freestanding facilities and hospital-based programs, it can be expected that there will be some form of upper caps on hospital-based general and administrative download. This will have a negative impact on the cost shifting that a hospital can benefit from under the current system.

PHYSICAL PLANT CONSIDERATIONS

Skilled nursing units are generally between 15 to 40 beds, whereas a freestanding unit is generally at least 100 beds. Hospital-based units will generally be completely focused on subacute services; freestanding facilities with few exceptions will not be. This will make placement of subacute patients, who are not able to be returned home, easier in the nursing home.

Many hospital-based subacute units try to redesign the interior decoration to fit the image of a long-term care facility. Ironically, freestanding skilled nursing facilities try to make their subacute units look like hospital-based units, down to hospital-like signage. The primary considerations on the design of the space are the availability of dedicated, adjacent space for therapy services, office space, and storage space.

Under the atypical cost report scenario, all physical plant development costs are reimbursable. The schedule for amortization of renovation costs should be very aggressive in case the financial paradigm changes and cost become important.

COMMON PROBLEMS TO AVOID

There are some common issues that present themselves to a variety of hospital-based subacute providers. Briefly, some of the problems that have created barriers to success for some subacute providers are thinking too narrowly about the services to be delivered, anticipation over internal resistance to the development of these services, and internal competition among the medical/surgical units, rehabilitation units, and subacute units.

SUCCESS FORMULA

The basic success formula for a subacute unit, as it is for any healthcare service, is to focus on high-quality services for patients. This service delivery should result in rigorous quality improvement with an outcome-oriented research component.

ADDENDUM

Specific Subacute Programs

Rehabilitation-Based Subacute Programs

Stroke rehabilitation program
Orthopedic rehabilitation program
Brain injury rehabilitation program
Pulmonary rehabilitation program
Neuromuscular rehabilitation program
General rehabilitation program

Medically Based Subacute Programs

Pulmonary management
Infusion support
Wound management
Surgical recovery program
AIDS
Nutritional support
Oncology management

Hospice
Renal program
Psycho-geriatric program
Post-ER program

These programs are defined by the following clinical capabilities:

Tracheotomy care/weaning
Intermittent IV therapy
Continuous IV therapy with or without medication
Continuous subcutaneous infusion
Continuous central line or port therapy with or without medication
Chest percussion and postural drainage
Gastrostomy or naso-gastric tube feeding
Enterostomal or fistual care (including patient and family teaching)
Intensive wound care
Post-op care
TPN therapy
Isolation
Coma or semi-coma status with tracheotomy
Respiratory therapy, that is, IPPB

Physical Plant Considerations

Floor layout (central nursing station, acoustics, proximity to therapies)
Call system
Emergency generator
Heating/ventilation, air conditioning
Isolation capabilities
Room size
Storage capacities
Environment (hospital high tech vs. residential)
Medical gas systems
Central vacuum system
Multiple IVs (track or poles)

Electrical demands
Unit location resident/patient mix
Physical, occupational, speech therapy space
Office space

Equipment/Products/Services

Ventilators
Dialysis
Wound care
Pharmaceuticals
Beds
EKG
PCA pumps
Pulse oximetry
Monitors
Laboratory
Ambulance

Chapter 10

Subacute Care
The Integration of Care and the Clash of Cultures

Gary W. Singleton, PhD
*Senior Vice President–Strategic Planning and Development,
Integrated Health Services*

The concept of subacute care began in the mid-1980s in response to consumers' calls for a more cost-efficient, result-oriented healthcare delivery system that would help patients through every step of the recovery process. The subacute approach offers a wide variety of medical, rehabilitative, and therapeutic services, at quality comparable to hospital care, yet at greatly reduced cost.

As the legitimacy of subacute care grows and its benefits are noted, an increasing number of long-term care facilities have opened subacute units to accommodate those patients who need extended skilled medical or rehabilitation attention before discharge to home. Indeed, creating specialized subacute units within already existing long-term care facilities appears to be the most logical answer to a pressing need expressed by patients, payors, and providers.

This chapter discusses the process that occurs when the subacute culture is introduced into a stable, long-term care environment. We will examine the obstacles and conflicts that arise, and contrast the different types of cultures and their values. Next is a discussion of those actions that facilitate a successful integration. Two case studies illustrate the dynamic involved, in its various stages.

THE TRANSFORMATION OF NURSING HOMES

The trend toward subacute care has served to reinvent the typical long-term care center in a far different, more dynamic light—as virtual "mini-hospitals" where medically stable patients *of all ages* and with a variety of needs can receive the equivalent of traditional hospital care, without the associated price. In this setting, the advanced technology of a hospital is combined with the efficient operation of long-term care facility to achieve an optimal balance between quality of care and value.

Numerous benefits are realized by the operators of this type of hybrid facility. These centers enjoy more prestige, a higher profile, greater expertise, increased census and ancillary use, improved revenue, and a wider variety of patients. Positioning themselves as healthcare centers clearly indicates their capacity to support a broad-based continuum of care, and it removes the "nursing home" stigma. By upgrading their public image, these facilities are much more aligned with the public's demand for top-quality, cost-efficient care.

An additional benefit is the expanded opportunity to attract highly skilled healthcare workers. These days, physicians, nurses, and other coveted specialists usually associated with acute care now welcome the opportunity to work in subacute settings. This reflects a recognition of a major—and inevitable—shift in the nature of healthcare delivery in this country.

THE INTEGRATION OF DISTINCT CULTURES

The implementation and long-range success of subacute programs can be difficult and disruptive to a facility's ongoing operation, in that it requires integration of acute care and rehabilitation cultures that usually are very different from the traditional long-term care setting. The resulting culture clash requires careful management to minimize conflict and staff turnover. Many subacute programs have failed or been less than successful because they neglected this aspect of the subacute introduction plan. However, an organization that can successfully overcome natural resistance to change and new concepts, emphasize team collaboration and empowerment, and encourage a commitment to high-quality, cost-effective, discharge-oriented outcomes will find itself at the forefront of the most influential movement in healthcare today.

MAJOR BARRIERS TO MAKING THE SWITCH

The challenges faced in establishing a subacute care culture in a skilled nursing environment are immense and often inevitable, but always surmountable. They can include obtaining necessary clinical and reimbursement expertise; establishing unit support systems; securing adequate capital for the initial investment of construction, equipment, and unit renovation; maintaining cash flow to support the investment until cash flow turns positive; and meeting the needs of a unique long-term care environment in terms of reimbursement and state regulations.

All of these problem areas are relatively objective and can be overcome with adequate financial support and organizational commitment. There is, however, one barrier that is a "soft issue," less quantifiable: the installation of a new culture within a facility, and the mixing of several different cultures, which results in a culture clash and conflict among staff and within the organization as a whole. Major changes in the organization's philosophy of care and staff organization are therefore required. Inattention to this potential conflict can result in poor or ineffective program installation and, perhaps, ultimately contribute to its long-range failure.

THE INHERENT CULTURE CLASH

A subacute culture is built around providing quality care for medically compromised patients, utilizing a rehabilitation philosophy under which patients are in a *less* institutional environment and for whom we seek *more* autonomy and independence than we could for traditional acute patients. Integrating acute care, rehabilitation, and skilled nursing facility cultures results in a clash of competing traditions, expectations, perceptions of staff, and role definitions, as groups of staff members come together from very different orientations, often bringing with them negative perceptions of the other cultures and its members. Part of this conflict results from competition for limited resources among different groups, in a setting and with people traditionally less experienced with conflict resolution.

The success of the unit absolutely depends on resolving this conflict. It is an unavoidable issue that must be addressed by the subacute care team members as they work to build their own culture. By creating a unified, common vision for the facility, different from anything the groups could have envisioned individually, multiple cultures are integrated into a cohesive working entity with its own visions, goals, and traditions.

THE SEPARATE CULTURES INVOLVED

Any organizational culture reflects the common experiences and traditions that develop among a group in order to meet the unique needs of its customers, which in the case of a long-term care facility includes residents and their families, as well as staff members. A subacute culture results from the integration of several different backgrounds, including *acute care, rehabilitation,* and *long-term care* cultures, each of which have evolved to meet a distinct set of circumstances and needs. Successful integration results in a unique environment in which the best aspects of each discipline are combined, while addressing the inherent weaknesses of each. Let's now look at each of the areas of specialization that will ultimately combine to form a subacute culture.

The Acute Care Culture

Typically, staff moving into subacute programs have acute care experience, often in an emergency room setting or in intensive care or critical care units. The staff represent a culture that reflects the needs of patients in those settings, the type of staff required to care for them, and the organizational structure that supports the entire process.

Acute patients experience shorter lengths of stay, and often experience life-threatening episodes. They may also experience a sudden change in medical status requiring rapid response time. Typically within an acute care setting, patients are relatively passive—constantly having something done to them, whether getting medication or undergoing lab tests or surgery. This culture revolves around the need for quick, standardized responses and for patients who are relatively passive to the system, giving up a fair amount of their independence, autonomy, and decision making so as to facilitate diagnosis and intervention.

Nurses and staff working in an emergency room or in critical care tend to be the most highly trained within the healthcare industry; they often work in the high-prestige end of their professions. These individuals are aggressive and capable of making quick decisions in response to the needs of their patients. They have very little tolerance for delay and are accustomed to having physician support readily available.

Their personal rewards are governed by relatively short-term events, as patients either live or die, get better or have surgery, and go home. Feedback time is therefore relatively short, and these staff are oriented toward meeting immediate clinical needs. There is less need for the ability to delay gratification. In an acute care environment, attention is more focused on clinical needs of the patients than on the patient's comfort and concerns, and only peripherally on the family and support systems of the patient.

The organization that evolves from this, the acute care hospital, is typically a heterogeneous environment with multiple professional groups brought together to perform their own particular tasks individually, less as a member of a cohesive team. The team model is more multidisciplinary than interdisciplinary. This culture is also designed to manage large and diverse organizations, high technology, and human resources with greater depths of back-up support than are found in other medical environments.

The acute care environment tends to be more institutional; rules and regulations are based on the need to make immediate decisions and are much less patient- or customer-oriented. It is a culture very much built on the classic medical model. The culture is experienced at resolving conflict among diverse sophisticated professional disciplines and specialty groups that are each competing for limited resources and recognition.

The Rehabilitation Culture

This culture is less driven by the traditional medical model and more by educational and interdisciplinary team models. Patient needs are very different. They have fewer medical complications and are not on the verge of sudden death. The rehabilitation environment focuses on the need to regain physical function following trauma or illness and to relearn skills necessary to promote greater autonomy and independence.

A rehabilitation patient's length of stay is longer, improvement is slower, and feedback for staff is less immediate. However, there is a much more active involvement among staff, patients, and their families. Staff tend to get very involved in a patient's progress, not only professionally, but often on a personal and emotional level as well. Frequently the staff members become community-level advocates for the rights and opportunities of their patients. In the acute care model, on the other hand, staff tend to put up barriers to such closeness because of the possibility of death or failure beyond their control. The poorer the short-term prognosis, the more barriers tend to appear.

Rehabilitation staff members are concerned with patient motivation and education. This culture's motto might be: "We don't just do something to people and they get better; rather, we educate, motivate, and nurture patients." For example, instead of simply pushing them in a wheelchair, the staff members teach patients how to use the wheelchairs and expect them to wheel themselves down the hall. The rehabilitation culture revolves around the interdisciplinary team, which is accustomed to working together and including patients and families in the development of their goals.

From an organizational perspective, the management of a rehabilitation facility and culture reflects the emphasis on a more educational and motivational model of care in which the patient and support system must play a much more active role. The organization must therefore actively encourage and support an environment that provides for greater patient independence and autonomy. This requires fewer restrictions imposed by the institution, which results in less control and standardization of activities. Patients and families are more likely to be included in the interdisciplinary team's goal setting, and likewise, staff members are more likely to be involved in the organization's goal setting and direction.

Conflict resolution is prevalent within the rehabilitation culture but takes a somewhat different form than in the acute care culture. Though conflicts occasionally emerge among professional disciplines when role boundaries become less well defined, more conflict is generated among interdisciplinary teams as they compete for the limited available resources. This is particularly prevalent as specialty programs are introduced, which tend to have more resource allocation as a result of more favorable reimbursement or the demands of more aggressive staff members who are attracted to the more specialized and prestigious programs.

The Long-Term Care Culture

This culture model is distinctly different from acute care or rehabilitation. It is driven not so much by patient acuity as by resident needs and extended lengths of stay. These factors result in a very different kind of culture. Traditionally, the long-term care facility serves a geriatric, end-of-life population, experiencing few sudden changes and having little need for an organizational culture that has to respond quickly to rapid developments. Changes tend to be more slowly paced over a period of time—which means that resources can be allocated with less urgency than typically found in the acute care setting, and decisions are made at a much slower pace.

The long-term care culture is shaped by the needs of residents and the healthcare resources they receive. From a staff perspective, this is a culture characterized by staff who receive their rewards from building strong relationships with their residents and families and from helping to enhance the quality of residents' lives. However, it tends to be a group with somewhat less training and lower on the prestige and pay continuum within the healthcare professions. These staff are accustomed to little resource support and have learned to make do with the limited resources available. Their primary focus is on good physical care and the rights of residents.

This is a much more homogeneous organizational culture than found in an acute care or rehabilitation facility, requiring less conflict resolution in day-to-day operations. The long-term care culture is further defined by stringent state regulations that can result in facility closure if adequate attention is not paid to the healthcare needs and the rights and safety of the residents as defined by these regulations. This culture therefore tends to be characterized by more autocratic management styles.

CULTURE STRENGTHS AND WEAKNESSES

In summarizing these three different cultures, it should be recognized that none of them are inherently "good" or "bad"; rather, each culture has evolved to meet the needs of those who are either being treated, or who are providing the treatment within that environment. Certainly, the strength of the *acute care culture* is the ability to quickly bring adequate resources to bear on life-threatening situations, by staff who are aggressive and do not tolerate delays in patient treatment. It's a culture in which response to the patient's needs is the primary concern, and patient autonomy, independence, and freedom are necessarily restricted to meet those needs. However, from the patient's and family's perspectives, the acute care culture is also more regimented and institutionalized and perhaps not responsive to their social and psychological needs. The acute care model focuses on medical intervention to a relatively passive patient.

Whereas the acute care culture is multidisciplinary in nature, the *rehabilitation culture* excels in working together as an interdisciplinary team with somewhat less commitment to their professional disciplines and more identification with their individual teams. The rehabilitation team's focus is on improving the physical functioning and independence of the patient. Treatment, education, and motivation are provided to patients who are expected to be active participants. However, this culture tends to be not as strong at meeting the needs of medically compromised patients.

With the *long-term care culture,* respect for resident rights and a less institutionalized environment emerge as strong positive aspects. The organization and staff are accustomed to working with minimal resources and are able to establish long-term emotional bonds with residents and their families. However, staff members here again have little experience working with medically compromised patients or with conflict resolution.

Bringing together such diverse groups that have little experience working with each other in a heterogeneous organization creates a climate of major cultural change, in which conflict resolution becomes a primary concern.

FOSTERING A SUBACUTE ENVIRONMENT

The goal of a subacute program is to create an environment that provides high-quality medical or rehabilitative care to medically compromised patients and that utilizes an interdisciplinary team approach to maximize the independence and autonomy of the patient and family in a less institutional environment and at a lower cost.

Having examined the strengths and weaknesses of the acute, rehabilitation, and long-term care disciplines, we next look at what happens when the three cultures are combined to create such an environment.

Problems That Each Group Faces

Introducing such diverse cultures into a stable, existing organization can disrupt the culture, organization, and role expectations of all involved. As new staff from different cultures are introduced, differing knowledge bases, language, prestige, and role expectations come together, resulting in a significant culture clash.

Though it is essential that staff with more acute care experience be utilized in the subacute environment, their initial introduction into a subacute facility tends to be traumatic for them, other staff, and the management team. They are accustomed to relatively rigid role definitions and expectations, multiple physician support, and plentiful and immediate resources for every contingency. Suddenly, they are thrust into an environment that is more nursing and therapy intensive, and less physician intensive. Though they have the guidance and support of the unit's medical staff, they are required to work more autonomously and to utilize their clinical skills and judgment to the fullest extent of their training, experience, and licensure. They are confused by new systems for resource procurement and unsettled that everything they could possibly require is not immediately at hand. Though they are accustomed to working with other disciplines, they are unsure of how to interact with other members of an interdisciplinary team. They are dismayed to learn that their monitoring of, intervention, and interaction with patients is now governed by a different set of regulations, which in many ways is more restrictive than the acute care environment.

All of these changes can be overwhelming. In addition, they come to the subacute setting with the expectation that they will be warmly welcomed and appreciated for their clinical skills and experience. Instead, they may be resented and isolated by the existing staff members who are experiencing significant organizational changes. They may find their clinical skills questioned by staff whose acute care experience is out-of-date. As they then turn to management for direction and support, they may discover confusion with the complexities of new programs, resentment at the unaccustomed aggressiveness and demands of the new staff, and inexperience in coping with the internal conflicts that were nonexistent in a simple environment only a short time before. They have left the prestige of working in an emergency room or critical care setting to come to work in a facility that has not yet developed a new reputation, but rather is perceived to be less prestigious. No wonder that the initial introduction of acute care staff can be so traumatic.

Rehabilitation nurses and therapists often have very similar experiences. They have been accustomed to the availability of the most sophisticated therapy equipment available and now must function without such luxuries. They may have little experience with beginning the therapy process earlier with more medically compromised patients. They are frustrated with the acute and long-term care staff who are less experienced working as an interdisciplinary team, and they are frustrated with the efforts to compare rehabilitation services within the long-term care environment with those they have practiced as part of a comprehensive interdisciplinary rehabilitation program. It is here that the clash of the medical, education, and resident models can become the most prevalent or the successful integration the most rewarding.

The professional lives of the long-term care management and staff are disrupted as well. Their long-standing culture is threatened, and their security is at risk, particularly in high-occupancy facilities. Some staff will need to learn new skills and work with more acutely ill patients or face possible job elimination. Perceiving the new staff as condescending and demanding, they feel unappreciated and undervalued. Long-term care staff see the new programs as receiving all the attention and resources, while they have had to struggle for everything that they have gotten. Seeing the new staff members as uninformed about state regulations and reimbursement requirements, they are fearful of negative consequences for themselves and the facility as sicker patients are admitted to it.

Facility management can be overwhelmed by confusion with the implementation process. They may be apprehensive about the ability of the new staff to care for patients in a nontraditional setting and how any failures will be perceived by the state and their community. They may perceive a loss of control as the subacute implementation proceeds, and they resent the demanding, aggressive nature of the new staff. Just at a time of maximum activity and confusion, they are all called upon to develop a whole new knowledge base of technical, clinical, and reimbursement information. And in the midst of all of this, a previously stable and smoothly operating organization is faced with heretofore unheard-of conflicts among the staff. Their experience has most likely not prepared them for this conflict or how to resolve it, typically leaving all of the staff dissatisfied with the process of conflict resolution or the outcomes.

Creating a Cohesive Team

With such disparate experiences, perceptions, and culturally bound expectations, change does not come easily. It is amazing that it comes at all. Creating a unique and dynamic subacute culture does not simply emerge from the combination of acute care, rehabilitation, and long-term care cultures unless one is willing to think in terms of evolutionary time frames and Darwinian concepts.

Initially what exists in the newly created subacute program are three separate cultures with very little commonality and very rigid boundaries. The cultures do not share a common language. People value the members of their own culture more highly and devalue the members and traditions of the other cultures. They seek comfort levels with their known culture and attempt to avoid others. They rigidly pursue the vision and methods of their culture to the exclusion of those of other cultures. Our challenge is to structure sufficient direction and interaction among the members of these cultures so as to combine their strengths and foster a common language, while reducing the rigid boundaries and forcing interaction until new comfort levels are achieved. Figures 10–1 and 10–2 diagram the expectations and realities of merging separate cultures.

FIGURE 10–1

Subacute Culture Expectation

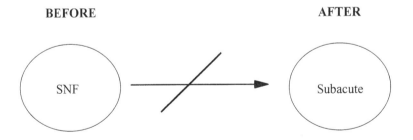

FIGURE 10–2

Subacute Culture Reality

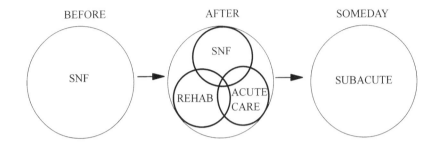

A Cross-Cultural Perspective

We should not be surprised that new cultures automatically and immediately emerge from the combination of several disparate cultures. If we look at what happened in this country as different ethnic groups immigrated here, we quickly come to the realization that a uniquely *American* culture didn't suddenly emerge. Rather, what happened more than 200–300 years ago was that immigrants from varying cultures moved to the New World, lived together in small pockets, continued to speak the same language, and had little interaction with other groups. It took multiple generations for the differences to diminish, for common languages to be spoken, and for these groups to move back and forth among one another before a unique American culture was created. The greater the differences between cultures, the more generations that were required for assimilation—a process that continues to this day.

Facilitating the Process

There are several ways to facilitate cultural assimilation within the subacute environment. One way is to allow the acute care, rehabilitation, and long-term care cultures to gradually merge over generations of staff. In this instance, a generation is defined by turnover of key staff. The goal may be achieved eventually, but not without significant disruption and casualties. This method is inefficient and assures maximum turmoil and frustration. Cultural integration and program success are threatened, and some are terminated as unexplainable failures.

Another way is to develop a common exterior enemy that forces the cultures to work more closely together. In the case of the subacute facility, the common enemy may be the competitive forces in the marketplace, community resistance of alternative care sites, or the corporate office. This may be effective if all members of the team share a common threat and perceive the external enemy as more threatening than internal members of the other cultures. The usefulness of this method is limited by the mobility of staff who have no commitment to the vision and who can easily remove themselves from the external threat by seeking alternative employment. Additionally, the effectiveness of this method before a cohesive group has developed is diminished by the tendency to regress to prior cultural norms once the external threat is removed.

A third way is to actively facilitate and develop a culture in which people can work together. Here, it is essential to anticipate and plan for conflict. It must be viewed as a normal part of the process; everybody coming into the new environment must recognize that conflict will arise, and be committed to working together to overcome it.

Strong management leadership within the facility is essential. Leaders who can keep people focused on the vision, who can deal with diverse populations of staff coping with a totally new environment, and who can bring conflicts out into the open with an eye toward resolution are imperative if the new culture is to develop. Lack of leadership is the single most prevalent reason for the failure of such units and the frustration of staff.

Beyond the management of all of the complexity of associated detail, the facility management must understand, be committed to, and champion the vision of a subacute program within the facility. They must subordinate their *own* anxieties to the needs of the staff for strong leadership. At the same time, strong managers will include the staff in decisions that affect them. They must be able to recognize the strengths and skills of all of the varied staff as well as their weaknesses and subsequent need for training and support. Depending on the abilities of the leaders, the culture clash will be minimized or will result in cultural warfare.

Staff Selection

All of the best management practices in themselves, however, cannot make a subacute culture work—human resources are key to subacute success. Staff selection is very important, and not only for the technical expertise that each member brings. Seeking individuals who have a greater degree of flexibility, who are not rigid in their expectations and their approach to problem solving, and who are willing to persevere and arrive at solutions versus giving in to intolerance and frustration levels is crucial. People who will ride out the storm to achieve common goals can make a subacute team work, despite obstacles. Developing a staff with commitment to the vision is essential—you need team members who are champions for the culture and the programs being developed within their facilities.

Because the subacute culture combines talent of acute care, rehabilitation, and long-term care staff members, the resultant "ideal" staff is essentially responsible for mastering a new specialty—and thus, must be capable of and willing to learn. In addition to understanding the new specialty, cross-training between acute care, rehabilitation, and long-term care staff is critical; this again promotes the necessity of hiring people who are willing not only to learn, but to learn from each other—and for this, of course, communication is essential.

Education and Training

Once the staff with these skills has been selected, attention must be focused on education and training. This is important, first of all, so that a common language is spoken; just because individuals are in the same industry doesn't necessarily mean they communicate in the same way. This commonality needs to be encouraged and strengthened.

The subacute vision must be understood and owned by all, and training plays a critical role here. There needs to be a particular focus on building a coordinated team within the facility, rather than letting the teams develop separately and maintain their unique cultures without any integration. Various staff roles and responsibilities must be clearly defined so that the acute care and rehabilitation staff coming into the facility understand their roles, understand the roles of the long-term care staff, and know what they need to learn from one another.

It is likewise essential that the long-term care staff understand and appreciate the clinical skills that others bring into the facility, and that they understand what they will gain from this process. There's also a need to educate the acute and rehabilitation staff on long-term care regulations and documentation—what can and can't be done within this setting.

Space Design

One method of facilitating the new culture is through space design to force communication among the teams. For example, placing team members in proximity so that they are forced to interact and speak with one another will encourage communication and the development of common goals and expectations. On the other hand, physical separation tends to create pockets of cultures whose members don't walk down the hall and interact with each other. Placing various therapy groups in proximity to each other or in the same space and close to nursing staff facilitates communication. Assigning key staff members in the same office serves as a catalyst in building common goals. These staff members don't always like it at first, but their enthusiasm increases as the interdisciplinary team is established. Later in the process, this is much less of an issue and space can be assigned more liberally.

UNDERSTANDING FAILURE—A CASE STUDY

When the subacute culture fails, it often does so because of an inability to bring the competing cultures together into one single, new and unique entity. How facilities manage this process of culture clash will determine the ultimate success or failure of the subacute program. What follows is the story of two facilities, one that failed and one that succeeded in managing the culture shock and subsequent clash. Both experienced all of the initial difficulties previously discussed, but the outcomes were very different.

At the first facility, the management team did not understand or develop ownership of the subacute vision. They operated a fairly basic long-term care facility for many years, with an administrator experienced only in managing a homogeneous group unaccustomed to questioning any decisions. This management team did not understand the demands of caring for sicker patients within the facility, and so they did not support the subacute concept, let alone serve as champions for it.

In the process, they went through renovation and hired both acute care and rehabilitation staff to work in the facility. New staff members and nurses coming in felt that the management team was not supportive; there was very little communication with the director of nursing or others. In a sense, the management team hoped that it would stumble and fail so they could go back to what they had done prior to the subacute venture.

The acute care staff were somewhat nervous about bringing in their first patients, the long-term care staff being resistant to treating patients any sicker than the residents to whom they were accustomed. The long-term care staff did not assist the acute care staff to make them knowledgeable of regulatory issues or even the admissions process. Indeed, they fully anticipated state survey and reimbursement difficulties and withheld information because of the perceived condescending attitude of the subacute staff.

The subacute staff began to challenge the facility management, which was slow in making decisions or unwilling to provide supportive decisions. The acute care staff progressively became more aggressive and more frustrated, and as they did, the management team became even more resistant.

Finally, the first patients arrived. The acute care staff, although unaware of documentation issues and resident rights issues, began to care for the patients, doing an adequate clinical job; however, there was consistent conflict within the facility. The long-term care staff were angered by the resources that the acute care staff received for renovation, staffing, and other support; at the same time the acute care staff were concerned with the lack of systems, direction, and vision.

The team did not function as an interdependent unit. It was a case of individual staff groups trying to provide care for patients, with nobody bringing it together. The result for this facility was that over a period of time census was low and turnover among the subacute staff was high. When the state officials came in to survey the facility, they found that a number of documentation issues had not been addressed and that the staff was unaware of resident rights issues. The facility received a bad survey, which resulted in staff in one portion of the building saying, "I told you so," and staff in the other side saying, "You never told me or trained me right." Ultimately the program closed down. The lack of leadership, vision, and commitment prevented even the inclusion of alternative cultures, let alone their assimilation.

ANOTHER WAY—ACHIEVING SUCCESS

The other side of that is a story of a facility in which the culture was nurtured. Initially, the facility experienced many of the same circumstances as the one that failed, with one exception. The management team, even though apprehensive about the changes and somewhat resistant to them, was committed to moving forward and learning about the program as they went. When any conflicts arose, the management team sat down, sometimes on a daily basis, and worked through the issues. Team members discussed what subacute care meant for the facility as a whole, what the facility's future would hold, and how the long-term care staff would be affected, not only by renovations of part of the building, but ultimately by additional revenue generated by the new program and by the overall better working conditions throughout the facility.

The administrator of this facility was able to manage the frustration levels and aggressiveness of the new staff and to channel their energies toward the subacute vision. As the divergent staff cultures worked through each of the issues and problem areas that arose, they began to trust each other. The director of nursing learned to trust the clinical expertise of the new acute care nurses and began to develop a comfort level with them; at the same time, even though the DON did not feel she was as knowledgeable or experienced as the new nurses, she gained their trust for her support and willingness to share information. The subacute staff felt supported and trained in the essential issues and how to access resources available within the facility, and there was daily communication among all of the groups.

The facility was configured in a way that facilitated communication, and staff members regularly interacted with one another. Eventually, the subacute nurses and the long-term care nurses were spending much work and personal time together. Some of the long-term care staff members wished to upgrade their skills; appreciating this interest, the subacute staff began to train them, while recognizing that there were things to be learned from the long-term staff as well. Documentation for reimbursement and survey purposes was well done, and ultimately all involved were able to yield a product that represented the best efforts of an interdisciplinary team—a productive and profitable healthcare environment.

FROM THE PATIENT'S POINT OF VIEW

The benefits to patients of care provided in a well-managed, professionally competent subacute unit are numerous—that's the result when all the elements described here come together. This case concerns a patient that I'll call "Joe"—a 70-year-old retired police officer. Joe had been on a ventilator in an intensive care unit at an acute care hospital for 10 months, with chronic obstructive lung disease. He was a terminal patient.

The culture at the hospital was such that staff members focused on the most critically ill patients in their unit. Joe was no longer critically ill—that is, he was not on the verge of sudden death nor were any sudden changes in medical status expected, so the staff spent most of their time with other patients.

The nurses would come in a couple of times a day to see how he was doing. His doctor would come in briefly to say hello. Joe had his meals served to him, but he always had to eat alone. He got only sponge baths during this period. Some of his relatives would visit from 5:00 until 7:00 in the evening, two at a time, but nobody under age 16. This was basically his life experience for those 10 months.

After a time, Joe was told that he would not be able to get off of the ventilator or get up and walk around. There was no reason to pursue these goals. It was expected that he would live for approximately six months and that attention should be focused on just making him comfortable during that time. In time, the hospital's case manager proposed transferring Joe to a local subacute unit that had been achieving outstanding results with a wide range of patients. The interdisciplinary team was committed to the vision of high-quality care with a rehabilitation philosophy at a lower cost. They wanted Joe to be not only comfortable, but also as independent and autonomous as possible. That is, they wanted to maximize his quality of life for the remaining six months he was expected to live. They began to work on weaning him off of the ventilator, with the respiratory therapist and nurses working closely together.

The other goal was get him out of bed to socialize with other patients within the unit, rather than being constantly confined to his bed. They were soon able to wean him off the ventilator for 12 hours a day. They were then able to get him up out of bed and ambulatory, about 300 feet at a time, which meant that he could get up, go down the hall, and take his meals while socializing with other patients.

They got him into the tub room, which had a recumbent tub, and gave him regular rather than sponge baths. Joe's family was able to visit whenever they wished, in groups as large as they wished, including his great-grandchildren, who were very close and important to him and whom he had not seen in the previous 10 months. Even his dog visited him during this time! Because of the facility's ability to make him more independent and autonomous, Joe was even able to go home for short stays on two occasions. He also went to his family reunions, spending time with his family and loved ones.

Although Joe died after approximately six months, the quality of his life during this time was much improved from what it would have been had he remained in the intensive care experience, which certainly reflected the accomplishments of a diverse group of professionals working as a team—not only to meet his medical needs, but to provide him with the opportunity to be as autonomous and independent as possible in a less institutionalized environment, and at a much lower cost. This was the result of the best of three cultures merging into something greater than any could have provided independently of the others.

SUMMARY

Although the challenge of combining multiple healthcare cultures into a coherent, collaborative team is not the most obvious barrier to establishing effective subacute units, it can create the most disruption within the organization. Unless management diligently addresses the issue and creates a completely new culture through emphatic vision, leadership, and communication, such units will be less effective and could fail entirely. When assembled and managed properly, subacute units offer, to patients and staff alike, rewards that are unequaled by any other healthcare setting.

RECOMMENDATIONS

- Understand that as facilities take on subacute capabilities, three distinctly different cultures are at work among employees: acute care, rehabilitation, and long-term care cultures.
- Know that from these three separate mind-sets, a singular culture will ultimately emerge: subacute care.
- Recognize the potential for a culture clash within the facility, and prepare both the existing and new staff for this, in order to minimize the impact of changes.
- Prepare a plan for communicating the unique focus and attributes of the facility to your employees.
- To expedite the planning and implementation process, seek the assistance of those experienced with subacute programs.

Chapter 11

Rehabilitation Service Delivery Issues in a Managed Care Environment

Linda Berezny
Therapy Management Innovations, Inc.

Janet Howells
Vice President, Therapy Management Innovations, Inc.

R ehabilitation services are provided in institutional, industrial, community, and home settings and offer restorative and preventive care. Managed healthcare has become an integral part of rehabilitation services across all practice settings. It has evolved to curtail healthcare expenditures while assuring quality healthcare delivery.

The rehabilitation service delivery issues discussed in this chapter refer to managing the care of patients whose acuity is at a subacute level, who are cared for in a skilled nursing facility, and whose reimbursement comes from a managed care organization.

For providers of rehabilitation, clinical care is the primary focus. As managed care expands its scope, clinicians too are becoming increasingly involved in the financial management of services to patients. This is a new area of accountability for those who have retained a clinical perspective and kept themselves at arm's length from management functions.

This chapter will address some of the measures rehabilitation providers utilize for quality care, as movement toward limiting costs and services emerges. Resource utilization analysis and an effective case management approach are presented as tools for planning and delivering services. A need for financial analysis of care delivery systems is identified and strategies for implementation are offered.

QUALITY

Current Practice Trends

What is quality healthcare? What is the relationship between quality and cost? How can high quality consistently be achieved while meeting cost control constraints? Parameters to define quality have been emerging and they require provider management and accountability in new areas. These include:

Payor limitations. Payors are limiting both the amount and reimbursement of services. One possible result of the inability to define quality objectively is the noticeable limitation by payors for prescribed rehabilitation services. Rehabilitation quality is currently ill-defined. Does quality mean positive outcome for that length of stay, or the ability to maintain the outcome over a period of time? Does quality relate to the cost to achieve the outcome or to patient satisfaction? Or are other factors involved? Providers equate quality with their ability to provide all services they identify as medically necessary. It is usually a "more is better" approach. Philosophical differences among consumers, payors, and providers can be seen in the few high-profile legal decisions that have favored consumers when care has been withheld for "experimental services."

Limited outcome data. Outcome prediction and reporting are important to payors who direct referrals and to providers who must demonstrate quality results for lower costs. Predicting and reporting outcomes with clinical (functional) and cost data is needed for providers to be able to "win" the referral battle. Effectiveness data can help clinicians, payors, and consumers make better decisions about needed care. Using outcomes to assess quality requires standardization in data collection and reporting.

Accounting for variables such as case mix, socioeconomic factors, clinician competency, treatment protocols, and practice setting is needed.

Regulations and standards of care. Regulations such as Ombudsman Budget Reconciliation Act (OBRA) exist for skilled nursing facilities. OBRA does not however, address levels of care. The law requires that services identified as necessary for residents to improve function or to prevent decline must be provided. Reimbursement for these services is not addressed.

Subacute care as a level of care is an industry category rather than a regulatory category at this time. There is no separate category for payment nor does the Health Care Finance Administration (HCFA) intend at this time to create one. Subacute care is provided in institutions that may vary from skilled nursing facilities, long-term care hospitals, and acute rehabilitation hospitals, to acute hospitals with transitional care wings or swing beds.

Many states are considering their own healthcare reform measures. They are proposing legislation to define subacute level of care. Research reveals that 16 states have specific laws or regulations that mainly describe reimbursement rates for the diverse subacute population.

Industry standards for subacute care have been developed by trade associations or providers until just recently.[1] Now, both the Joint Commission on Accreditation of Health Care Organizations (JCAHO) and the Commission on Accreditation of Rehabilitation Facilities (CARF) have finalized definitions or established subacute standards. For facilities and programs seeking subacute accreditation, the survey standards have been being implemented since January 1, 1995, by both accrediting bodies.

Liability. Rehabilitation providers are concerned about quality when services are limited by payors. Providers also fear that they will be held liable for unsuccessful outcomes with patients. Will providers be more vulnerable as they care for more acute patients? Ethical concerns also prevail. According to therapists, there are two levels of care in place. One level, the traditional one, allows medically necessary skilled services. The services are initially determined by the provider and retrospectively determined by the payor. Historically, payment has been assured. The other level of care appears to limit services in amount and duration to contain costs. Providers of care find themselves struggling during this transition from fee-for-service and managed care reimbursement. The struggle occurs as attempts are made to define parameters of quality.

Future Issues

Limited services authorization. Limitations on services will become more widespread, and therapists will need to become knowledgeable and creative in managing both clinically and financially to provide the most efficient, highest-quality care. Knowing the costs of care in the traditional delivery system and utilizing lower-cost alternatives will be necessary for all providers. They will need to learn skills to manage the limitations of reimbursement.

Quality-based outcome data. Providers must be able to anticipate outcomes critically. Currently, providers establish long-term and short-term goals that encompass the full rehabilitation spectrum of care. In the future, as care is managed from the start, this continuum of care will be provided in a variety of settings.

Payors perceive that quality healthcare consists of medically necessary services that result in a cure, a significant measured improvement in the patient's condition, such as alleviation of pain, or other desired outcomes. Rehabilitation outcomes will need to be oriented to functional improvement and not necessarily a return to normal function. Rehabilitation providers will need to measure and analyze outcomes to help choose the most effective treatments and contain costs.

Payors will no longer accept that rehabilitation services are specialized and that no two patients are alike. Long-term studies of statistically significant numbers of patients are needed so that risk-to-benefit ratios can be determined. Co-morbidities (risks) and restored or improved functions (benefits) must be examined. Then the risk benefit and cost benefit can be compared and realistic practice guidelines developed.

Value and cost to the payor. Cost/value ratio will be measured by improvement of the patient, and payor and family satisfaction by the services and outcomes. Improvement of the patient related to the cost of the care will be analyzed. Solid data consisting of charges and length of stay are needed. Cost per unit of improvement is a quantifiable measure of resources utilized. Quality will be measured by the following outcomes: functional improvement, decreased complications, fewer admissions to acute hospitals, short-term stays, and postrehabilitation healthcare needs. Outcomes will contribute to the payors' evaluation of provider performance, another of the new measures of quality.

Provider profiles. Profiles of providers will be established to determine economy and efficacy of service delivery. Providers will need to meet the criteria for cost-effective, outcome-focused, high-quality service delivery. Providers whose service delivery practices can successfully withstand scrutiny will be competitive in their treatment protocols, their costs, diagnoses treated, quality of services, utilization compliance, outcomes, and comparisons with other like entities. More sophisticated data collection will be necessary to accurately compare provider outcomes with those that are cost-based, such as treatment efficacy of selected protocols.

Regulations and standards of care. Federal and state regulatory agencies can be expected to devise more regulations as more state medical aid programs and more payors define subacute care by developing tiered levels of care and tiered reimbursement, based on acuity levels.

As previously mentioned, the JCAHO definition, standards, and protocols for subacute care and CARF standards for subacute rehabilitation care are complete and have been distributed. (See Figure 11–1.)

Liability. Liability considerations will continue for providers. Coverage in written contracts must not be so limited that services authorized for treatment are insufficient to meet clinical standards of care. Preauthorization requirements might potentially expose the facility to risk regarding negligence or abandonment of patients in the event of nonpayment. Payors and providers will need to negotiate and assure themselves and their patients that appropriate, medically necessary, quality services will be provided to avoid liability in the future.

FIGURE 11–1

CARF's Comprehensive Inpatient Categories 1 through 3

Category	Category 1: Acute	Category 2: Subacute	Category 3: Subacute
Location	Hospital	Hospital; hospital-based SNF; SFF	Hospital; hospital-based SNF; SNF
Medical needs	Risk for medical instability is high	Risk for medical instability is variable	Risk for medical instability is low
Rehab physician needs	Across all categories, regular, direct, individual contact determined by medical and rehabilitation needs		
Rehab nursing needs	Multiple or complex rehab nursing needs, potential for high medical acuity skilled nursing	Multiple or complex rehab nursing needs, potential for high medical acuity skilled nursing	Routine rehab nursing needs, low potential for high medical acuity skilled nursing
PT, OT, speech, SS, psych, TR	Should receive, determined by need, minimum three hours	Should receive, determined by need, minimum one to three hours	Should receive, determined by need, minimum one to three hours
Availability of core team	Five days a week minimum	Five days a week minimum	Five days a week minimum
Outcomes expected	Progress to another level or community with support as needed	Progress to another level or community with support as needed	Community with support as needed
Education/ training of patient/family	Ongoing	Ongoing	Ongoing
Examples of patients, not limited to those listed	CVA, SCI, TBI, neurological dxs, multiple trauma, etc.	CVA, multiple trauma, TBI, neuromuscular diseases, etc.	Uncomplicated total hip replacements, amputations, uncomplicated multiple trauma, etc.

Reprinted with permission.

Case management. Case management will be the process for systematic patient care delivery. It focuses on the achievement of outcomes within an identified time frame and with appropriate use of resources. It encompasses an entire episode of illness across all settings in which the client receives care. An individually customized interdisciplinary or transdisciplinary care plan is developed around the needs of the client and is revised on an ongoing basis as the needs of the client change. All team members are accountable for the outcomes by monitoring quality, use of resources, and length of stay. Ultimately, the case management process allows for the achievement of quality care and cost savings. It also allows tracking of variances that might require immediate care plan changes or future critical pathway changes, which could ultimately result in changes in clinical practice and standards of care. The process is dynamic and will contribute to shaping the future delivery of rehabilitation services.

Strategies

Facilities can use a variety of strategies to improve the quality of care in the future while managing with fewer resources. These strategies address the following issues.

Limited reimbursement issues. If clinicians are to be accountable for the financial component of the delivery of rehabilitation services, they must have information about the contents of contracts negotiated with all payors of rehabilitation services. They must know the specifics of each contract in detail, regarding rehabilitation services authorized or restricted. The amount, frequency, and duration of treatments, equipment and supplies covered, limitations to providing services, utilization and reauthorization requirements, and documentation requirements for medical record keeping and billing needs must be known to the providers. This knowledge will impact how providers design the system of care for each patient. (Delivery systems will be addressed later in this chapter.)

Contract information can be made available to the rehabilitation staff in synopsis form, or the entire contract can be provided for reference purposes. Ideally, this will occur prior to the admission of patients so that input to the admission decision will be from all providers of care, and reflect the ability to provide essential care for the patient.

Cost- and quality-based outcomes. Quality measures will be built on outcomes and demonstrated value. Each provider must be able to evaluate their delivery system and refine and enhance it to meet regulatory and payment criteria. Mechanisms need to be developed to monitor and report data that can best demonstrate value through outcomes. These may include daily patient specific charges, charges by diagnosis, or length of stay. The cost per unit of improvement is a quantifiable measure of resources utilized. A quantifiable tool such as the Functional Independence Measure (FIM)[2] can provide patient information since it describes a patient's functional progress numerically. There are many variations of functional measurement tools available from outcome data management and consulting companies.

Monitoring of services delivered versus services negotiated needs to be ongoing. Costs, effects of treatment, and time frames can be monitored and reported to the payor. A case manager who is the single point of accountability for the resident's outcomes should be responsible for this reporting and needs the input of all providers of care.

Regulatory and liability issues. Skilled nursing facilities that provide a subacute level of care in the post-acute continuum of care will continue to be required to comply with OBRA. Expert legal counsel should review contracts for subacute care patients to ensure that the services authorized for treatment are sufficient to meet clinical standards of care and to minimize risk for the facility. Contract language should avoid shifting all liability to the providers of service. Pre-authorization requirements must also not expose the facility to risk. Contracts need to provide for shared legal and financial risk between the institution or provider and the payor. This is particularly true when reimbursement is not cost-based. The following example serves to demonstrate a remedy for the above concerns.

A neurologically impaired patient with severe abnormal muscle tone is at risk for developing contractures that will be painful, will impair personal hygiene, and place him at risk for pressure ulcers. There is a predictable need for skilled intervention by an occupational therapist, at least on a quarterly basis, for splint fabrication and modification. There is also a need to establish a positioning program and to instruct nursing in contracture management. Since skilled intervention can be anticipated at an undetermined frequency, negotiations for intermittent, skilled coverage should be reflected in the contract at the time of admission. This will assure that the patient receives the necessary essential services, that the facility is in compliance with OBRA, and that there is reimbursement for the skilled level of care, which will ultimately prevent serious and costly complications.

The payor will likely impose some reasonable limits regarding medical necessity and skilled intervention required, as well as payment limits for the services that will contain costs, but should not place the facility totally at financial risk for the care.

Case management. This important function can be utilized to determine patient needs, the best service delivery system to meet those needs, and the most cost-effective way to provide the care. Persons outside of the care setting will be managing care, such as payor-based or contracted case managers. Patients and families will be involved in understanding the care proposed, the setting for the care, and the reasons for both. Extending teamwork beyond the treatment setting can invite necessary partnerships and alliances with referral sources, families, and payors to achieve the above common goals.

RESOURCE UTILIZATION

With the move to cost containment, effective utilization of limited resources in providing rehabilitation services is imperative. Fewer overall healthcare dollars means servicing fewer patients or changing the delivery systems to reduce the cost of services to each patient. This incorporates appropriate use of human resources, technology, and service delivery (e.g., six to seven treatment days per week versus the traditional five days per week).

MANAGEMENT OF HUMAN RESOURCES

With almost all of the direct costs of rehabilitation services in skilled nursing facilities spent in the area of manpower, human resource utilization and practices are critical focus areas.

Past and Current Practices

Historically, skilled nursing facilities had limited capabilities in delivering rehabilitation services. Most facilities contracted for therapy services with individual therapists or local hospitals. Rehabilitation services were delivered when physician orders were received, whereupon the therapist would respond to that patient's needs. Rarely was there more than one therapist in the facility to foster an interdisciplinary approach. Rehabilitation was not viewed as a profitable area, and contracted therapists were discouraged from spending time in the facility beyond providing the physician-ordered services. Most patients were admitted with the goal of long-term placement, and discharge planning was infrequent.

With the implementation of the Medicare prospective payment system in acute care hospitals, patients were discharged more quickly to home or to a transitional environment such as the skilled nursing facility for recovery. Beginning in the 1980s, contract therapy service organizations and some facilities developed a more dedicated rehabilitation approach to meet the needs of the long-term care industry. A commitment to participate with the nursing staff in identifying and meeting the rehabilitation needs of all residents is now present. Many facilities have moved to contracting all rehabilitation services from a single therapy vendor company, resulting in an improved rehabilitation presence in the facility and the beginning of an interdisciplinary approach.

With the development of a true interdisciplinary rehabilitation model in skilled nursing facilities, and the competitive positioning of many facilities in the subacute arena, has come the opportunity for direct employment of therapy staff. Hiring an in-house rehabilitation staff has also enabled the development of a cohesive rehabilitation approach. Financially, contract services charge on a fee-for-service basis for occupational and speech/language pathology services, and the salary equivalency method is used for physical therapy. The fee-for-service model encourages increased utilization of services and limits the financial risks to the facility for dedicated staffing costs. Facilities recognize the financial value of rehabilitation services in attracting more private-pay patients, allowing quicker patient turnover and shifting costs of operations to Medicare reimbursement. The practice of discharging patients from the skilled nursing facility to lesser levels of care is occurring.

Future Trends

Rehabilitation professionals now consider the skilled nursing facility as a potential site for employment. In addition, managed care contracts on a per diem or case rate basis have forced facilities to critically evaluate and control their ancillary costs, of which rehabilitation is significant. This will be discussed further in the care management and financial analysis areas.

The future human resource issues in a managed care environment include the following:

1. Staffing costs as related to each unit of rehabilitation services. These must be monitored and decreased to enhance profitability. Inherent in this issue are the following points:
    *   Determination of appropriate productivity levels, for example, for treatment hours per day, according to therapy service or classification of personnel. A physical therapist may be expected to deliver 4 hours of treatment in an 8-hour day (50 percent productivity); whereas a physical therapist assistant may be expected to deliver 6 hours per 8-hour day (75 percent productivity). The physical therapist may have a lower productivity requirement due to involvement in admission decisions, care planning, and case management processes.
    *   Identification and utilization of an appropriate mix of staffing levels within a therapy discipline with consideration of limitations based upon state therapy practice acts.
    *   A change in financial incentives for contract service vendors from increased utilization to risk sharing and outcome-based criteria.
2. Recruitment and retention of rehabilitation staff in a limited supply and competitive market.
3. Establishment of regional and national networks among contract rehabilitation vendors.

Strategies

The following approaches should be considered in dealing with the above mentioned issues:

1. Risk sharing with the therapy contract vendor. If the facility does not hire its own staff but contracts for therapy services, the development of an alternate fee structure for services should tie the risk of overutilization to the contractor's payment. The monitoring of clinical outcomes and quality-of-care indicators should be included in this arrangement. When considering the impact of lowering the contractor's fee for managed care patients, it must be understood that charges must be equally imposed on all patients as per Medicare requirements.

2. Hire an in-house rehabilitation staff. Developing a recruitment plan with staffing levels, job descriptions, and recruitment activities is necessary. Consideration should be given to the development of a competitive wage and benefit package. Awarding facility scholarships to current employees and/or students for professional training with a commitment to facility employment upon graduation is a long-term strategy for recruitment. The current therapy vendor should be given ample prior notification of the intention to go in-house, and there should be sufficient transition time to prevent interruptions in service delivery, which may produce negative patient outcomes.

   Recruitment and retention strategies for rehabilitation staff must focus on factors that contribute to job satisfaction, such as work schedules, patient population, and autonomy of practice.[3]

3. Develop service delivery guidelines for all levels of therapy personnel. The appropriate utilization of support staff can indeed reduce the costs of delivering rehabilitation services. Policies and standards from the professional associations, the American Physical Therapy Association, the American Occupational Therapy Association, and the American Speech-Language-Hearing Association are beneficial. In addition, obtain each the state practice acts that apply to each therapy, which generally define the scope of services and supervision requirements for all levels of rehabilitation staff.

4. Decrease organizational complexity. By structuring all the therapy services within one department and combining many of the personnel and administrative functions in a rehabilitation director's position, duplicate efforts are eliminated. This model may also help promote improved patient care through the enhancement of team communication and coordination of treatment strategies.

5. Develop and monitor productivity standards. Industry standards for rehabilitation services vary by setting. Subacute facilities have not published their productivity definitions or experience. Currently, 75–80 percent of the total clinician's time is spent delivering billable services. To establish fair guidelines that are acceptable to staff, the facility's managers should collect and analyze data from time studies. "Time wasters" in the system, such as, waiting for patients, should be identified by the rehabilitation staff, and an active quality improvement process should be developed to eliminate them.

6. Simplify documentation systems. Significant clinician time is spent in documenting patient care delivered and information required by regulatory and reimbursement agencies. When evaluating documentation systems, allow flexibility to meet multiple users' needs. Consult with fiscal intermediaries and managed care organizations to make forms "user friendly." Investigate the computerization of documentation so critical data entered can be used for multiple purposes. If computerization is not feasible, consider checklists or critical pathways that may allow documentation by exception. Simplification of data collection will assist in productivity. However, make certain that the impact of changing forms and systems is studied from all documentation aspects: medical, legal, and reimbursement.

TECHNOLOGY

Consumers and clinicians alike are infatuated with the latest medical technology available.

Current Practices

In a fee-for-service reimbursement model, new technology is favorably viewed through the generation of additional revenues by delivering a new service. Return on investment projections accompany capital expenditure requests attempting to justify the outlay of monies. The latest technology is often promoted by facilities when differentiating services through marketing techniques such as open houses and colorful, glossy brochures.

Though "high tech" may influence the consumer to select a facility, it is ultimately "high touch" that leads to customer satisfaction.

Future Trends

New equipment will capture a significant portion of valuable resource dollars allocated for rehabilitation services. Clinical managers will need to make critical decisions about where dollars are best spent.

The following issues relative to the role of technology on rehabilitation services in the future must be addressed:

1. Clinicians' belief that they must have the latest technology to compete.
2. Consumer insistence on high-tech services.
3. Third-party reimbursement coverage limitations on new technology, especially equipment with limited clinical efficacy studies.

Strategies

Options for addressing the above-mentioned issues include:

1. Clinicians must know the efficacy of new technology. Clinical research studies must be critically reviewed for reliability, validity, and generalizability. Therapists need to query the equipment manufacturers about studies published in professional journals investigating the clinical effects of their new technology. Manufacturers may financially support clinical studies to assist in demonstrating efficacy of their equipment.
2. Dialogue with reimbursers must occur to investigate insurance coverage for new types of treatment. Third-party payor resistance to reimbursement of treatment using new technology may be countered with strong clinical research studies. In addition, it is important to know the FDA labeling for new equipment use, as this may be used to establish coverage limits by insurance carriers.
3. Justification for equipment expenditures needs to focus on how the technology will save service delivery costs through the

reduction of length of stays and/or improvement of patient outcomes. The generation of new revenues through new equipment is a vision of the past. With managed care reimbursement, financial rationale will focus on decreasing expenditures for all resources.

4. Versatility of equipment will help to justify capital expenditures. For example, an electrical stimulation unit that delivers more than one mode of electrical current may be more expensive than a single-mode unit but ultimately more cost effective than purchasing multiple devices, each dedicated to one form of current.

CARE MANAGEMENT

Figure 11–2 compares and contrasts the traditional service delivery system to the care management system.

FIGURE 11–2

Service Delivery Comparisons

Traditional Services	*Care Management*
1. Begins with admission and inquiry process	Begins prior to admission with clinical on-site screening
2. Individual discipline care planning on a regular basis or schedule	Case manager and transdisciplinary team determine initial care plan intervention; communication and monitoring of variances in relation to care plan are ongoing by the interdisciplinary team
3. Reimbursement is based on medically necessary services without specific time limits per case	Reimbursement is negotiated case by case, and time limited per case
4. Accountability for clinical and financial outcomes is retrospective	Accountability for clinical and financial outcomes is determined prior to start of care
5. Service delivery is multi-disciplinary in focus	Service delivery is transdisciplinary in focus
6. Quality assurance focus: Variances are identified and analyzed retrospectively; corrective action addresses future interventions	Quality improvement focus: Variances are identified, analyzed concurrently, and corrective action is taken to eliminate them on an ongoing basis

FIGURE 11–2 *(concluded)*

Traditional Services	Care Management
7. Outcomes are a return to prior function or to highest attainable functional level	Outcomes are functional for discharge to next level of care
8. Fee is billed for individual therapy service	Negotiated per diem rate or capitated rate is established to include all services
9. Traditional service delivery system typically involves each discipline treating each resident 1–2 hours/day	Service delivery is redesigned per resident need and may include group therapy, co-evals, co-treatments, and so forth
10. Denial of service is determined retroactively regarding length of stay	Length of stay must be renegotiated over time
11. Discharge planning/goals process begins just prior to anticipated institution discharge	Discharge planning is based on outcome achievement and determined at the time of assessment

Rehabilitation service delivery is experiencing changes for many of the same reasons that other healthcare areas are. This has become most apparent as reimbursement changes have occurred. It began with employers inquiring about alternatives to decrease the cost of employee health coverage.

Rehabilitation services were not directly affected by early changes. However, in a relatively short time, consideration has been given to altering the rehabilitation services delivery system primarily through reimbursement limitations.

Current Practices

Admission. In the traditional method for rehabilitation services, patients are admitted on physician referral. Patients are then screened or evaluated by the appropriate healthcare givers to determine what discipline-specific needs each has, also according to physician referral. The delivery system is physician-directed. The approach may be fragmented, as each discipline, independent of one another and of other department staff, assesses each patient and develops a plan of care for him or her.

Goal setting and care plan development. Discipline-specific goals are established with or without patient input. In a well-coordinated setting, the various care providers meet on a regular schedule and report on the patient's involvement in their individual therapy sessions and determine when they anticipate discharge from each specific therapy. It is a fairly autonomous process requiring minimal input from other team members or the patient. There are no incentives to limit the services that are needed by the patient. Needed services are identified and provided in the amount judged to be appropriate by each individual clinician. If equipment is needed, it is ordered for the patient. The payor is traditionally billed for the services provided with the expectation and realization of full payment for these services.

There is minimal standardization of treatment protocols or therapeutic equipment used, so practitioners are free to utilize what they know from experience, and to use newly acquired knowledge or skill learned from continuing education courses. Integration of care plans is not essential. The traditional return on investment calculation is utilized for department budgeting of new equipment or for continuing education. This results in a charge-driven system. There appears to be little or no accountability imposed on the providers of care, and therefore no incentive to change the system to deliver care.

Future Trends

Evolution of the transdisciplinary team. The key to future healthcare delivery will be in how teams evolve to provide and manage each case. Figure 11–3 defines the evolution from unidisciplinary to transdisciplinary teams.

Unidisciplinary intervention has become self-limited, and professionals now recognize the support needed by other caregiver team members in order to achieve total quality. Competency in one's own discipline, as the unidisciplinary role is defined, is not enough. The step into a multidisciplinary role shows an awareness of others' important contributions to ensuring comprehensive service delivery.

Jointly planning care as a team is the next evolutionary phase, the interdisciplinary team. Responsibility for care remains discipline-specific. In the final evolution—the transdisciplinary model—traditional discipline boundaries are crossed in favor of efficiently and effectively providing patient care.

FIGURE 11–3

Evolution of a Transdisciplinary Role in the Intervention Process

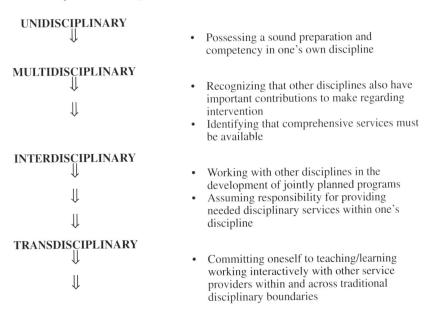

UNIDISCIPLINARY

- Possessing a sound preparation and competency in one's own discipline

MULTIDISCIPLINARY

- Recognizing that other disciplines also have important contributions to make regarding intervention
- Identifying that comprehensive services must be available

INTERDISCIPLINARY

- Working with other disciplines in the development of jointly planned programs
- Assuming responsibility for providing needed disciplinary services within one's discipline

TRANSDISCIPLINARY

- Committing oneself to teaching/learning working interactively with other service providers within and across traditional disciplinary boundaries

Pre-admission planning. In care management, the process of *pre-admission* begins with an inquiry and a clinical on-site visit for screening of the patient in the acute setting. A representative of the transdisciplinary team, typically a registered nurse with acute care experience or rehabilitation nursing expertise, is the usual on-site evaluator. Rehabilitation staff are also involved in the pre-admission screening, depending on the aspects of care needed by the patient. There may be a case manager involved who is from the facility or from a managed care organization, another payor organization, or an independent consultant. The transdisciplinary team will determine the initial care plan. In the care management model, from pre-admission to post-discharge, the service will be patient focused and the service delivery will be transdisciplinary.

Predicting outcomes. Predetermined functional outcomes will direct the transdisciplinary approaches to care. Today's opinion-based practice guidelines will either become validated by research or more effective treatment protocols will emerge. Deviations from the predicted outcomes will be continuously monitored and the treatment approach concurrently modified. Outcome monitoring will be necessary to document these protocols and cost of care. The outcomes achieved will need to justify dollars spent by the payor.

Reimbursement. Reimbursement may be negotiated on a case-by-case basis and be time or services limited. Another option, the case rate agreement, requires that the facility accepting the patient assumes financial risk for prenegotiated areas of needed care. Capitation is a reimbursement method that provides prepayment for services anticipated for a specific population. With these reimbursement scenarios possible, the clinical and financial outcomes will be determined prior to the start of care.

Expanding knowledge and thinking. A significant task ahead is that of training staff in this new way of thinking. For subacute programs in long-term care settings, the larger task is that of helping staff to recognize opportunities for patients who have opted for benefit plans that are different from the traditional ones with full service agreements. It is very difficult for therapists to realize that services that they were once able to offer to all patients, based on their clinical decisions and without financial considerations, will now be potentially more limited for some patients. New knowledge is needed for financial forecasting and tracking, outcome prediction and monitoring, and redesigning of service delivery. At first, trainers will not always be able to successfully answer questions. In fact, new questions will arise. Trainers will continue to be challenged and may feel like this anonymous source: "In some ways I feel we are as confused as ever, but I believe we are confused on a higher level and about more important things."

Strategies

The following strategies may be employed to help cope with and successfully deliver rehabilitation services in the managed care reimbursement arena:

Pre-admission activities/care plan development. Rehabilitation providers must be involved from the time of an inquiry regarding potential admission so that input into the total management of each patient admitted can be considered. Mutual decision making is needed about who will perform on-site preadmission screening. Patients' rehabilitation needs and the ability to meet these needs must be determined prior to admission. Clinical treatment and equipment requirements can also be discussed at this time. The move toward a transdisciplinary approach needs to emerge. In the care management model, discharge planning is begun prior to admission.

To establish the care plan for a potential admission, the treatments that the patient needs must be identified initially without regard to which discipline will provide them. Time frames for each treatment must also be determined. Then, the respective caregivers can be identified. The individual treatment procedures should be performed by persons who are trained and who can perform them safely and effectively. The lower-cost provider that can accomplish the above is the likely and reasonable choice.

Functional outcomes. Outcomes should be developed by the team for discharge to the next level of care. This may not be achievement of total independence and discharge to home, but may be a discharge from a skilled nursing facility to an acute rehabilitation setting, outpatient services, or home healthcare. Discharge outcomes will direct the care plan development. It will require communication and coordination efforts by each member of the transdisciplinary team.

Cost determination. Delineating which treatment procedures will be performed, amount of time for each one, and which staff member will provide the treatment will assist the staff to calculate the cost of care for a potential referral. Other financial information is needed by the staff to accurately calculate the per diem costs of care. Hourly wage and labor dollars for each category of staff is needed so that the cost of each treatment for a given period of time can be determined. Having this information allows the cost of each rehabilitation treatment to be calculated. This does not include the use of any equipment or supplies that may be a cost to the facility, nor does it include an efficiency calculation.

A decision regarding admission cannot effectively be made without cost predictions. Changes in staffing, the care plan, or the patient's condition will likely result in changes in the cost of care, so recalculations will be necessary when this occurs. Clinicians will need to (1) critically analyze functional progress in relation to treatment approaches, (2) consider alternative treatments, and (3) recalculate costs as needed.

Using the above factors to calculate costs prior to admission is necessary to remaining financially viable. See Figure 11–4 for a sample of a per diem worksheet (cost-calculation tool).

FIGURE 11–4

Per Diem Worksheet

Patient Name _____   Facility _____

Date _____   Primary Payor _____
                                                                    Secondary Payor _____
Diagnosis _____   Payment Limits (policy) _____

Referral Source _____   Tentative Discharge Date from Hospital _____
                                                                    Anticipate Length of Stay _____

THERAPIES	NEGOTIATED UNITS	RECOMMENDED UNITS AFTER SCREENING		COST
PT	_____	_____ @ _____	/unit Sub–total	_____
OT	_____	_____ @ _____	/unit Sub–total	_____
SLP	_____	_____ @ _____	/unit Sub–total	_____
Respiratory Therapy	_____	_____ @ _____	/unit Sub–total	_____
Wound Care	_____	_____ @ _____	/unit Sub–total	_____
Others (specialty programs)	_____	_____ @ _____	/unit Sub–total	_____
_____	_____	_____ @ _____	/unit Sub–total	_____
_____	_____	_____ @ _____	/unit Sub–total	_____

		1.	TOTAL	_____

SUPPLIES / EQUIPMENT	COST
Respiratory	_____
Wound Care	_____
DME	_____
Orthotics/prosthetics	_____
Nutrition	_____
Pharmaceutical	_____
Lab	_____
Radiology	_____
Other	_____
_____	_____
_____	_____

FACILITY STAY	COST
Daily room and board	_____
Additional nursing hours	_____
3. TOTAL	_____

2. TOTAL _____

TOTAL COSTS	
1. Ancillary services	_____
2. Supplies/Equipment	_____
3. Facility stay	
4. Total Stay	_____
(per diem)	

SUMMARY	
Proposed Rate	_____
Negotiated Rate	_____
Margin ($)	_____
Percent Margin	_____

Post-admission activities. Monitoring costs on a regular basis continues post-admission to assure that the cost initially determined is not being overrun. To assist the manager in this function each department that is accountable for their costs should have a tracking tool.

To assist in controlling the costs of rehabilitation, therapists will need to consider alternative ways to deliver services. Some examples of alternative service delivery methods are described below.

1. *Group therapy.* One variation for rehabilitation service delivery is providing group therapy sessions. This includes treating more than one patient at the same time. The patients who are grouped have similar needs. The plan is established by a skilled therapist and is focused on the individual's needs. Group therapy is an adjunct to the therapy treatment plan and not the sole plan of treatment. Charges may be fairly established to reflect the time spent with each patient (e.g., in a one hour group session for therapeutic exercise with four patients, each patient is charged for 15 minutes; or a group charge, lower than an individual treatment charge, may be employed).

2. *Co-treatment.* Co-treatment is another option, but must be used carefully because treatment is provided by more than one discipline at the same time. The charge is for the time spent treating the same patient by each discipline. It may be combined with a group or provided individually. It is often a potent way to provide needed stimulation to neurological patients, and is also effective for short-term patients. Co-treatment may be provided at a lesser frequency and often less treatment time is needed per session.

3. *Removing discipline barriers.* The transdisciplinary approach. The transdisciplinary approach, where service providers work across traditional disciplinary boundaries, is also a novel way to offer services. To prevent turf battles, it may be wise to engage in team-building activities. The essential services and safety needs of each patient must prevail as alternative service delivery is explored. Some essential services that lend themselves to a transdisciplinary approach are:

   • Dysphagia management
   • Feeding management
   • Cognitive problems

- Wound care
- Mobility training
- Energy conservation
- Safety issues
- Physical agents

Viewing nursing staff as active members of the rehabilitation team can enhance the rehabilitation environment because they are available 24 hours a day, seven days a week. In service education and ongoing consultation for nursing services, a staff to carry out patient activities will be needed. This is a further extension of the transdisciplinary approach to care.

As mentioned, post-admission data collection and monitoring to review the effectiveness of the treatment plan is necessary. The purpose is to ensure that the length of stay and discharge status are not jeopardized because of deviations occurring. The monitoring process alerts clinicians to deviations and the need to make necessary changes to the care plan.

Financial outcome measures can be easily determined if there is regular, ongoing monitoring. Information that will be important to have is the cost of individual treatments, average length of stay, and average cost of stay by diagnosis. Post-discharge surveys of patients, on satisfaction and retention of outcomes, can give providers useful information about their services. The goal of tracking outcomes is to show positive, functional, and measurable results, to demonstrate cost-effective quality results to payors, and to validate treatment protocols and quality care.

Collecting preliminary clinical outcomes information is an important beginning if treatment protocols will be developed. The FIM has already been mentioned. It is a relatively simple data collection tool that has the advantage of a large database to which institutions can subscribe and participate. The quantitative nature of this tool adds to its appeal; it allows information to be reported to managed care organizations, other payors, and case managers.

In summary, managing care is a very proactive approach. It is patient-focused and outcome-oriented and requires resources to be managed and tracked. The process of this delivery system experiences frequent change.

FINANCIAL ANALYSIS

Current Practices

With the vast majority of rehabilitation services within skilled nursing facilities being billed to the Medicare program, cost reimbursement methodology is currently the dominant payment source. The direct and indirect costs of rehabilitation services are reimbursed as long as the costs do not exceed the charges and the costs meet certain tests of reasonableness, such as prudent buyer and salary equivalency limits. Indirect costs, such as capital equipment, are allocated to each cost center on a statistical basis. The reimbursement of indirect costs shifts costs toward the Medicare program. Since there is no true profitability in a cost-reimbursed program, the shifting of costs toward the Medicare program lowers costs allocated to the private-pay sector and enhances profitability in this area.

Financial analysis of rehabilitation services delivered in a Medicare cost-reimbursed method requires ongoing monitoring of the cost-to-charge ratio, productivity, and disallowed costs.

Future Trends

Managed care reimbursement for rehabilitation services within skilled nursing facilities has become a significant percentage of the volume in some regions of the country. Medicare beneficiaries with increasing frequency are signing over their benefits to managed care organizations (MCOs). The development of subacute levels of nursing and rehabilitation care has allowed the skilled nursing facility industry the opportunity to demonstrate to MCOs that they are the most cost-effective providers.

Negotiation of fees with managed care payors may include discounted fee for service, all-inclusive per diem rates, per diem rates plus ancillary service charges, case rate, and capitation arrangements. Except for fee-for-services arrangements, limited total charges place a financial risk on the provider and are an incentive to carefully monitor resource utilization.

The following issues need to be considered:

1. Rehabilitation charges are historically based upon markups established in a cost-reimbursed system. Since charges are not

what is ultimately reimbursed by Medicare, they may not be reflective of competitive pricing in a managed care environment.

2. Financial systems were developed around cost-shifting reimbursement, for example, increasing square footage allocated to rehabilitation.

3. Per diem and case rates require monitoring the total cost of care and not each individual service department.

4. There is a lack of cost data per case to negotiate risk-based contracts with MCOs. Cost-based reimbursement is based upon the aggregate and is not case dependent.

5. The negotiation process with MCOs may not involve a rehabilitation representative or the results may not be communicated to therapy clinicians. This may result in higher utilization of rehabilitation services or not knowing or meeting the case manager's expectations of the desired patient outcome.

Strategies

The following strategies may be used to address the issues mentioned above:

1. Know the costs of delivering care. If historical data is not available, begin to collect data to know the costs per unit of service or treatment and costs per case (based on ICD-9 codes or impairment groups). The Medicare cost report can be used to identify overall costs and then costs per case can be extrapolated from there.[4]

   A per diem worksheet (Figure 11–4) can be used to develop a cost analysis prior to admission and then on a concurrent basis when there are changes in the patient's clinical needs and resources are utilized.

2. Include the rehabilitation manager in negotiating managed care contracts. Because ancillary costs make or break the profitability of a risk-based contract, it is critical to involve a representative of the rehabilitation department when negotiating services with a managed care organization for patients with rehabilitation needs. In addition, this process will assist the rehabilitation manager in understanding the need for developing alternate delivery models for providing more cost-effective care.

3. Monitor the care that is delivered versus what was negotiated. Since there will be no penalty to delivering more care to non-risk-based contracts, such as Medicare, it is natural for clinicians to deliver whatever amount of service the Medicare patient needs and tolerates. Managed care patients will require additional authorization to change the intensity of services. Having dual systems will require close monitoring of how much service is being delivered to MCO patients.

4. Monitor the payor mix. Even a small percentage of managed care patients will have a significant impact on the true "profitability" of the rehabilitation department. The movement from cost shifting to cost containment operations may occur long before a majority of services are managed care reimbursed. The critical point in payor mix, and movement to cost containment systems can be evaluated with the assistance of the facility's reimbursement department or accountant.

5. Monitor productivity. Because the highest percentage of costs in rehabilitation are for personnel, it is critical to establish and monitor productivity levels. Staffing decisions in regard to hiring, approving time off, and establishing the appropriate staffing mix should be considered with reference to productivity levels.

6. Consider rehabilitation an ancillary cost versus a revenue center. The shift in viewing themselves as a revenue generating department to an additional ancillary cost is difficult for rehabilitation staff. In a true managed care environment, rehabilitation becomes another cost of delivering care. Departmental revenue generation will no longer exist with per diem and capitation contracts.
   Because there will be a plurality of payors within the facility, revenue will still be tracked for ancillary services. However, moving away from focusing on revenue production and increasing utilization of services will assist in managed care success.

7. Monitor the profitability per case versus per department. The inclusion of rehabilitation along with all other patient-related costs in comparison to negotiated charges will give a truer picture of the profitability of managed care patients than the traditional profit and loss statement of departmental profitability. This profitability exercise should be done on a concurrent basis versus retrospectively. The patient-related costs must reflect what the patient is actually receiving versus what services were negotiated as previously discussed.

SUMMARY

Providers of healthcare can no longer only provide services, they must manage care on prospective, concurrent, and retrospective bases. The shift in the skilled nursing facility's rehabilitation department from a primarily Medicare to a managed care reimbursed service has been discussed in this chapter. This shift in payor source has a dramatic impact on the daily operations, the model and goals of care, and the extent of services provided. These differences are summarized in Figure 11–4. Rehabilitation staff must be willing to move toward a patient-focused, outcome-oriented process, with emphasis on resource utilization in order to adapt to the managed care environment.

FIGURE 11–4

Rehabilitation Service Delivery Comparison

Issue	Medicare	Managed Care
Model of care	Service-focused care planning	Patient-focused care managing
Goals of services	Increase functional ability, capped at "prior level of function"	Predetermined; move to established discharge setting
Amount of services	Unlimited: medically necessary, requires skills of a therapist	Limited: directed toward discharge goal
Reimbursement	Cost reimbursed, prudent buyer, salary equivalency	Negotiated rate reimbursed, financial risk sharing
Financial incentive	Cost build, intensity oriented	Cost contain, productivity oriented
Financial monitoring	Markup: charges/ direct + indirect cost ratios	Margin: net revenue/direct + indirect costs

BIBLIOGRAPHY

Boland, Peter. *Making Managed Healthcare Work: A Practical Guide to Strategies and Solutions.* Aspen Publications, 1993.

Boland, P. "Joining Forces to Make Managed Health Care Work." *Health Care Financial Management*, December 1990, pp. 21–31.

Browdie, R. "Ethical Issues in Case Management from a Political and Systems Perspective." *Journal of Case Management*, Fall 1992, pp. 87–89.

Capitman J. "Case Management for Long-Term and Acute Medical Care." *Health Care Financing Review*, December 1988, Special no, pp. 53–55.

Carolova, J. "Could This Alternative to Hospital Care Help Your Patients?" *Medical Economics*, September 1988, pp. 105–9.

Coffey, R. et al. "An Introduction to Critical Paths." *Quality Management in Health Care*, 1992, pp. 45–54.

Coile, R. C., Jr. "Transitional Care: Redefining Long-Term Care for a Managed Care Marketplace." *Hospital Strategy Report*, April 1993, pp. 1–5.

Cox, M. P. "The Changing Healthcare Delivery System: The Long-Term Care Perspective." *NLN Publications*, September 1985, pp. 148–53.

Egenberger, T. "The Challenge of Managed Care." *Rehab Management*, February/March 1993, pp. 85-86.

Froisness, R. "The Financial Path to Managed Care." *Provider*, April 1994, pp. 47–48.

Kane, R. A. "Case Management: Ethical Pitfalls on the Road to High-Quality Managed Care." *Quality Review Bulletin*, May 1988, pp. 161–66.

Kerr M. H., and J. M. Birk, "A Client-Centered Case Management Model." *Quality Review Bulletin*, Sept. 1988, pp. 269–83.

Kongstvedt, Peter. *Managed Health Care Handbook.* Aspen Publications, 1993.

Schroeder, R. et al. "Pricing Medical Services in the Managed Care Environment." *Topics in Health Care Financing*, Winter 1992, pp. 58–64.

Scott, Joy. "Long-Term Meets Managed Care." *Nursing Homes*, November/December 1993, pp. 10–13.

Weinstein, M., and N. O'Gaga. "Managed Care Strategies for the 90s." *Healthcare Financial Management*, August 1992, pp. 42–46.

Notes

[1]American Health Care Association, *Subacute Care, Medical and Rehabilitation Definition and Guide to Business Development*, Washington, DC, courtesy of Golden Care, Inc., and Pinnacle Rehabilitation, 1994. See also American Transitional Care, Inc., *Standards for Subacute Healthcare*, Nashville, TN.

[2]Uniform Data Service (UDS), Research Foundation, State University of New York, 82 Farber Hall, SUNY-Main Street, Buffalo, NY 14214.

[3]American Physical Therapy Association, *Resource Guide: Recruitment and Retention of Physical Therapists in Long-Term Care,* 1992.

[4]Froisness, Robert, "The Financial Path to Managed Care," *Provider,* April 1994, pp. 47–48.

Chapter 12

Managed Care Contracting: The Subacute Provider

J. Mark Waxman, JD
Principal, Weissburg & Aronson, Inc.

The continuing pressure to reduce the costs of acute inpatient hospital services, together with the rapid expansion of managed care contracting, has led to a high level of interest in managed care contracting for subacute care services. These services, provided in subacute care units, transitional care units, or defined areas of skilled nursing facilities, pose special problems for managed care contracting, particularly if payment is to be made on other than a fee-for-service basis. This article discusses several of the key issues in managed care contracting for subacute care services.

DEFINING THE PRODUCT

The initial challenge in preparing for managed care contracting for the delivery of subacute care services is to define the bundle of goods and services to be grouped as subacute. Included in the definition of the subacute product will be an identification of three principal components. First, the criteria to determine the specific conditions or identifying characteristics of the patient capable of being admitted to the subacute care unit must be established. Typically, subacute patients are those who no longer require acute care services, but still require a high level of medical and nursing care and treatment, including the use of services that a typical freestanding nursing facility may not be capable of delivering, such as IV services, ventilator services, and so forth.

The second definitional component of the product will be the setting in which the services will be rendered. Various states have already established specific criteria for subacute care units. Among the typical requirements are that the setting be in an identifiable unit of the facility, approved by the relevant regulatory agency as a subacute care unit.

The third component will be the specific level or levels of care and equipment to be provided. Defining this component will include specifying the level of nursing intervention required, both in terms of hours and types of treatment, as well as the licensed status of the personnel involved (e.g., registered nurse as opposed to licensed vocational nurse). Any continuing care obligations must be included as well.

It is critical to managed care organization (MCO) contracting to properly define the scope of the subacute care program. It is only with this program definition in mind that both parties to any MCO contract can ascertain the services that are the subject of the contract and avoid controversy as to which patients will receive those services.

ASSESSING THE TRUE COSTS OF THE SUBACUTE PROGRAM

After carefully defining the subacute service product, the provider is in a position to determine the price levels at which the services will be provided. In determining that price, the provider should ensure that it has properly considered all of the costs to be incurred in providing the defined subacute care services. This will include not only appropriately determined capital costs and direct staffing costs, but other costs that should properly be allocated to the subacute service, including a pro rata allocation of facility professional staff such as the medical director, nursing director, and administrative assistants. The costs inherent in complying with the administrative requirements of a managed care contract, such as those incurred in properly filing claims, providing utilization data, and participating in a utilization review and quality assurance program, must also be considered. Finally, any continuing care services, whether through home visits or follow-up therapy sessions, must be costed as part of the overall pricing analysis.

PRE-CONTRACTING CONSIDERATIONS

With a clear definition of the product and the price to be charged in mind, a provider of subacute care services is ready to begin the contracting process. That process, however, actually begins with a variety of pre-contracting considerations.

First, before commencing negotiations, the parties to the contractual arrangement should be clearly identified, with the responsibilities of each of the parties outlined. Second, the provider should carefully appraise the risks and potential rewards, both economic and otherwise, associated with this particular MCO. Due diligence in this area should include research concerning the past financial performance of the MCO, the compatibility between the MIS systems of each of the parties, and an understanding as to who the key players on each side of the relationship will be.

Assuming that each of these issues has been carefully reviewed, the parties may then turn their attention to negotiating specific contract provisions.

COVERED VERSUS NONCOVERED SERVICES

Under the agreement, the provider will provide "covered services" that meet the criteria for the subacute care program defined by the contract. The MCO will seek to define covered services as broadly as possible. From the provider prospective, it is therefore critical to define precisely what is covered, as well as what is not. This is because noncovered services are typically paid by the subscriber at ordinary and customary rates. It is also important to identify services that are not available through the provider or any of its subcontractors.

One important aspect with respect to the definition of the services to be covered relates to ancillary services or supplies. The extent that these are not covered should be specifically indicated in the contracts.

COMPENSATION AND TERMS OF PAYMENT

After determining the costs of the subacute product, the provider is in a position to commence negotiations of pricing methodologies and terms of payment. Given the newness of subacute care programs and the variability of costs that may be incurred, it is probably in the best interests of the provider to initiate the contracting relationship on a discounted fee-for-service or a global-fee basis, as opposed to capitation or another type of risk-based contracting. Whichever arrangement is selected, however, the contract must clearly specify the rates of payment, whether by formula or otherwise, and the terms and conditions upon which payment will be made. To the extent that co-payments or deductible obligations exist, the contract should specify the obligation of either the MCO or the providing entity to collect these amounts.

While the pricing of subacute care services is critical, a clear understanding of the procedures for billing for covered services is also important. In the ordinary course, payment will be conditioned upon the submission of a "clean" claim, which should be defined in the agreement.

The contract should also cover timeliness of payment and any applicable late penalties. Providers should keep in mind that once the negotiations are completed, and the subacute program commences its operation, the failure to make timely payments requires immediate attention. This is particularly important where continuing care obligations may exist.

TERM AND TERMINATION PROVISIONS

A typical managed care contract provides for a fixed term, such as one or two years, with automatic renewal without notice to the contrary. Contracts also typically contain two types of termination clauses: one that allows termination for specified causes (a "for cause" termination), and one that allows termination "without cause." Typically, terminations for cause will allow parties to cure breaches of the agreement within a defined time period; those without cause will simply require notice of termination within a specified period—often as short as 90 days.

In addition to negotiating termination provisions, the provider should also carefully negotiate post-contract responsibilities and obligations. In this regard, the provider should require specificity of care obligations and the obligations to pay for the delivery of services following any termination. MCO contracts also discuss the ability of each party to continue to contact patients following termination and the need for confidentiality of exchanged information.

UTILIZATION REVIEW AND QUALITY ASSURANCE

Managed care contracting requires participation in a defined utilization and quality assurance program. Each contract should identify that program, the type of review allowed (prospective concurrent or retrospective), and the procedures to be used for any services rendered on an emergency basis. To the extent appeals will be allowed for utilization decisions, an appeal mechanism should be specified that is expeditious and fair. Finally, the contract will require compliance with all applicable laws, including antidumping legislation.

ADMINISTRATIVE PROVISIONS

There are a wide variety of so-called administrative provisions that should not be perceived as boilerplate items in contract negotiations. Among the most important are the following:

- Exclusivity and territoriality provisions—part of the negotiations may pertain to whether the provider has an exclusive arrangement within a given geographic territory.
- Dispute resolution clauses—the parties will negotiate whether disputes will be resolved by arbitration or litigation.
- Insurance requirements—the parties will specify the type of insurance each party must have as well as give consideration to "stop loss" provisions as an alternative to accepting unlimited risks in risk-based contracting areas.
- Data requirements—reporting and data requirements are particular areas of concern, and costs should be carefully identified.
- Whether any part of the contract may be assigned or subcontracted by either party.

Parties should also review the contract to ensure it does not violate any state or federal laws related to fraud and abuse or antireferral prohibitions. In addition, reimbursement mechanisms should be carefully studied to ensure the contract has not compromised the ability of the parties to maximize any third-party pay or reimbursement that may be involved.

CONCLUSION

Subacute care contracting poses a variety of challenges. They will require that any "form" agreement be significantly modified to match the particular circumstances under review. This mandates that providers understand each of the critical areas for negotiations.

Chapter 13

Medicare

A Payor Source and Reimbursement Methodology for Subacute Units within Long-Term Care Facilities

Kenneth F. Raupach
President and CEO, AmCorps, Inc.

The Medicare program has been a significant payment source for many of the successful subacute units in operation today. Since Medicare is a cost-based payment system, these successful units have had to be even more diligent in cost identification, accounting, and collection of financial data than the typical Medicare provider. Many of these subacute units have used Medicare as a stepping-stone into higher-acuity services and allowed the program to assist with subsidization of other payors during the start-up of a unit. However, while Medicare does provide certain avenues to step up acuity and shift certain costs, it is still a cost-based system and therefore not the ultimate desirable payor source. It does afford a methodology of pricing services by using the fully loaded costs as a factor to calculate minimum service charges for other charge-based payors.

This chapter will provide an overview of operational and financial steps, procedures, and suggestions that have proven effective with providers using Medicare as an initial payor source. Several providers continue to use Medicare as a supplemental payor for higher-acuity patients needing both complex medical and intensive rehabilitation services found in more sophisticated subacute units. Several of these providers have found that the Medicare cost allocation methodology becomes a basis for pricing services to managed care organizations.

Medicare guidelines are continually changing and being updated. The most significant change is scheduled to occur on October 1, 1995, when a prospective reimbursement system is mandated to be implemented. At present, subacute providers that utilize the program effectively will likely have a greater opportunity to continue to enhance Medicare revenues once the prospective system is implemented.

MEDICARE PATIENTS AS PRIMARY/INITIAL PATIENT RESOURCE

Once a subacute unit has been developed, a facility may recognize that Medicare patients may be the primary source of utilization. With this being the case, subacute units should be located within the Medicare certified distinct part (CDP) of the facility. Depending on the type of subacute services being provided, many providers find that this unit, while Medicare certified, might be separate and identifiable from the general geriatric Medicare certified unit. There are several reasons that these specialty beds should be certified (refer to Figure 13–1 for an example of a subacute unit within a Medicare CDP):

1. Hospitals are usually willing to discharge only the patients that are beyond their DRG length of stay, while keeping their more lucrative managed care patients. This may provide a referral source that is not normally available to the long-term care facility due to the unique medical needs of patients whom physicians are unwilling to discharge to facilities other than a subacute unit, where higher than average nursing services are available. The subacute unit able to relieve the hospital from these DRG Medicare "outliers" are often prime locations for partnering opportunities.

2. Managed care case managers will want to see that a facility can provide appropriate services to specialized subacute patients. Because Medicare beneficiaries are often some of the first patients on the unit, these patients help prove that higher-acuity services can be rendered in the subacute unit located within the long-term care facility.

FIGURE 13–1

XYZ Nursing and Rehabilitation Center

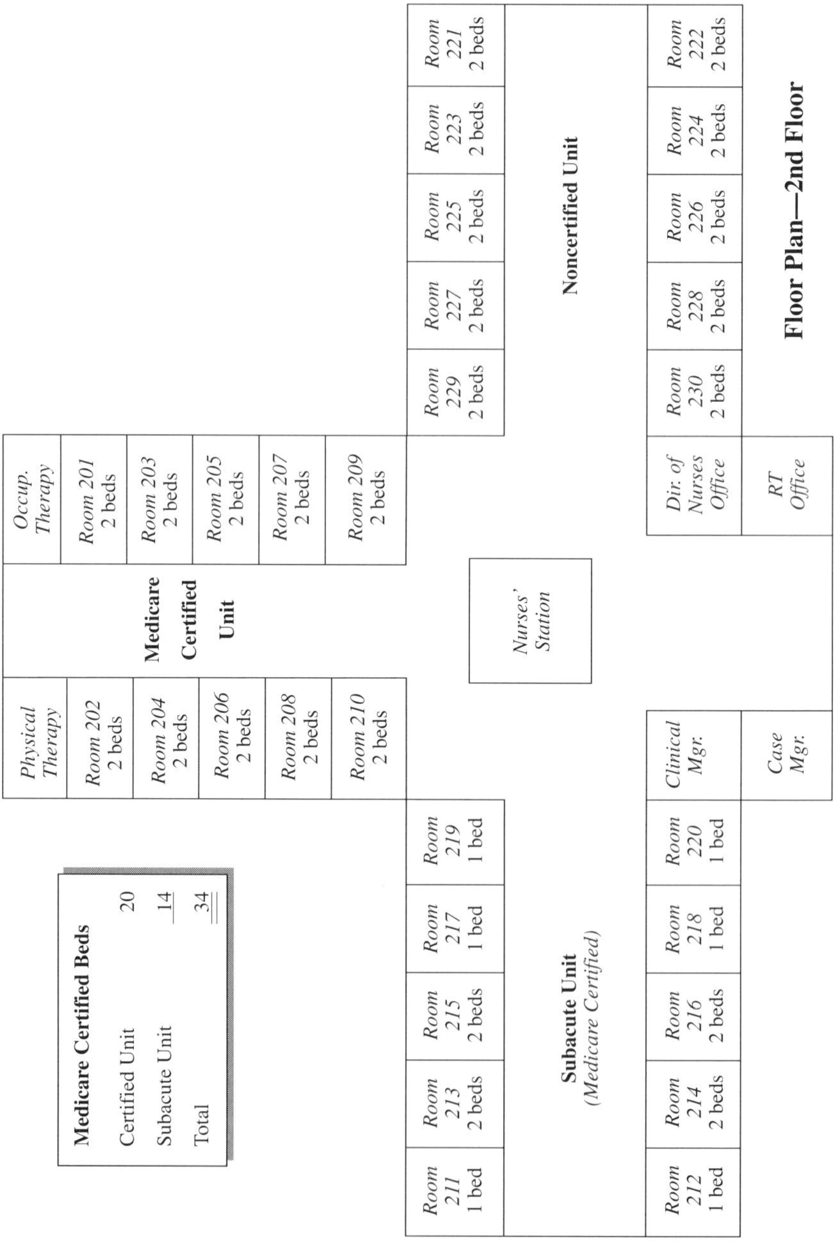

Medicare Certified Beds	
Certified Unit	20
Subacute Unit	14
Total	34

Floor Plan—2nd Floor

3. Medicare will pay its share of the costs associated with the development of the subacute unit during the initial start-up and development phase. Although there has been discussion at the federal level, the Medicare program currently does not recognize special care units located within the nursing facility setting or within the CDP. Therefore, the costs associated with the care of the specialized patient will be part of the total certified unit cost.

4. During the start-up period of the unit, subacute patients may be integrated into the general population of Medicare or other CDP patients. However, this is not the optimum configuration. Some providers find that expanding into subacute or specialized services is done through attrition of other long-term care patients. In some cases, this can take months to accomplish. Having a separate subacute CDP may not be realistic during this growth.

5. For medical care, diagnosis, and age considerations, many of the mature subacute units segregate the subacute patients from the general geriatric patients within the CDP. Often, acute care nursing personnel are required to provide the specialized care that the patients need. To avoid duplication of staff and other higher costs associated with subacute patients, a dedicated unit is often located within a CDP that caters to the high-acuity patient.

MAXIMIZING MEDICARE REIMBURSEMENT

When entering into subacute services, maximizing Medicare revenues is an initial primary goal for the provider. The facility management team should focus additional efforts on several factors that directly affect reimbursement. Some of those are:

1. Maintain the proper cost data related to the Medicare certified unit. Properly recording and documenting the cost of providing direct patient care is critical to assure the maximum legitimate reimbursement from Medicare.

   Clinical issues related to the direct cost of caring for these subacute patients are as follows:

   • The nursing personnel required to provide the specialized care are not readily available in a long-term care facility. Professional nurses, with specialized training and educational backgrounds necessary for the care of the residents require higher salaries and benefits, in many cases, more than the typical director of nurses in the SNF setting.

• The daily services required by these residents can only be provided by licensed nurses, thus materially increasing the cost of routine care. While a Medicare certified unit may provide an average of, perhaps, 3.5 hours of nursing care per patient per day, the medical needs of these residents may require in excess of 5 hours of primarily professionally licensed nursing care per day. The typical skilled unit is staffed with 25 to 30 percent RNs and LPNs while certified nursing assistants comprise 70 to 75 percent. A subacute unit may be staffed at 60 to 65 percent with licensed professional nurses and the remaining 40 percent by certified nursing assistants (refer to Figure 13–2 for a comparison of daily staffing levels).

2. In addition to the direct nursing service personnel, there may be a need for additional nursing supervision and support services. This will assure adequate care of these residents as well as the general facility population. The use of proper cost finding statistics, such as time studies (with proper prior approval of the fiscal intermediary—must be requested 90 days prior to the start of the provider's fiscal year), will assure that the cost of various departments such as nursing administration, social service (which might include the admissions personnel), and medical records are allocated based on the actual time spent (refer to Figure 13–3 for the applicable statistical basis of allocation).

3. The care of these residents increases the cost of the facility's ancillary services. Not only will physical, occupational, and speech/language services increase, but so will the use of supplies and staff to provide services to these higher-acuity patients. In addition, the specialized third generation medications or treatments patients receive will also increase. It becomes imperative that the provider has accounting systems and procedures that will capture all ancillary supply costs and increased service costs.

FIGURE 13–2

Daily Nursing Staffing (hours per patient day), Certified Unit versus Subacute Unit

Certified Unit

Hours/Shift	AM	PM	NOC	Total
RN	0.15	0.20	0.20	0.55
LPN/LVN	0.15	0.15	0.00	0.30
CNA	1.00	0.75	0.75	2.50
Total	1.30	1.10	0.95	3.35

Calculation	Total Hours		Average Wage Rate		Total Cost
RN	0.55	×	$17.00	=	$ 9.35
LPN/LVN	0.30	×	$13.50	=	$ 4.05
CNA	2.50	×	$ 7.00	=	$17.50
Total	3.35				$30.90
	Hours PPD				Cost PPD

Subacute Unit

Hours/Shift	AM	PM	NOC	Total
RN	0.75	0.75	0.75	2.25
LPN/LVN	0.50	0.75	0.50	1.75
CNA	1.00	1.00	1.00	3.00
Total	2.25	2.50	2.25	7.00

Calculation	Total Hours		Average Wage Rate		Total Cost
RN	2.25	×	$19.00	=	$42.75
LPN/LVN	1.75	×	$15.00	=	$26.25
CNA	3.00	×	$ 8.00	=	$24.00
Total	7.00				$93.00
	Hours PPD				Cost PPD

FIGURE 13–3

Medicare Rate Calculation Components

Direct Cost	

Nursing labor cost
Nursing registry cost

Allocated Indirect Cost	Statistic
Capital cost	Square footage
Employee benefits	Gross salaries
Administrative & general	Accumulated cost
Plant operations & maintenance	Square footage
Laundry & linen	Pounds of laundry
Housekeeping	Hours of service (square footage)
Dietary	Meals served
Nursing administration	Time spent (monthly time studies)
Medical records	Time spent (monthly time studies)
Social services	Time spent (monthly time studies)

4. Since Medicare will pay its fair share of the certified unit costs,
    the inappropriate placement of non-Medicare or lower-acuity (and
    therefore lower-cost) patients should be monitored. However,
    with the advent of the OBRA regulations, this task becomes more
    difficult since residents cannot be forced to move from a unit
    against their will. Assuming that there is an equal number of
    patients among Medicare, insurance, and other payors, the
    following scenarios will illustrate this point:

	Scenario I, Routine Cost PPD	Scenario II, Routine Cost PPD
Medicare patients	$150.00	$150.00
Managed care/insurance patients	$175.00	$175.00
Lower-acuity/other patients	$100.00	0
Average cost PPD	$141.66	$162.50

    The Medicare program would reimburse the average in either
case. However, in the first scenario, Medicare would pay less
than the average cost of Medicare patients alone. In the second

scenario, Medicare would pay more than the Medicare average cost, thus subsidizing the cost of the higher-cost insurance patient. This will ultimately assist in the profitability of the unit.

As a result of the additional cost related to the care of these high-acuity patients, the following issues should also be considered:

- What additional claims review issues will have to be dealt with?
- Is there any specialized documentation necessary for these services?
- What are the cash flow implications?
- Will these increased costs cause the facility to exceed the Medicare routine cost limit?

There are two categories to analyze when answering these questions:

Audit/Reimbursement Issues for Routine Costs

As a result of these higher-cost patients, when reporting certified unit costs on the Medicare cost report, a provider must be aware that the fiscal intermediary (FI) will use certain benchmarks to evaluate the reasonableness of routine nursing costs. One of these is the ratio of nursing certified costs to the nursing noncertified costs on a per patient day basis. The typical SNF may have a ratio of $2.00 of certified costs to $1.00 of noncertified costs, which may or may not be reasonable from the intermediary's perspective. With the increased cost of this high-acuity patient, the ratio may be in excess of $3.00 to $1.00 due simply to the higher cost of acute or specialized nursing staff and a higher-than-average ratio of professional to nonprofessional staff. A facility must assure that documentation is maintained to substantiate the nursing hours and costs in the unit. This documentation would include the monthly nursing schedules, the daily sign-in sheets, time cards (or computerized records if electronic clocks are used in lieu of time cards), and payroll records. Proper documentation is critical in proving to the FI that your costs, and therefore your ratio, are reasonable.

With these higher ratios of staffing, the FI may wish to audit not only the financial records, but also a random sampling of clinical records, which clearly show the need for the higher staffing.

Claims/Medical Review Issues and Billing Issues

The second point to consider is in the area of claims and medical review. These issues are grouped into two categories. First, what will the FI expect in the way of documentation to support the claim? Generally speaking, it is felt that the specific nature of the services is not the critical component. The basic provision of Revision 262/280 becomes the significant issue, and that is, "Does the beneficiary meet the criteria of requiring daily skilled services?" Nurses' notes or therapy treatment and progress notes need to not only support the daily skilled requirement, but identify any specialized or intensive treatments or programs that the patient requires as ordered by the physician.

HCFA has mandated that the intermediaries perform "focused reviews" related to specific services that may be prevalent or unusual in that region. Providers are not informed in advance of what areas will be focused upon. However, as requests for documentation filter into the facility, the focus issues become clear. For example, the use of air-fluidized therapy will initiate the request for a physician certification for this ancillary equipment. With the increased volume of other high-cost equipment and supplies needed for the care of subacute patients, the intermediaries will be requesting added documentation to support the need for these procedures. These requests may delay the processing of claims and thereby the payment to the facility.

The second category relating to Medicare billing issues is in claims review. How do providers get paid quicker with less cash flow delays? The care of the high-acuity residents puts a strain on both human and financial resources. A couple of options are available to minimize the cash flow impact of delays in claims processing. The first is to bill the intermediary using electronic media claims (EMCs). EMCs, if not already implemented through the provider FI, soon will be. These EMCs are submitted electronically using a variety of methods as outlined and approved by the FI. However, the main benefit of EMCs is that the system assures that the data submitted is complete, avoiding technical denials and rebilling of claims. This speeds up claims processing, and the facility will receive claims sooner. Second, facilities might consider utilizing the mechanism of periodic interim payments (PIP) to provide consistent and predictable Medicare cash flow. PIP reimbursement does require, at a minimum, quarterly updates that provide the intermediary with both projected Medicare utilization and Medicare cost data. This benefits the facility as well, by assuring that the increased costs of providing any increased ancillary services to the higher-acuity patients will be reflected and paid on a more timely basis. This is especially true during the start-up phase of a subacute unit.

Whether PIP is utilized or not, it is critical that the interim payments are reviewed at least quarterly to assure that payment levels are consistent with the increased cost. Most subacute providers are producing (either internally or through their cost report preparers) at least quarterly mini cost reports. The provider with a mature unit may even integrate monthly cost reports into its financial systems. By coupling EMC and PIP with this periodic review of costs, a substantial reduction of outstanding Medicare accounts receivable will occur.

By continual monitoring of the reimbursable costs, a provider will be aware of the relationship of its routine costs to the routine cost limits that are frozen for the period from October 1, 1993, through October 1, 1995. As the number of high-acuity patients increases, the costs will get closer to and eventually exceed this limit, which is based on geographical indicators.

ROUTINE COST LIMITS AND EXCEPTIONS FOR ATYPICAL NURSING SERVICES

The routine costs of a provider are comprised of those cost centers that are not ancillary or capital related. The predominate costs are the direct care nursing costs. However, depending on the nature of the specialty being offered by the provider, there may also be increases in other routine costs, such as administration for additional billing personnel and so forth. Generally, the care of the higher-acuity residents will increase the costs of Medicare services to a point that will exceed the Medicare routine cost limit (RCL). Under provisions of 42 CFR 413.30 (f), a provider may request an exception to the RCL if it can demonstrate that costs are in excess of the limit as a result of atypical nursing services or atypical patients being cared for on the CDP.

Prior to July 20, 1994, this process was time consuming and posed a significant delay in cash flow from Medicare. However, effective for all requests filed with the fiscal intermediary after July 20, 1994, and received by HCFA after August 9, 1994, this process has been expedited. The following is a synopsis of the revised policy for requesting an exception:

1. The provider should file the exception request prior to or after the close of its cost reporting period. However, at the latest, the exception request must be filed not later than 180 days after the receipt of "Notice of Program Reimbursement" (NPR) from the FI to be considered.

2. The FI must then make a recommendation on the acceptability of the exception request within 90 days of receipt. If it has no need for clarification or requests for additional information, it will pass it to HCFA under certain conditions.

3. If it is an initial exception request or a repeat request that has exceeded the standard variances (noted below), HCFA must make a determination on the exception within 90 days of receipt. If HCFA fails to make a timely decision, the FI recommendations are approved.

4. If the provider is experiencing substantial cash flow problems, it can file an interim request prior to the end of the cost reporting period. But the provider must meet the following conditions:

   • It must file the cost report within the time period specified in the guidelines.

   • The cost report must be accompanied by the completed exception request with all supporting documentation.

   • The cost report is accompanied by a request to revise the interim exception amount to reflect the actual data for the cost reporting period.

   If these conditions are not met by the provider, the FI has the right to ask for all exception amounts to be repaid immediately. For some providers, this may mean hundreds of thousands of dollars.

5. The interim exception may be tentatively approved and payments made to the provider prior to HCFA approval.

6. General exception request requirements include the following:

   • A cost report must be submitted with the exception request for the period in which the exception is being requested, including a home office cost report for chain organizations.

- If an initial prospective request is being sought and no previous cost report exists (e.g., a new subacute ventilator unit with no services being provided in prior cost reporting period), a pro forma interim cost report must be submitted.
- If a cost report exists from a preceding period where an exception has been previously granted, it must be included and compared to current exception report data (both financial and medical).
- If a repeat request is being sought and there is no substantial change in exception request methodology, and costs do not exceed prior approved exceptions by 20 percent in any per diem cost center and nursing hours do not exceed 25 percent in any classification, then the FI may make the approval without HCFA approval.
- There must be a certification statement by the provider's representative that states that there has been no significant change in the acuity levels compared to the previous period.

The exception request contents should include both quantitative and qualitative analyses. The atypical patient profile is demonstrated in various ways, as follows (refer to Figure 13–4 for a sample patient profile form and Figure 13-5 for ADL needs):

- Diagnostic data (case mix analysis).
- Average length of stay.
- Discharge domicile profile.
- Ancillary services utilization.
- Competitor peer group analysis.
- Analysis of patient ADL requirements.

An analysis of labor cost is performed to:

- Demonstrate that higher staffing levels are due to atypical nursing services or patients rather than excess staffing (refer to Figure 13–6 for an example).
- Comparison to HCFA standard staffing levels.
- HCFA uniform peer group comparison.
- Competitors peer group analysis (refer to Figure 13–07 for an example of the updated uniform peer group derivation).

FIGURE 13-4

Medicare Certified Unit Patient Profile

Medicare Certified Unit Patient Profile

Month/Year _____   Page ____ of ____

Facility Name _____

Resident ID # / Name or Room #	# NSG Trmts	# Meds	Units Therapy	ICD-9 Code #	Diagnosis	Diagnosis Cat. (a)	Total # of Diagnoses	Admission Date	Discharge Date	Dischg. Loc # (b)	Total Pat Days
			PT								
			OT								
			SLP								
			Total								
			PT								
			OT								
			SLP								
			Total								
			PT								
			OT								
			SLP								
			Total								
			PT								
			OT								
			SLP								
			Total								
			PT								
			OT								
			SLP								
			Total								
			PT								
			OT								
			SLP								
			Total								

Diagnosis/treatment Categories: (a)

1. Renal/Urological
2. Non-Vent Trach
3. Respiratory
4. IV/Antibiotic Therapy
5. Tube Feeding
6. Central Lines/Hyperal
7. Cancer/pain mgt.
8. Diabetes
9. CVA
10. Cardiovascular Disease
11. Decubitus/Wound mgt
12. Orthopedics
13. Amputations
14. Neurological
15. Gastrointestinal
16. Hemorrhagic
17. Electrolyte Imbalance
18. Opthalmic Disorders
19. Other

Discharge Location: (b)

1. Home
2. Hospital
3. Expired
4. This Facility
5. Other Facility

AmCorps, Inc.

08/02/95

FIGURE 13–5

Patient Profile: ADL Needs

Directions: Check off all ADLs that apply (only one check per category). All patients listed on patient profile must be listed.

ADL Description	Name or ID#: Admit Date:	Name or ID#: Admit Date:	Name or ID#: Admit Date:	Name or ID#: Admit Date:	Name or ID#: Admit Date:	Name or ID#: Admit Date:
Aids used:						
Eyeglasses or contacts						
Hearing aid						
Bathing:						
Requiring assistance						
Dressing:						
Requires assistance; incl. those who do not dress						
Continence:						
Difficulty controlling bowels						
Difficulty controlling bladder						
Difficulty controlling bowels and bladder						
Ostomy						
Mobility:						
Walks with assistance						
Chairfast						
Bedfast						

FIGURE 13-5 (*concluded*)

ADL Description	Name or ID#: Admit Date:	Name or ID#: Admit Date:	Name or ID#: Admit Date:	Name or ID#: Admit Date:	Name or ID#: Admit Date:	Name or ID#: Admit Date:
Transferring:						
Requires assistance						
Eating:						
Requires assistance (includes those who are tube or intravenously fed)						
Hearing:						
Partially impaired						
Severely impaired						
Completely lost						
Unknown						
Vision:						
Partially impaired						
Severely impaired						
Completely lost						
Unknown						
Using toilet room:						
Requires assistance						
Does not use toilet room						

FIGURE 13–6

XYZ Nursing and Rehabilitation Center, Atypical Nursing Salary Per Diem—Fiscal Year Ended 12/31/93

This schedule demonstrates XYZ Nursing and Rehabilitation Center's atypical nursing cost per diem per HCFA guidelines, and it supports the facility's excess over the limit of $31.56 as calculated on page 1.

	RN	LPN	CNA	Total
1. Direct patient care nursing hours, general routine	11,209	23,617	49,635	84,461 (p. 30)
2. Total inpatient general routine days	17,991	17,991	17,991	17,991
3. Man-hours per day	0.62	1.31	2.76	4.69
4. Average man-hours per day*	0.54	0.34	2.35	3.23
5. Atypical nursing service hours	0.08	0.97	0.41	1.46
6. Average hourly general routine salary (weighted average)	$18.98	$14.53	$7.22	(p. 30)
7. Atypical nursing salary (line 5 × line 6)	$1.52	$14.09	$2.96	$18.57
8. Routine employees health and welfare (EH&W) cost per dollar of direct general routine salary	0.217139	($18.57 × .217139)		$4.03
9. Routine administrative and general costs associated with atypical nursing and EH&W Costs	0.132472	([$18.57 + $4.03] × .132472)		$2.99
				$25.60†

*This format is from the HCFA office of reimbursement policy and procedure. Line 4 was developed from HCFA data and represents the averages of 561 freestanding urban SNFs.

†May not add due to rounding.

FIGURE 13–07

XYZ Nursing and Rehabilitation Center, Uniform Peer Group Derivaton—Fiscal Year Ended 12/31/93

	(A) 1992 Base Breakdown Per Diem Amounts	(B) Per Diem Adjustment Ratio	(C) Providers Cost Limit Times Ratio (B)	(D) Providers Adjusted Actual Cost Per Diems*	(E) Amount of Actual Cost Over Cost Limit	(F) Amount of Actual Cost Under Cost Limit
Direct expense	$37.20	0.439145	$44.34	$59.78	$15.44	
Indirect expense						
Employee health & welfare	$7.16	0.084524	$8.53	$10.69	$2.15†	
Administrative & general	$6.55	0.077323	$7.81	$6.63		($1.18)
Maintenance/operation of plant	$5.10	0.060205	$6.08	$6.72	$0.64	
Laundry	$2.05	0.024200	$2.44	$1.79		($0.65)
Housekeeping	$4.05	0.047810	$4.83	$4.36		($0.47)
Dietary	$12.25	0.144611	$14.60	$22.37	$7.77	
Nursing administration	$5.20	0.061386	$6.20	$8.70	$2.51†	
Central supply	$1.36	0.016055	$1.62	$5.31	$3.69	
Pharmacy	$1.02	0.012041	$1.22			($1.22)
Medical records	$0.76	0.008972	$0.91	$0.41		($0.49)†
Social services/activities	$2.01	0.023728	$2.40	$5.77	$3.37	
Total	$84.71	1.000000	$100.97†	$132.53	$35.57	($4.01)

Certified days = 17,991

Direct cost over or (under)		$15.44
Indirect cost over or (under)		$16.13†
Total cost over or (under)		$31.56†

	B Part I	B Part II	Operating Cost	Less: Pvt Rm Cost Diff. $35,770	Adjusted Operating Cost
Direct expense	1,091,632	0	1,091,632	16,134	1,075,498
Capital	383,953	(383,953)	0	0	0
Employee benefits	195,160	0	195,160	2,884	192,276
Administrative & general	127,254	(6,215)	121,039	1,789	119,250
Maintenance/operation of plant	140,785	(18,087)	122,698	1,813	120,885
Laundry	42,068	(9,390)	32,678	483	32,195
Housekeeping	84,288	(4,686)	79,602	1,176	78,426
Dietary	478,066	(69,592)	408,474	6,037	402,437
Nursing administration	163,655	(4,705)	158,950	2,349	156,601
Central supply	100,563	(3,538)	97,025	1,434	95,591
Medical records	7,596	(26)	7,570	112	7,458
Social services/Activities	132,075	(26,700)	105,375	1,557	103,818
Total	2,947,095	(526,892)	2,420,203	35,770†	2,384,433†

*The adjusted actual cost per diems is the total general inpatient routine service cost net of the private room cost differential divided by total Medicare certified unit days of 17,991.

†May not add due to rounding.

The exception process is continued with an analysis of indirect costs by way of the following:

• HCFA uniform peer group comparison.

• Qualitative rationale—the narrative argument that provider services are atypical.

• Competitor peer group analysis.

Once a provider has substantiated, through this analysis and the supporting data, that costs are in excess of the limit due to atypical services or patients, HCFA may grant an exception to the RCL based on the fiscal intermediary's recommendations. The exception is granted for a specific per patient day amount and approval is for that year only. If costs exceed the limits in subsequent years, the provider must request and substantiate its claim of atypical services for each fiscal year.

Until an exception is requested as outlined above (even prospectively), the FI will not reimburse a provider through interim payments of any cost in excess of the limit. Therefore, a provider deciding whether to provide specialized subacute services must be willing to support the cash flow of these excess costs for a period of up to 12 months from the beginning of the development of the subacute program, assuming an interim exception is obtained. To expedite the process, even while subacute census is growing, an interim exception should be requested from the FI as soon as possible. However, the initial interim exception request would require three months of actual cost data and nine months of budgeted data. If an interim exception is not requested, an organization may end up supporting the cash flow of these excess costs for a period of up to nine months from the end of the cost reporting year. Granting of an interim exception does not eliminate the necessity to prepare a formal exception request at the year's end. It should be noted that once a year-end exception is granted, HCFA and the FI will generally grant an interim exception, moving forward, based upon the actual amount granted for the prior year.

One caution regarding RCL exceptions is that, once received, they are not a license to steal from the program. Proof of reasonable and necessary costs are still the responsibility of the provider.

ANCILLARY SERVICES AND SUPPLIES

Almost without exception, ancillary services and supplies will increase as the acuity of the patients increases. In some cases, depending on the specialty service, these costs can increase disproportionately. Some providers see ancillary costs at two to three times the costs of the routine costs.

One area that has become attractive to some subacute providers is service for ventilator-dependent patients. These programs may be chronic, chronic weanable, or a combination of both, in design. When this type of unit is developed, respiratory therapy (RT) often becomes an issue. If the subacute unit has a ventilator component, consideration should be given to the use of respiratory therapy services under contract with a hospital versus RT services on staff. Respiratory therapy services provided within the nursing facility must meet certain criteria for them to be reimbursed by the Medicare program as ancillary services. The cost of respiratory services is limited by a salary equivalency guideline. This guideline is applied similarly to that for physical therapy services.

There are separate, state-specific RT guidelines for certified as well as registered respiratory therapists. A facility should assure, for Medicare reimbursement purposes, that the amount paid does not exceed these guidelines. The basic requirement is that the services must be provided by a therapist who is an employee of a hospital with which the nursing facility has a transfer agreement. In evaluating the relationship between the therapist and the hospital, the FI will use the IRS definition of an employee. The employee must have access to benefit programs, and the hospital must withhold applicable payroll taxes. Subcontractors would not meet the definition and qualify as employees. If the therapist is determined not to be an employee of the hospital, the cost of services would be considered routine, and therefore, subject to the Medicare RCL. However, HCFA has issued a memo indicating that in order for RT services to be considered nursing services, they must be provided under the supervision of a registered nurse and the therapist must either meet the nurse's aide training and evaluation requirements or be an otherwise licensed health professional.

If the conditions of the patients on the ventilator unit necessitate utilization of RT services around the clock, seven days a week, it might be more appropriate to establish a relationship with a transfer hospital paid under this salary equivalency guideline. However, some area hospitals may not have the luxury of respiratory therapy personnel to support off-site ventilator units. Hospitals may also see nursing facilities as competitors and not be willing to contract for RT services. Regardless, respiratory therapy service is a critical part of the quality ventilator-dependent program. Some providers considering ventilator services have found it beneficial (both operationally and clinically) to contract with companies that specialize in providing ventilators and supplies, that provide respiratory therapists through hospitals, and that use proven policies and procedures. However, in the event that RT services are not available through the contract hospital or, for operational reasons the RT services are provided by the facility's staff, the costs become routine in nature and may help the argument that a patient population is atypical in nature.

The AARC has sponsored a bill that would remove the requirement for hospital employees to perform respiratory therapy services to be considered ancillary. The bill, known as The Nursing Home Access to Respiratory Therapy Act of 1991, was delivered to the Congressional Budget Office (CBO) in 1991. The CBO must perform a cost estimate on the proposed bill before it can be presented to the committee of Congress. In the interim, the intermediaries are scrutinizing RT services, both from the claims and the audit perspective.

As a final comparative note, under certain circumstances, assuming the RCL exception is obtained or that routine service costs are below the RCL, a facility may receive higher reimbursement of the costs for respiratory therapy as routine cost versus ancillary cost (refer to Figure 13–8 for an example).

This same theory may apply to the other therapy departments as well. An assessment should be made to determine if your contract therapy company is capable of providing the number of staff necessary to provide intensive therapy on a subacute unit. However, care should be given to costs related to contract therapy in the event a heavy managed care patient population is developed. Consideration might be given to hiring facility therapy personnel to control costs.

Third generation pharmaceuticals for subacute patients are a major consideration for cost in developing a specialty unit. Due to the complexity of the medical condition of many of these patients, third generation pharmaceuticals may be necessary, and they may be extremely expensive. During the nursing evaluation of the patient, cost factors for these third generation pharmaceuticals must be considered.

FIGURE 13–8

Respiratory Therapy Services—Routine versus Ancillary

Ancillary Services Cost

Direct cost	$200,000	
Indirect cost	$ 30,000	
Total cost	$230,000	
Total RT charges	$350,000	
Medicare charges	$175,000	50.00%
Medicare reimbursement ($230,000 × 50%)		$115,000

Routine Services Cost

	Medicare	Total	Medicare Utilization
Certified unit	4,500	6,000	75.00%
Ventilator unit	2,000	4,000	50.00%
Total certified unit	6,500	10,000	62.50%
Medicare reimbursement* ($230,000 × 62.50%)			$143,750

Respiratory Therapy Reimbursement

	Ancillary	Routine	Variance
Private/managed care	$175,000	$175,000	$0
Medicare	$115,000	$143,750	$28,750
Total	$290,000	$318,750	$28,750

*Assumes routine cost limit exception has been granted.

As a final comment on the use of ancillary services, some supplies paid for under Part A are not covered under Part B (ventilator supplies, for example). Often providers are entering into joint ventures or other types of alliances with suppliers to assist in controlling the costs of these ancillary supplies. While Medicare pays certain overhead costs related to ancillary services and supplies, most providers seeking managed care payors are looking for partners that are willing to assist in sharing the financial risk by buying the supplies at the lowest possible prices. This is the only way that overall costs can be controlled, which will allow the provider to maintain a competitive edge.

PHYSICIAN SUPPORT AND MEDICARE BILLING FOR FREQUENT PHYSICIAN VISITS

Physician support for the specialized subacute program is critical to its success. Prior to accepting that specialized services can be provided within a long-term care setting, physicians and managed care organization case managers may wish to evaluate the program's policies and procedures, the credentials of the facility's staff, and the availability of support services, such as a specialized medical director and other physician support, as well as other intensive ancillary therapy programs such as respiratory therapy services. Providers should attempt to obtain the services of a physician who is well respected in the community and specialized in the unit's area of emphasis (e.g., a physiatrist for an intensive rehabilitation program and pulmonologist for a ventilator unit) to serve as the unit's medical director. In addition, the services of other attending physicians should be secured to serve on care planning and policy committees. This will assure that the physicians in the community would visit the facility and observe, firsthand, the services being provided.

Physician Payment for Alternate Visits

Historically, one barrier to physician support of the specialized units in long-term care facilities was the limited payment that they could receive for their visits to the nursing home. Effective January 1992, the payment methodology for physician visits was modified to broaden the categories of codes based upon the AMA evaluation and management codes (E/M). More important, these codes were expanded financially to come more in line with other payments made for physician visits. They are detailed in Addendum E of the *Physicians Current Procedural Terminology*, fourth edition, copyright 1991 by the American Medical Association (CPT-1992), as well as in annual updates in the *Federal Register*.

    Several providers have found it advantageous to set up internal billing systems and procedures for the specialty physicians working in their subacute programs. These bills must be submitted to the intermediary using the physician's provider number and billed on HCFA form 1500. If this service is provided, the facility must keep accurate records of the time spent by its staff in billing for the physician. This time is not an allowable cost for the provider and must be eliminated from the provider cost report. However, the time spent is relatively insignificant in comparison to the value added by billing for the physician.

For an overview of this billing process, consider the following information regarding the levels of the E/M services:

1. The unique code number must be listed.
2. The place or type of service is specified.
3. The content of the service is defined.
4. The nature of the problem(s) is described.
5. The time required to provide the service is specified.

There are two subcategories of nursing facility services that are recognized: (1) comprehensive nursing facility assessments (post-acute visit) and (2) subsequent nursing facility care. Some providers have found it beneficial, and sometimes necessary, to provide specific education programs to inform the medical community of these reimbursement changes (i.e., physicians, both group and single practices; business office managers and directors of physician clinics; insurance groups that bill Medicare for their physicians; and so forth).

Both subcategories apply to new or established patients. Comprehensive assessments may be performed at one or more sites in the assessment process, for example, hospital, office, nursing facility, or patient's home. Refer to the following chart for the details of the billing codes to be used on the 1500 billing forms for services rendered within the nursing facility setting.

Billing Codes—Comprehensive

Code	History	Decision Making	Time
99301	Detailed	Straightforward/ low complexity	30 minutes
99302	Detailed	Moderate to high complexity	40 minutes
99303	Comprehensive	Moderate to high complexity	50 minutes

Billing Codes—Subsequent Visits

Code	History	Decision Making	Time
99311	Problem focused	Straightforward/low complexity	15 minutes
99312	Expanded; problem focused	Moderate complexity	25 minutes
99313	Detailed	Moderate to high complexity	35 minutes

The basis of payment to the physicians is determined by the frequency and type of services provided. Therefore, the physician can now make *multiple visits* to the patient in a nursing facility, particularly if the patient's condition is under continual assessment. This is frequently the case in the subacute unit that caters to the high-acuity, high-cost patient. The need for routine physician consultation and examination of the subacute patient, particularly those with new trachs and ventilators, is critical to the patient's well-being. The need to monitor such things as the patient's blood gasses and reactions to prescribed medications could require, in the early stages, almost daily visits. This expanded service requirement would allow for the payment for these visits, whereas in the past, it would not. As always, the Medicare program requires that the proper documentation must be maintained to support need for the frequency of the visits and the level of services provided by the physician.

In computing the specific payment to the physician, a calculation must be made to take the following factors into consideration (refer to Figure 13–9 for an example): (1) relative value units for each code and (2) geographic practice cost indices (GPCI).

MEDICARE COST FINDING AS PRICING MECHANISM FOR OTHER PAYOR SOURCES

To assure that the unit will be profitable, the patient mix must include those whose payment source is not cost based. The cost-based payors, for example, Medicare, will pay the cost of providing services plus a share of the fixed cost of the unit. The charge-based payors, for example, managed care organizations, will allow the unit to become profitable if it has

FIGURE 13–9

Physician Payment Example (effective 1/1/94)

Procedure:	Comprehensive Nursing Facility Care
Code no.:	99303
Location:	Dallas, Texas

		RVU				GPCI
(A1)	Work	2.32	(B1)	Work		0.996
(A2)	Practice expense	0.96	(B2)	Practice expense		0.971
(A3)	Malpractice	0.07	(B3)	Malpractice		0.504

Multiply values:

$$(A1) \times (B1) = 2.3107 \quad (C1)$$
$$(A2) \times (B2) = 0.9322 \quad (C2)$$
$$(A3) \times (B3) = \underline{0.0353} \quad (C3)$$

Add (C1) + (C2) + (C3):	3.2782	(D)
Conversion factor	$32.905	
Schedule amount per visit (multiply [D] by the conversion factor)	$107.87	

the right contract and patient. The ability to attract patients with insurance coverage, therefore, becomes critical to the economic success of the subacute unit and the facility as a whole. In deciding to place a patient in a particular facility, a managed care case manager must consider two factors: First, the facility's ability to meet the needs of the patient, and second (and generally most important), the price that the MCO will pay for the care. The goal of the managed care organization is to provide appropriate care at the least cost to it. Therefore, in marketing services to these organizations, a facility must be in a position to provide a cost savings over the alternate options, such as the acute hospital or other similar nursing facility units. Former marketing tactics of sending flowers, fruit baskets, and so forth won't get the quality patients needed to assure the financial success of the unit, but the price of subacute services will.

PRICING OF SERVICES

In the early days of subacute long-term care, a new provider would often underbid the existing acute care hospital by 30 to 40 percent per patient day. In other words, "get as much as it could" from the managed care organizations by pricing off of existing hospital rates. A 30 to 40 percent savings in the cost of a higher-acuity bed is quite attractive to case managers seeking placement for patients, and early subacute units were fortunate enough to have time to develop the pricing and cost methodology that is necessary to compete today. As more services in new sites become available, this method of pricing off of hospital rates may not work.

This has necessitated that providers develop a system to determine the cost of services and then price them competitively. This includes development of on-site assessments that determine, at least, such things as the following:

1. Pre-admission evaluation of the medical needs of the patient to detail, including:

   - Nursing hours of service.
   - Therapy hours/units of service (physical, occupational, speech/language, and respiratory services).
   - Medical supplies and equipment.
   - Oxygen utilization.
   - Specialized equipment, such as ventilators, AFT, and so forth.
   - Legend and nonlegend pharmaceuticals.

2. A pricing tool to summarize the daily needs identified above, the charges related to those services and supplies, and a cost basis to assure that the negotiated payment is not less than the actual cost.

One way to determine the cost of providing care is to utilize the Medicare cost-finding methodology. Each cost category, routine and specific ancillary costs, would have a cost factor that would identify the ratio of cost to charges. The ratio or cost factor would be based on fully loaded cost, that is, direct and indirect cost. These factors would be determined from the current interim Medicare cost report calculations, which could change as higher-acuity services were expanded or the physical plant was modified to cover a greater amount of space for performance of subacute services (refer to Figure 13–10 for an example of a subacute provider Medicare rate calculation).

EXHIBIT 13–10

XYZ Nursing and Rehabilitation Center Medicare Rate Calculation, Period 1/1/93 to 12/31/93

Cost Center	Direct Cost	Adjust	Adjusted Expenses	Allocated Cost $	PPD	Routine Charges/Ancillary Charges	Cost Factors
General service							
Capital related, building	1,509,385	(7,223)	1,502,162				
Employee benefits	780,959		780,959				
Administrative & general	688,329	(105,333)	582,996				
Plant operations, maintenance & repairs	401,389	(2,476)	398,913				
Laundry & linen	76,688	(18,574)	58,114				
Housekeeping	222,948		222,948				
Dietary	888,638	(29,096)	859,542				
Nursing administration	287,757		287,757				
Central services & supply	242,120		242,120				
Medical records	16,243		16,243				
Activities	161,401		161,401				
Routine service							
SNF-certified	1,091,632		1,091,632	2,947,095	163.81	240.00	0.682539
NF-noncertified	1,394,717		1,394,717	4,255,855	134.10	150.00	0.893984

Ancillary service

Radiology	39,018		39,018	42,821	2.38	47,257	.0906130
Laboratory	26,531		26,531	28,780	1.60	12,946	2.223080
Oxygen therapy	298,729		298,729	329,850	18.33	382,776	0.861731
Physical therapy	293,346		293,346	487,850	27.12	932,883	0.522949
Occupational therapy	168,704		168,704	191,293	10.63	270,910	0.706113
Speech language pathology	140,045		140,045	158,139	8.79	230,780	0.685237
Medical supplies	121,857		121,857	152,631	8.48	187,398	0.814475
Drugs	451,691		451,691	495,372	27.53	538,133	0.920538
PEN therapy	50,527		50,527	55,205	3.07	47,198	1.169647
Air-fluidized therapy	20,946		20,946	23,261	1.29	40,927	0.568353
Nonreimbursable							
Gift shop	4,330		4,330	16,118	0.90		
Barber & beauty shop	50,599		50,599	81,557	4.53		
Total	$9,428,529	($162,702)	$9,265,827	$9,265,827	$114.66	$2,691,208

Once the pre-admission evaluation is completed and the daily services are determined, the gross charges based upon the provider's established charge structure are calculated. The cost factors are then applied and the fully loaded cost of services is determined. In the negotiation of a fixed-rate or a percentage-of-charges contract, the provider would then know the upper limit (gross charges) and lower limit (net cost) to ensure that the rate agreed upon is not only competitive in the market, but also not less than the cost of providing the care (refer to Figures 13–11 and 13–12 for samples of pricing worksheets).

This Medicare methodology will also ensure that the established charge structure of the facility is appropriate. Too many times a negotiated rate for the special care patient will appear good when compared to the typical nursing facility rate. However, after using a pricing worksheet to establish the cost of services, supplies, and equipment actually used, the patient may not be profitable. If costs are determined to be too high to be competitive in the market, the service being provided must be reevaluated.

Once the relative high and low points are determined, the facility is in a position to negotiate the terms of a contract with insurance companies and managed care providers. Many managed care organizations would prefer to establish all-inclusive, fixed-rate contracts. This generally is not to the benefit of the facility providing the services since patient cost varies, depending on diagnosis and condition. The pre-admission evaluation and assessment of the patient now becomes a critical component in the process of admitting and caring for the patient. Several weeks or even days after admission into the subacute unit, care requirements of the patient may be entirely different than those determined at the time of the pre-admission evaluation. To protect the facility from having a potentially profitable patient become an extremely unprofitable one, the established payment rate should be based on a percentage of charges. This not only protects the facility but is also to the benefit of the insurance company. In reality, the insurance company will benefit as the patient's condition improves because its cost will be reduced.

If the common practice in the area is to have a fixed-rate contract, then there must be provisions in the contract for limits or exclusions. These would relate to a specific level of ancillary utilization, such as therapy, units of service, or cost of third generation pharmaceuticals and various specialized equipment rentals. Regardless, pricing the potential patient and responding to the managed care case manager on a timely basis (hours versus days) will be to the provider's advantage in securing the admission.

EXHIBIT 13–11

Specialty Unit

Pricing Worksheet

Patient Name: _____		Referral Source: _____
Insurance Company: _____		Length of Coverage: _____
Secondary Coverage: _____		Length of Coverage: _____
Medicare _____ Yes _____ No		

ROUTINE SERVICES:	Room Rate		Gross Charges	Cost Factors *	Net Cost
Private Room	_____		_____ X	_____ =	_____
Semi-Private Room	_____		_____ X	_____ =	_____
Specialty Bed	_____		_____ X	_____ =	_____
Special Nursing Charges:	_____		_____ X	_____ =	_____

ANCILLARY SERVICES:	Units per Day	Per Unit Charge			
Physical Therapy	_____	_____	_____ X	_____ =	_____
Occupational Therapy	_____	_____	_____ X	_____ =	_____
Speech Therapy	_____	_____	_____ X	_____ =	_____
Respiratory Therapy	_____	_____	_____ X	_____ =	_____

ANCILLARY EQUIPMENT AND SUPPLIES:

Oxygen:
- Liquid/Gas _____ _____ X _____ = _____
- Concentrator _____ _____ X _____ = _____

Equipment Rental:
_____ _____ X _____ = _____

Drugs:
_____ _____ X _____ = _____

Medical Supplies:
_____ _____ X _____ = _____

Other Services and Supplies:
_____ _____ X _____ = _____

TOTALS $ _____ $ _____

APPROVED RATE $ _____

Prepared By: _____ Date: _____	Approved By: _____ Date: _____

* To be provided by the Corporate Reimbursement Department.   *AmCorps, Inc. 7/93*

EXHIBIT 13–12

Specialty Unit

Pricing Worksheet

Patient Name:	Jonathan Q. Doe		Referral Source:	Bill A. Smith, M.D.
Insurance Company:	"The Blues"		Length of Coverage:	265 Days after Medicare
Secondary Coverage:	"Medi-Gap"		Length of Coverage:	530 Days after "The Blues"
Medicare	XX Yes	No		

ROUTINE SERVICES:	Room Rate			Gross Charges/day	Cost Factors *	Net Cost/day
Private Room	$325.00			X	0.682539 =	
Semi-Private Room	$150.00			$150.00 X	0.682539 =	$102.38
Specialty Bed	$150.00			$150.00 X	0.568353 =	$85.25
Special Nursing Charges:	<7 hppd			$25.00 X	0.682539 =	$17.06

ANCILLARY SERVICES:	Units per Day	Per Unit Charge				
Physical Therapy	8	$25.00		$200.00 X	0.522949 =	$104.59
Occupational Therapy	6	$45.00		$270.00 X	0.706113 =	$190.65
Speech Therapy	6	$45.00		$270.00 X	0.685237 =	$185.01
Respiratory Therapy	12	$30.00		$360.00 X	0.861731 =	$310.22

ANCILLARY EQUIPMENT AND SUPPLIES:

Oxygen:

Liquid/Gas	4 ltr/hr	$5.00/hr		$120.00 X	0.861731 =	$103.41
Concentrator				X	=	$0.00

Equipment Rental:

Suction Equipment		$25.00/day				
Ventilator		$75.00/day		$100.00 X	0.568353 =	$56.84

Drugs:

IV Antibiotics		$125.00/day				
Regular Meds		$37.50/day				
				$162.50 X	0.920538 =	$149.59

Medical Supplies:

Sterile Dressings		$22.00/day				
Catheters		$9.00/mth				
Sterile Gloves		$5.00/day		$27.30 X	0.814475 =	$22.24

Other Services and Supplies:

Lab - ABG		$55.00/mth				
X-rays		$120.00/mth				
Miscellaneous		$300.00/mth				
				$15.83 X	0.814475 =	$12.90

TOTALS			$	$1,850.63	$	$1,340.14

APPROVED RATE					$	$1,595.38

Prepared By:	Date:		Approved By:	Date:
Jim Willis, Case Manager	11/04/94		Sue Bass, Controller	11/04/94

* To be provided by the Corporate Reimbursement Department.

AmCorps, Inc. 7/93

SUMMARY

Medicare is strictly cost based and there are opportunities for shifting certain overhead costs to the Medicare program. However, the successful and profitable subacute units seek an appropriate mix of payor sources for patients on the unit.

Large subacute chain organizations work continually in refining and maximizing the Medicare program in their subacute facilities. They offer opportunities for making the charge-based patients (managed care organizations) more profitable by allowing Medicare to pay its share. It is almost always assured that the provider will exceed the routine cost limit. In doing so, considerable expense, either through contractual arrangements with consulting firms or through additional staff, will occur. These costs are considered part of doing business in making Medicare work for the provider of subacute care. There are very few programs or reimbursement methods more difficult to manage than Medicare, but serious consideration should be given to using Medicare as the stepping-stone into development of higher-acuity patient services.

Chapter 14

Strategic Alliances
Joint Ventures, Contracting, and Networking

Harry Dalsey, JD
President, Specialty Care Management

From the implementation of the prospective payment system (PPS) in 1993, pressure has continued to build on hospitals and physicians to reduce the use of acute inpatient services and redirect patients to ambulatory centers or lower-cost inpatient settings. The growth in managed care has enhanced the movement to find lower-cost alternatives, driving the development of a variety of subacute centers. These centers operating under hospital and skilled nursing licensure have created a whirlwind of interest in subacute care. This interest comes from:

1. The potential for reducing the cost of care for patients requiring continuing inpatient services.

2. The perception that higher operating margins are derived by subacute providers.

3. The opportunity for hospitals to utilize excess capacity to provide subacute care.

4. The higher trading multiples for stock in nursing home companies providing subacute care.

Even with phenomenal growth, the business is still embryonic, thereby creating many opportunities for other providers to enter the market. While the financial requirements for establishing a subacute program can approach $500,000, the real barriers to entry include:

1. Licensure: Maximum benefits for providers and patients come from utilizing either a skilled nursing or long-term hospital license. In many states, acquiring a new license may be prohibited by the certificate-of-need laws.
2. Learning curve and clinical care: The expectations of referral sources, physicians, payors, patients, and families are increasing. Cost of care and clinical outcomes will be critical indicators for successful subacute providers.
3. Cost of service: Controlling the cost of ancillary services will be essential for meeting the price demands of managed care companies.
4. Patient flow: Opportunities will increase for subacute care providers with the growth in managed care enrollment. Subacute providers will need to become contracted providers competing with other subacute centers.

Even though the healthcare changes proposed by the Clinton administration have been delayed and Congress is still debating how to reduce Medicare costs, the healthcare system is undergoing fundamental changes. Employers needing to reduce costs are encouraging enrollment in various forms of managed care. Medicare beneficiaries are joining health maintenance organizations and states are enrolling Medicaid beneficiaries in managed care programs. The responsibility for controlling costs is shifted to managed care companies that spread the risks to their contracted providers. Projections indicate that within the next five years most people will be enrolled in an aggressive managed care company. This will drive more patients into subacute centers as the managed care companies and their at-risk providers seek additional options for reducing the costs of continuing inpatient care.

Since the 1980s, hospitals and other providers have experimented with alliances and networks. Beginning in the early 1990s, other progressive providers began implementing cooperative ventures, frequently offering an insurance product or linking with a managed care company. Providers, being proactive are not waiting for congressional action, and are merging, acquiring competitors, and forming joint ventures or other strategic alliances to protect or enhance market position to assure a role in the local healthcare system of the year 2000.

Successful regional systems will utilize a combined clinical and financial database for decision making. Patients will be moved through various sites of care to environments where the level of care meets their individual need. Initially, the cost of care will need to be matched with the level of reimbursement, so that the provider can realize a margin on the care provided. However, as all providers begin to provide care under a uniform rate and assume the risk for utilization and cost of service within each level of care in the continuum, the margin on reimbursement per unit of service will be immaterial. At that point, revenue will be fixed and the provider will need to control utilization and manage the cost of care delivered within each level of care. The age of "case management" has therefore begun. In this new age, patients will continue to be downstaged to lower-cost alternatives as:

1. Insurers seek to reduce their costs through restricting access to high-cost acute inpatient programs.

2. Providers look to preserve a margin on patient care and downstage patients to owned or contracted subacute centers.

3. Integrated delivery systems linked with insurers will convert all care sites from revenue centers to cost centers. The clinical managers of care will have to identify patient needs and in a timely manner move patients to cost-effective alternate settings.

Alliances can also be used to control relationships with managed care or develop insurance products within the network. As hospitals and insurers become fully aware of the benefits of subacute care, they will use alliances to dictate the rules for this level of care. The new rules will involve using providers in the alliance for the subacute services. In addition, hospitals with excess capacity will attempt to operate hospital-based SNFs. Physicians, having recognized the benefits of subacute care (post-emergency room), will increase their referrals. This number will be further increased when at-risk physicians use subacute care instead of acute inpatient services. When the alliances or hospitals become fully capitated, all centers of care will shift from being revenue generators to cost centers. At that point, the role of subacute will change to that of a cost-effective component of the delivery system. Therefore, subacute will be a service site within a seamless delivery system, providing incremental system value to the integrated system.

STRATEGIC ALLIANCES

Throughout the country, healthcare providers, to assure their survival, are looking for new relationships through acquisition, merger, joint venture, or simple contracts. Hospitals in Ohio have merged with insurers and other hospitals, and their medical staffs are creating new structures potentially including joint ownership of the hospital. Large for-profit chains are continuing to acquire other nonprofit hospitals. Ancillary providers in Michigan are forming networks to bid on preferred provider contracts. Nursing homes in New Jersey, Connecticut, California, Wisconsin, Illinois, and Michigan are also forming networks to function as preferred provider organizations able to contract with managed care for subacute services. These providers appear to recognize the need to establish a variety of strategic alliances with other providers, both vertically and horizontally, to create seamless delivery models. Time does not allow for all providers to independently establish all the levels of care necessary to compete.

The pioneers in subacute care have been independent providers. Even the large national corporations that established subacute care services have implemented this level of care independently of the remainder of the delivery system. This entrepreneurship has created a new level of cost-effective care, but freestanding subacute centers have continued the historic trend of fractionating the delivery system. This is counter to the future trend of consolidating service centers within an integrated delivery system. Large, national for-profit subacute providers have recognized the need to link with other area providers (acute and subacute) and are developing alternative relationships with acute providers and insurers to assure their continued success. The initial rationale for a strategic alliance includes reducing the learning curve and time of market entry, assuring patient flow, and guaranteeing the ability to buy support services more cost effectively. Within two years, the major reason for developing strategic alliances in subacute care will be to assure a significant place in the future delivery system, thereby protecting investments and subacute franchises established by nursing homes and hospitals.

ALTERNATIVE SCENARIOS

To assure a place in the postacute market, skilled nursing home providers will need to assess alternative scenarios for establishing subacute programs and maintaining referral relationships with hospitals, physicians, and insurers. The consolidation that is occurring nationally is evolving at different rates within each regional market. Within the local market, each current subacute provider and each nursing home and hospital contemplating the initiation of subacute services should answer the following questions:

1. Can a "Lone Ranger" approach be successful in the local market?
2. If a cooperative relationship would increase the chance of long-term viability, then which partner or partners is appropriate?
3. What is the structure for the relationship given the objectives, corporate cultures, and time frames of each partner?

Each model needs to be reviewed by management and compared to the following criteria attempting to answer the associated questions.

1. Corporate commitments	Why is each provider entering the relationship? Are both organization's objectives compatible or mutually exclusive?
2. Mixing of cultures	How will the different cultures affect the relationship? Do all parties accept that the other brings value to the relationship? Are the parties negotiating from equal positions?
3. Time frames	Can the relationship be implemented in a timely manner to meet each party's time lines? Will the relationship reduce the costs of implementation and provide incremental value for future generations of subacute services?
4. Win-win relationships	Do all parties see short- and long-term benefits to the relationship? Are the benefits equal given the investments?

5. Assumptions of risk	How have the investments been evaluated? Has each party made a significant enough investment to be committed to the venture? Who owns what and who will control the relationship? What will be the continuing requirement of management to assure success, that is, will it have an active or passive role in the operation?
6. Reimbursement/cost	Will the new relationship maximize reimbursement? Under a fully capitated approach, when the new program becomes seen as a cost center rather than a revenue center, will the relationship be flexible enough to continue providing benefits to both parties?
7. Market attractiveness/ competitive position	Will the relationship or type of relationship improve the market attractiveness (price, location, outcomes) of the program? Will the competitive position of the provider be improved through access to more managed care providers?
8. Options	Have all possible scenarios been assessed? Will the option selected meet each party's corporate objectives?

Contracts

Establishing contractual relationships can be the easiest mechanism for developing a cooperative relationship. Frequently, all corporate objectives can be achieved through a well-constructed contract that avoids conceding ownership or by establishing a new corporation or joint venture. Examples of contracts that can be utilized by subacute providers include:

Lease arrangements. Under this arrangement, a postacute provider enters into a contract to lease space from a hospital or nursing home to develop and operate a new postacute program. This model generally requires the new subacute/postacute provider to obtain a new license and apply for Medicare and Medicaid certification as a new provider. In certain states, a lease will necessitate obtaining a certificate of need. This can be for a new nursing home or long-term care hospital, depending upon the state licensing requirements and other market dynamics. One benefit of the new provider status is that for SNFs, Medicare can grant an exemption from the routine cost ceiling for the first three years of operations, and for new long-term hospitals, a new TEFRA cap can be established. While the new program will be controlled by the operator, the landlord can influence the operation of the new program through a well-structured lease and a shared services agreement, whereby the landlord will, during the life of the lease, provide certain administrative, support, and ancillary services. The lessor benefits from the ability to have a new program/service available, receive rental payments, and shift fixed administrative and ancillary costs to the program through a shared services agreement. The risk to the lessor is the operator will control the program since it owns the license. After the term of the lease, the operator could move the program to another location. A lease arrangement may be a reasonable option where there is limited management capacity, the facility has limited capital, and the time frame demands a minimal learning curve. Also, the hospital needing capital will be receiving a guaranteed cash flow, while the lessee assumes the financial risks associated with the start-up of a new community service.

Bed holds or reserves. This type of contract provides an arrangement whereby a hospital or insurer pays a postacute provider to provide access for a fixed number of patients. Bed reserves and bed priorities have provided new revenue for the postacute provider. With the expansion of the need for subacute beds and with the availability of new providers, this vehicle will become less desirable, and postacute providers currently in this type of contractual situation should attempt to develop new relationships with the referral sources, possibly looking to develop a hospital- or nursing home–based subacute program, either through expansion of the contract or development of a joint venture.

Ancillary services—shared services. A conventional nursing home purchases a significant amount of ancillary services (therapy, pharmacy, laboratory), administrative services, and temporary staffing. A nursing home that establishes a subacute program can increase the use of ancillaries by $1,000,000 per year. Generally, these services are purchased from a group of unaffiliated ancillary providers. Hospitals can reduce lengths of stay by selecting appropriate placement options. They can also reduce the operating cost for providing care to the remaining acute care patients by spreading the high fixed costs in many ancillary departments through the sale of ancillary services to physicians and nursing homes. By developing a hospital-based program or by working with local nursing home providers, the hospital will benefit from downstaging patients but can also achieve an additional benefit from the provision of the ancillary services. The current profitability on ancillary services in the subacute center will be reduced with the increase in the number of patients covered by managed care. The profitability on all-inclusive per diem rates negotiated with managed care companies is dependent on controlling the ancillary services costs. Hospitals have the incentive to reduce the costs of the ancillary services provided to the nursing home and subacute program, as the hospital's overall goal is to reduce the length of stay while building a seamless continuum.

Management services. A hospital seeking to establish an on-site program can contract with a management company for the development, management, and marketing of a subacute service. The hospital retains ultimate control of the license, and through the Medicare program the hospital may be able to maximize its reimbursement through allocation of overhead to the new program. The magnitude of this allocation will probably exceed the amount of overhead designated under a lease arrangement. Medicare will continue to pay costs to the new postacute providers (exemption) and continue the exemption process for existing providers. The allocation of costs to the program by the hospital or nursing home will continue to be a successful strategy and cover certain diseconomies in the hospital or nursing home system. Many observers believe that within five years, all patients (including Medicare beneficiaries) will be covered by an aggressive managed care program. At that point, revenue generation on specific business units and cost allocation will be eliminated, as the driving force will be to become the manager of the healthcare dollar for an enrolled population. Then, as an "at risk" provider, the key will be providing care at the site where the care meets the patients' needs and the cost of care allows for a margin for the system. Also, hospital-based programs still need placement options for patients requiring continuing care. Therefore, working with local nursing home providers to develop a postacute network will assist the timely movement of patients.

Joint ventures. Under a joint ownership model, providers (hospital, nursing home, physician, ancillary companies) form a new legal entity that will be owned and governed by the incorporators. This new entity could buy an existing skilled nursing facility, develop a new skilled nursing facility, enter into a lease or management contract, develop and operate one or more subacute units in hospitals or nursing homes, or jointly develop a preferred provider organization to assume risk for providing care to an enrolled population. The partners in the venture would jointly capitalize the new company. Depending upon the needs of the providers, the new entity could be established as· a partnership, a stock corporation, or in certain states, a limited liability corporation. In whatever legal structure chosen, governance of the new corporation will be shared among the parties. While the business of the new venture can be controlled by certain parties (e.g., a hospital leasing to the new venture), the venture will need separate management to assure achievement of its goals. Fraud and abuse rules, reimbursement considerations, securities laws, antitrust guidelines, and related party issues and tax considerations must be reviewed with legal and accounting counsel. For these ventures to be successful, the parties must answer the above questions and establish clear objectives for their respective boards.

Networks With Other Postacute Providers

Another option is the establishment of a network. As an intermediate step, providers are forming networks to achieve a critical mass for contracting. Generally, these networks are governed by contract, but over time they can evolve into other structures, including a new corporation that creates a more integrated system and provides comprehensive care throughout the continuum. Network membership may also be available. Membership provides certain market protections while offering access to new markets, managed care contracts, and purchasing power for acquiring equipment, supplies, or ancillary services.

Potential Partners

In different markets, different partners will arise to assist with the development of strategic alliances. Patients do not self-refer to a subacute center. Ninety-nine percent of the patients today come to the subacute center having been referred from an acute hospital. While the number of patients referred from other locations (ERs, physician offices) will grow as payors recognize that subacute can substitute for acute care for patients with exacerbations of chronic conditions, subacute patient flow will be controlled by third parties. In many communities, a conveniently located and appropriately priced subacute program that provides an acceptable level of care will be successful. In the future, the criteria for success will not only include price and outcome, but also more formal linkages with hospitals, physician groups, and managed care companies will be required, even for the Medicare patient. Attempting to be a solo provider, whether in acute or subacute services, cannot be a successful strategy given the pressures in the system to purchase services from captive or sister companies or in-plan providers.

Hospitals. Hospitals are potential partners in strategic alliances. Even hospitals that have subacute programs (hospital-based SNFs or subacute units in nursing homes) need partners to complete the postacute continuum. The typical 250-bed hospital with 80 percent occupancy needs access to more than a 20-bed subacute unit. The subacute unit needs to discharge patients to provide continuing access, and since some patients require an inpatient stay of 1 to 90 days, there is a need for continuing subacute or conventional nursing home service. Individual hospitals are forming networks to protect their acute care base. In choosing a potential hospital partner, a subacute provider needs to identify the likelihood of that hospital providing the resources necessary for a successful, mutually beneficial long-term relationship. This would include hospitals with strong clinical programs, links to managed care companies, and strong medical staffs. Volume of referrals can be elusive, here today and gone tomorrow. There is an obvious need to assess hospitals for both today and tomorrow.

Insurers. Insurers are potential partners in strategic alliances regarding subacute care. Given the experiences in Ohio, it is apparent that to maintain a cost-effective delivery model, insurers must investigate the potential of also being providers. Given the benefits of subacute, a larger managed care company may make a reasonable partner.

Physician group practices. Physician group practices become likely partners for the subacute provider, given the increasing power of the group practices in the managed care model. As the physicians accept more risk through a capitated program, the physicians begin to assume a more predominant role. Since physicians have always needed to approve the discharge to subacute, they have a greater incentive to use the lower-cost center. The stark rules will need to be reviewed if this becomes a likely option.

Other Postacute Providers (SNFs, Ancillary Providers)

One option beginning to gain popularity is the postacute network. Payors or employers have determined that they can contain costs through selective contracting with niche providers. This is based upon the assumption that a focused contract with the preeminent cost-effective provider will achieve the cost reductions that are required, without limiting access. Again, these consortia cannot exist and flourish without linkages into the remainder of the healthcare continuum. This may be an effective strategy, whereby the postacute provider establishes a critical mass, negotiates with employers or managed care companies, achieves a contract, and then leverages that contract into more mutually beneficial relationships with large physician groups, hospitals, or integrated systems needing the postacute continuum.

LEGAL AND REGULATORY ISSUES

1. Fraud and abuse: Generally, the Medicare antikickback statutes prohibit the knowing or willful offer, payment, solicitation, or receipt of any remuneration, directly or indirectly, in cash or in kind, for the referral of a person for the provision, items, or services for which reimbursement may be made under the Medicare or Medicaid program. Illegal remuneration may be the distribution of profits by a joint venture or other entity to its owners, for the purpose of inducing the owners to refer Medicare or Medicaid patients to the venture. In establishing a new corporate structure, the parties will obtain legal counsel to ascertain if the proposed venture violates the antikickback statutes, if the proposed venture falls into the "safe harbors" that have been established, or if the risks associated with the venture are minimal. Risks can be minimized through appropriate capitalization, or a business purpose that reinforces public and Medicare policy (e.g., reducing healthcare costs).

2. Tax considerations: In reviewing the tax consequences associated with the new venture, it is necessary to assess the business implications (e.g., the double taxation associated with a corporate structure). Just as important is the review of the tax consequences if one or more of the parties is a tax exempt hospital or nursing home.

3. Related parties: Under Medicare regulations, costs applicable to services furnished to a Medicare provider by organizations related to the provider by common ownership or control are able to be included in the allowable costs of the provider, at an amount equal to the cost to the related organization, provided that such cost does not exceed the price of comparable services available for purchase elsewhere. For the near future (until all Medicare beneficiaries are enrolled in risk managed care programs), Medicare will be a major payor for the services to be provided through these ventures. Cost is defined as the fully allocated cost (direct plus certain indirect). In many cases where the transactions occur within a healthcare system seeking incremental system value, the shifting of cost can be very advantageous. But when outside parties become involved, as with new ventures, the related party issues must be assessed. If parties are determined to be related, the payments to the provider (e.g., nursing home) will be reduced

to the cost of the services provided. If the nursing home has paid cost plus a markup, then the nursing home will be financially disadvantaged. The potential step down to cost needs to be identified early in the negotiations and may be a significant factor in defining the final type of relationship established, as well as the final corporate structure and financial benefits.

4. Tax-exempt status and measurement: Ventures between for-proft and nonprofit providers need to be reviewed for potential problems associated with the use of funds from the nonprofit provider to benefit the for-profit provider.

5. Antitrust: A September 1994 statement by the Federal Trade Commission appears to have had a positive impact on the establishment of the type of relationships discussed here. The statement describes "antitrust safety zones," under which the federal antitrust law enforcement agencies will not challenge certain collaborative activities by hospitals, doctors, and other healthcare providers. The statement clearly indicates that joint ventures need not be concerned with antitrust enforcement unless the activities threaten competition, consumers, or healthcare providers seeking to improve efficiency, reduce costs, or otherwise benefit consumers. This does not preclude needing to have counsel review potential new ventures, but it does appear to support cooperative ventures that will improve access to certain levels of care while reducing the costs of care.

CONCLUSION

Currently, many solo providers, hospitals, and nursing homes have established successful subacute programs. The trend in healthcare delivery, however, is toward consolidation of services in efforts to create critical masses of cost-effective providers better able to compete in the future managed care markets. The hurdles for entry into the subacute market are low, and there has been an explosion of new providers. All will not survive, as even though the market is large (between 10 percent and 20 percent of all hospitalized patients), it has a natural ceiling and the cost of entry is low for a hospital (especially if the CON rules and licensure issues disappear). Also, hospitals with excess capacity and supportive state regulators will enter the market, and since the patients generally originate within the hospital, the flow to freestanding centers will be reduced. To assure the maintenance of their subacute programs in an environment of less growth, organizations must develop cooperative ventures with hospitals, nursing homes, physicians, and insurers. Organizations wanting to provide subacute care will need to clearly state their objectives, determine their capital requirements, and then identify potential partners for the future.

Chapter 15

Immediate and Future Challenges

Marshall W. Kelly
President, Rehab Partners, Inc.

The growth and development of subacute services parallels the implementation of market-based healthcare reform. In many ways, the widespread acceptance of subacute services is a signal of an increased emphasis on the cost containment focus of the market-based reforms. The utilization of subacute providers by managed care organizations, the desire on the part of hospitals for early discharge to increase profitability, and the focus on the resource utilization and patient outcome are all signs of pressures for market-based reforms.

As the nature of the service delivery evolves into integrated systems and networks, and the movement toward capitation and risk sharing intensifies, the changes in the healthcare marketplace will affect subacute services. As the physician, hospital, and ancillary support industries adapt, so will subacute services. These changes, particularly with the impact of capitation, will create a new financial paradigm in which subacute services will have to redefine their role among the players along a new continuum of services.

The financial justifications and the positioning under this system will change as we move away from licensure and process issues to focus upon efficiency, the overall cost to the system, the lowering of inpatient utilization, and the primacy of the risk assumption under global capitation scenarios.

The biggest issue and challenge for the participants in the marketplace reforms will be the ability to adapt to the new realities. There will be winners and losers under the new alignment. The losers will try to protect their current position and will fight or deny the possible changes as long as they possibly can. The shrewd ones will move to position themselves as a survivors, particularly since there will be a lesser need for inpatient acute beds and specialist services.

The essential issues for subacute providers will be to overcome the set of assumptions that made them successful in the recent past, and to become involved in the local healthcare marketplace as the conditions evolve. For example, if a program has been geared toward providing services to patients funded by the Medicare program, with a focus on cost and process, the shift to a cost competitive market will be important. Subacute providers must monitor market conditions and participate in its evolution.

Every local healthcare marketplace is unique. The evolutions in the different marketplaces across the country are in varying stages. It is interesting to note that the areas most would presume to be in the lead, say major sophisticated metropolitan areas, are actually behind the learning and evolution curve of some rural systems.

In some areas, hospitals have been successful in delivering systems in which they will have significant controls. In other locales, capitated primary physician groups are becoming the drivers of systems, with all other providers becoming vendors to the physicians' global capitation. In other areas, managed care organizations are the drivers of the systems. Whatever the local models present, subacute providers will need to participate or they will not thrive.

The areas that subacute providers need to address are successful integration with other providers both up and downstream, measurement of cost effectiveness, cost containment, risk participation, and convenience.

PARTICIPATION IN LOCAL DELIVERY SYSTEMS

The healthcare system will be organized horizontally by large enrolled populations in managed care organizations (MCOs). These MCOs will look to serve these large populations through alliances with vertically integrated networks or local delivery systems (LDSs). An LDS is a linkage of providers led by the "central risk assumer," who will arrange the providers in a simplified, integrated, and cost-conscious system. The LDS leader will probably require its partners to share risk with it. This would encourage the use of internal utilization reviews versus external reviews.

In the past, the healthcare service delivery system was for the most part done in an unorganized fashion, focusing on episodes of care. Under the new financial and service delivery paradigm, the focus will be on taking care of a population base in the most efficient system of care. This focus will stimulate integration, simplification, and participation among providers.

Local delivery systems are a vertical integration strategy. Relationships among physicians, hospitals, ancillary providers, and managed care companies will be carefully designed, emphasizing cost containment, co-ownership, mutuality, risk sharing, and participation. The clinical services will target preventative care, aggressive inpatient utilization practices, and self-care. Customer satisfaction will be an analytic measurement of services.

The financial incentives for providers will have to be considered. This would mean favoring contractual over collegial relationships, and risk participation over cost- or charge-based reimbursement. Inefficient, redundant, profligate, unnecessary, overpriced, and overmanaged providers will be identified, attacked, and wrung out of the system. Managers of the LDSs will have to have no protectionist tendencies for any one point along the continuum.

SYSTEM INTEGRATORS

The problem for subacute providers that stand alone (without direct hospital affiliation) is that they cannot, from their strategic position, easily become the integrators of a service delivery system. Traditionally, providers have been reimbursed for costs; this will evolve into assuming their risk for the service delivery. The major centers of healthcare expenditures are now the physicians and hospitals.

The key to an integrated service delivery system is an organization that assumes the capitated risk (medical loss or the premium benefit monies minus the managed care overhead) for a service delivery. Subacute or postacute providers are not at the center of the healthcare continuum. They are too far down the chain in the service delivery to be the controller of risk, such as a managed care organization, a physician group, or a hospital. Therefore the subacute, postacute, or home healthcare provider must strike a *strategic alliance* with a *system integrator* in the local healthcare environment.

NEW PRICING STRATEGIES

There is going to be a very rapid evolution in the pricing of subacute services to health insurance companies from "usual and customary" fee-for-service billing to more cost-containing methods of payment. The sum of this evolution will be unique to the subacute industry primarily because many providers do not have a tradition of the extensive fee-for-service billing systems used by hospitals. Most subacute sites will not want to replicate these systems and will instead look to establish all-inclusive per diems instead of quantifying all items and services utilized for patient care.

Identifying an all-inclusive per diem for cases will ease the amount of billing paperwork and will give a more predictive financial exposure for the insurance company. Of course from the insurer's perspective an all-inclusive per diem does not give prediction of length of stay, and therefore the exposure for the insurance company is more open-ended than desired. The next step in the evolution will be to go by care per diem, similar to the Medicare DRG payment system.

The final schema for payment will be prepayment, also called *capitation*. This means that a provider will be prepaid to take care of the needs for a specific patient population for a specific type of medical problem. An example would be a $3.50 payment on a PMPM (per enrolled member per month) basis for all types of inpatient rehabilitative services. The provider is at risk for all inpatient rehabilitative services for that 50,000-patient population. The provider receives a monthly check of $175,000, in this case, as a fixed budget.

With the potential exception for high-cost, nonpredictive patients, the capitated per case basis will be the eventual payment method. These outlier populations could include very high-acuity patients, catastrophically injured patients, or those with chronic problems, which could mean exceptional financial liabilities to a financial sponsor. For a relatively small number of patients, a sponsor may potentially have a large financial liability. Therefore, a provider that is willing to manage these cases on a per case basis would have the attention of the insurer.

MOVEMENT TOWARD EFFICIENCY

As a service evolves and matures, increased staff experience leads to efficiencies and practice patterns become normative.

If you follow the reimbursement trends of the movement away from usual and customary to all-inclusive per diems, a fixed-per-case reimbursement, and finally capitation, the drive is irreversibly toward a more efficient provision of service. All of the incentives through this evolution are toward lowering the financial liability of the payor and increasing the risk of the provider for the cost of the service delivery. This focus will drive providers to become more efficient in dealing with staffing costs, ancillary costs, overhead chargebacks, and lengths of stay. The goal will be to become the most efficient provider delivering the desired patients' outcome.

All current relationships, assumptions, and traditions will become variables in the drive toward efficiency. An outcome-oriented service delivery will question all of our process-oriented assumptions. Examples of this change are many and have to be answered. For instance, in the rehabilitative service area, will unlicensed staff under the supervision of licensed staff be able to deliver the outcome, and if so, does this add efficiency in lowering the cost? Would teaching a patient about self-care allow an earlier discharge? Is it less expensive to outsource a service or provide it in-house? How can we more fully integrate a continuum of care to provide more efficient care?

How these decisions will be made and the timing of them will become critical. One process to be employed should be TQI or CQI (total quality improvement or continuous quality improvement) methods that are becoming normative in the manufacturing sectors and increasingly visible in the service arena. These processes will focus the organization on customer concerns, and in this case the customer concerns are the payor's interest in lowering the cost of care. These processes will focus the attention of staff on patients' needs, will ease acceptance, and will be an excellent source of new ideas about becoming more efficient.

The pace of these efforts will be unrelenting as the alignment of the financial incentives will change with evolution of pricing to the marketplace and the mix of payor sources. The increased enrollment of Medicare recipients in managed care products, the pricing models desired by managed care, the provider interest in market share—these all indicate the need for efficiency in the service delivery in the marketplace.

PURCHASING POWER

The potential federal cuts in Medicare and Medicaid funds will be compounded by indivudual states' efforts to control the inflation spiral of their contributions to Medicaid programs. In local healthcare marketplaces, buying co-operatives will use their purchasing power to control, limit, or roll back payment to managed care organizations, which in turn will pass these cuts through to providers. Providers must recognize the eventuality of this monetary resource reduction. The drive toward efficiency will become the norm.

GLOBAL HEALTHCARE BUDGETS

There is strong evidence to believe that, over the long term, we will be moving to a global budget for healthcare services on a localized level. In other words, there will be a fixed pool of monies from which to pay for services. Market-based reforms are already pushing down premium rates as purchasers wield their clout.

Many of the initiatives for government-sponsored payment of healthcare come from Medicaid and Medicare. Movement into managed care is an example. Block grants are another.

The implications of global budgets are many and widespread. Increases in one area will require reductions in another. Stronger incentives will be created for efficiency. Profits will come through cost reductions as opposed to revenue enhancement. More costly innovations will come under greater scrutiny. Inefficient providers will have a poor prognosis. Basic care will be emphasized over esoteric procedures. Expectations for unlimited services will be controlled, because the larger group needs will be emphasized over the individual.

INFORMATION REQUIREMENTS

To conserve resources within our healthcare system and to improve the patient outcomes, we will have to develop and continually refine our assumptions about the care we deliver. Patients will seek efficacy of the treatments they receive; financial sponsors will want to understand the outcomes and costs; and staff members will need feedback on the effectiveness of their interventions.

The analysis of medical care requires objective tests using scientific methods. Clinical and laboratory studies are the foundation of medical training. Uses of these methods range from evaluating pharmaceutical interventions, procedures, and protocols to focusing on disease treatment and functional status. In many ways, we have not studied the larger issues of management, sites of service, cost of the service, and the effects that overall healthcare practices have on the system. This will change. In the marketplace of ideas, one that has high currency is the dialogue about outcomes. At the basic level, outcomes are the functional or health statuses of patients after intervention. And in today's cost-conscious healthcare environment, one goal is the measurement of resources utilized to meet those outcomes.

BUSINESS CYCLE

According to the Boston Group business cycle model, the cash flow stage of a business is that period during which supply does not meet market demand. When supply meets or exceeds the demand, margins become harder to justify to purchasers. This is inevitable in a market-driven capitalistic society.

A service or product in its initial stages of development will generally not meet market demand. At some point, given the laws of supply and demand, the capacity will catch up to the needs of the marketplace.

During the initial stages, differentiation of the service or the price of the service is not as significant as it becomes when market share matures.

For subacute providers, the differentiation of the service might be patient outcomes, cost, location, array of services, and probably most important, the willingness of the subacute provider to enter risk-sharing agreements.

Predictably, the market has experienced this maturity in several areas of the country, where the profits for subacute providers have become compressed. One important signal has been initial pricing. Like many other types of services, for example, home infusion, subacute services initially set their prices lower than those of inpatient acute hospitals, a form of shadow pricing. Once this level of care was widely known within a marketplace, providers were forced to price their services according to those of the competitive subacute provider, not the acute hospital cost structure. This significantly compressed profit margins.

The business cycle is an important strategic element that demands monitoring. When subacute care matures industrywide, development options will change, consolidation will be important, costs premier, and pricing essential.

The business cycle of the subacute industry has been rapid, primarily because of low barriers to entry and attractive financial incentives. Compared to other medical services like in-house psychiatric or rehabilitation, subacute services have low physical plant entry barriers. The conversion of an existing physical plant in a nursing home or hospital to accommodate subacute services is not very costly or time consuming. In short, the business cycle for subacute care has been rapid, with the product finding broad marketplace acceptance.

WINDOWS OF OPPORTUNITY

There are several windows of opportunity for subacute services. The first one is the open market stage, during which a provider can be the first to develop subacute services in a market. Establishing credibility is the major focus in this stage. However, this window is closing in most marketplaces.

The next window of opportunity appears when the market demands a newer and better mousetrap; at theis stage, a sophisticated provider with better allegiances, a more programmatic approach, better clinical resources, and more data can gain market share. Many of the successful providers in the open market stage are caught unprepared for the competitive forces in this stage and can lose their referral base and market position to better-prepared facilities. It is at this stage that hospitals will begin to react to the presence of subacute providers.

The final window of opportunity is the mature stage, which we are entering in most areas of the country. This is when sophisticated providers with a strong national, regional, or local market presence (as exemplified by the sophisticated for-profit providers) can succeed in integrated service delivery. Those companies and facilities that have transitioned themselves culturally and intellectually to successfully operate in the world of acute care services will outperform others. This final stage will be the arena in which there is separation between managements with vision and the ability to intellectually grow and those companies that see only short-term opportunities. Many of the companies professing this integration have not really made the adjustment. They rely on success formulas used in other industries and have failed to grasp the range of activities it will take to be successful in the emerging world.

The biggest danger here is the mind-set. When adjusting to a new set of assumptions, one must not to rely on past accomplishments. Generally a successful person's instinct is to return to what has made him or her successful to date. Breakout leaders see the new set of biases required for success in the new paradigm. This takes will, intelligence, and nerve.

COMPLETE ARRAY OF SERVICES

One of the issues a facility must address is the array of services it chooses to provide. This relates directly to the needs of the customer, in this case the managed care organizations and hospital referral sources. A facility interested in serving only one area of the spectrum of care, for example, subacute rehabilitation services, could be entering a competitively dangerous situation. A competitor with other medically based services may have an ongoing relationship with a shared referral source, which would allow it at some point to bundle its services for one-stop shopping.

Many providers, in anticipation of such a threat, have established themselves as full-service providers in one location or have established a complete service spectrum within a geographic area with a sister facility or through a cooperative agreement. This can help in meeting your referral sources' needs and protect the service delivery your facility has targeted.

As the spectrum of services that will be provided in subacute settings expands, delivering the capacity to offer it all will become more difficult. Making sure that your facility or your network of cooperative facilities can provide all levels of care within your catchment area will become more important as the industry matures and the market becomes more competitive.

REACTION BY HOSPITALS

If the market for subacute care is projected to be 15 to 20 percent of hospital discharges and the lengths of stay of subacute patients are significantly longer than acute stays, it is possible that subacute services could equal or exceed 40 percent of total inpatient patient days. Will hospitals sit still for this diminution of their inpatient medical/surgical or rehabilitation beds? Survival is linked to the answer. If the hospitals of the future will include only ICU towers and emergency rooms, then their administrators will have to drastically rethink their mission, size, management practices, and position in the health continuum. Not many hospitals are eagerly embracing this vision of their future. The only way that hospitals will accept this image of themselves is if the marketplace forces these restrictions upon them.

Will the market forces be strong enough to create this scenario for the hospitals? In some environments, I can already see this vision of the future. Depending upon the growth/reduction of the availability of funds to drive the healthcare system, the incentives of the central risk assumers, the local politics between providers, and the strengths/weaknesses of the hospitals, this vision can become a reality. But in the interim, hospitals will look to creating subacute units in their structures, on their campuses, or as a satellite facilities. They will primarily do this under a skilled nursing licensure in order to work the Medicare DRG system. The main barrier to entry for most hospitals will be a certificate-of-need process, if there is one, for conversion from one licensure to another.

In states with no certificate-of-need process, many hospitals have already converted licensure. In the Los Angeles basin, over 60 percent of the hospitals have relicensed their beds. The hospitals are able to download their general and administrative overhead onto the subacute for Medicare reimbursement. In the Los Angeles area, the Medicare rates for these units are very high. For price-sensitive patients, managed care organizations are moving out of hospitals into freestanding skill nursing facilities at half the hospital cost. This looks to be the competitive paradigm for hospital-based and skilled nursing facilities.

The issue of dealing with subacute services for hospitals is a matter of timing. Whether hospitals can become leaner and compete with skilled nursing facilities on price is the essential question. This would be a tremendous break from the traditional cost structure and mind-set of hospitals. A more likely scenario is that hospitals will try to purchase, operate, or contract with a freestanding skilled nursing subacute center.

Hospitals have high costs associated with their operations. Their general and administrative expenses range between 25 and 40 percent of any cost center. In addition to high management costs (over one manager per occupied bed), hospitals have traditionally done cost shifting among patients and services, have high capital cost components (buildings and equipment), and run at limited capacity.

WINNING SCENARIOS FOR SUBACUTE PROVIDERS

Capitation Risk Sharing

It is likely that by the year 2000 a significant percentage of reimbursement for healthcare services—some are predicting up to 70 percent—will be on a capitated, prepayment basis. Providers of healthcare will be assuming some of the unpredictability of the costs of providing these services.

An important element will be the use of internal utilization review processes, principally by primary care physicians in a "gatekeeper" or "care manager" role. Having physicians at risk helps them internalize the role of cost-conscious and cost-effective providers of healthcare. Internal utilization review, using peer judgment, has greater acceptance and utility than the use of external case managers provided by managed care organizations through their utilization review. This role reinforces the fundamental element in healthcare, the ongoing relationship between physician and patient. This enduring relationship, developed and maintained through trust, is essential.

An Integrated, Full Continuum of Services

One of the challenges facing the subacute industry is to integrate the subacute service delivery downstream and upstream along a continuum of care. Downstream means home healthcare services and outpatient rehabilitation centers. By integrating upstream, a subacute provider will have to align with acute care providers, possibly managed care organizations, outpatient surgery centers, and physician networks, both primary and specialists.

The primary emphasis in this strategy is for the providers to offer a system of care rather than one component, which is important when you intend to offer capitation strategy to managed care or subcapitation to a primary physician, hospital, or a combination thereof. This system will integrate the care, simplify the process, measure it, assist components with risk assumption, and compete with other provider networks. Cost containment will be a heavy theme of the process.

The vertical integration of the patient flow demands a definition of the continuum of care. Each unit is prepaid for one step along the continuum. Utilization patterns depend on each unit's capacity to handle the patient flow from the previous step. Defining the role of each part of the continuum will be critical.

Full Spectrum of Services

When your facility moves from an open referral to a contractual risk basis, the issue of services offered becomes more critical. Should you provide selected services within an integrated service delivery system or a broad spectrum of services? If you offer only certain types of services, the primary risk contractor has to find a competitor to provide the other services that may be required, which creates unnecessary potential competition for you. If you can't or are unprepared to provide the full spectrum, one solution is to identify another facility with which you can divide services. Also, since the subacute field is relatively new, it is difficult to predict what the spectrum of services will include. For instance, facilities under capitated contracts see a pattern of direct admissions into subacute sites from emergency rooms. These patients, such as stroke victims, have been directly admitted to subacute rehabilitation programs. There is no acute care admission, the rehabilitation is at an earlier intervention (which in the past has led to better outcomes), and hospital stays are shortened, resulting in lower costs.

Many subacute centers have focused on particular programs for financial reasons, personnel prerogatives, technical problems, or planning issues. The major divisions seem to be between rehabilitative services and medically based services. Rehabilitative services generate at least 30 to 40 percent of the volume of services currently delivered in subacute settings. The nature of the service delivery, the culture of the programs (nursing or therapy-driven), the physical plant requirements, staffing availability, managerial biases, and other issues dictate these service choices. The development of new programs will probably involve medical services, as the rehabilitation populations have been fairly defined.

Clinical Evolution of Services

As subacute providers gain more experience and acceptance, there will be a refinement of the clinical service delivery. The use of clinical pathways and various measurements of service delivery will allow it to be better focused and more cost-efficient.

New service modalities will be program-specific. Instead of a rehabilitation program, you'll find a stroke program, and possibly within it you will find a stroke program early in its development to further differentiate it. Other examples would be different types of services for ventilator-dependent patients, depending upon expectation, diagnosis, and desired disposition. Postsurgical programs will be defined specifically by the surgical intervention.

Participation in subacute conferences, close working relationships with the referring physician, and agreements with major innovative providers can keep smaller entities abreast of these developments.

Increasing Management Capacities

As a subacute provider becomes successful, the capacities of its management must keep abreast of the changes in the industry, the local marketplace, and the culture of its own facilities. New financial concerns, clinical leadership, staff development, basic support functions, therapy departments, billing issues, MIS support, marketing functions—all will require increased capacity and in some cases higher competencies to meet more sophisticated demands. Management inclusion in marketing activities will assume considerable time away from the facilities and operational duties.

Hospitals will face new regulatory requirements and new reimbursement models, but for the most part they have the management resources to deal with these. Freestanding skilled nursing facilities, on the other hand, may not have had such intense management requirements. However, facilities with 20- or 30-bed subacute units will probably have to double their management ranks to meet the demands. The traditional administrator and director of nursing roles will change, and new skills and additional resources will be required to meet the demands of communication, leadership, and shorter time frames.

Controlling Costs

A large part of the impetus for healthcare reform stems from the percentage of our economy associated with healthcare expenditures. Many other elements of our economy have already undergone restructuring. International competition and overcapacity in production and service areas have rung out many inefficiencies in various business segments. Healthcare has been somewhat isolated from these pressures, but it is clearly gaining widespread attention.

Many of us as healthcare professionals know of inefficiencies, abuses, and profligate expenses in our field. An oversupply of healthcare professionals in certain areas and disciplines, a built-in overcapacity in our hospital beds, redundancies, inappropriate financial incentives, and the overburdensome costs of regulatory compliance contribute to astronomical costs of healthcare.

In the subacute arena, we should be looking to provide our services more cost-effectively. If only for self-preservation, providers must try to offer cost-effective products to cost-sensitive purchasers of healthcare. This must be an ongoing effort.

Many of the issues involve reimbursement. For instance, under a cost-based system, there is little incentive to control costs. Process-oriented regulations (which specify how to do something, rather than outline an outcome) provide little opportunity to find better methods to deliver more cost-efficient outcomes. For the most part, the current Medicare regulations are both cost-based and process-oriented.

When we move to an outcome-oriented and price-sensitive payment system, the focus of the service delivery will be on delivering effective, cost-efficient patient outcomes. There will be many ways in which professionals can experiment with service deliveries, including earlier interventions, staffing adjustments, patient self-care, new teaching methods, more efficient equipment, new methods of family involvement, better integration or different levels of services, or just focusing on an outcome.

Whatever your orientation toward these issues, it is almost certain that the providers that develop high-quality services at the lowest cost will, as they have been in every other economic sector, be the eventual survivors in a competitive market.

In-House Ancillary Services

Many of the larger publicly traded subacute companies have attempted to control their ancillary service costs by establishing or buying separate companies that can, for instance, provide therapy or Medicare billing services or supply pharmaceuticals or durable equipment. The reasons for this strategy are to control costs, supply other providers with services, and create enough volume to be able to bill themselves at arm's length. In some areas, ancillary services have a more predictive and higher rate of profitability. Owning such companies gives healthcare providers stability that they lack as solely vendor companies.

There is a reason providers maintain the separation of the companies. It allows potential competitors to contract at somewhat arm's length; that is, the provider, as parent company to the ancillary service, can sell that service, and thus indirectly do business with a competing provider. Moreover, there are certain circumstances in which a company can bill its parent company at arm's length, given owners' equity percentages of the company's services outside of the parent company's ownership.

Most long-term publicly traded companies approach the industry from a perspective of real estate. Long-term care is a relatively predictive industry in terms of cost and revenues, so the principal financial component is the physical plant. Subacute companies have become management services and ancillary companies, since that is where the profitability lies. The understanding of executive managers to this subtlety is an indication of their potential success in the subacute field.

From Subacute to Postacute

As the subacute industry evolves, we are seeing innovative providers expand into new areas of services to which they can refer patients to complete the continuum of care. They are primarily home healthcare companies, outpatient rehabilitation centers, and durable medical equipment vendors. Providing such services moves a company from being subacute-focused to postacute-oriented. The stimulus for this change is a simple vertical integration strategy in preparation for capitation and risk assumption. The question is, If you are preparing for risk assumption for inpatient subacute care, why not provide the other services with which you will need to integrate? Owning these services primarily helps to control costs and gain market share downstream. They include home healthcare services, community-based services (e.g., vocational programs, social services, residential services), durable medical equipment providers, and other agencies required in a service delivery system.

ALIGNMENT WITH PHYSICIAN GROUP PRACTICES

As capitation becomes the dominant reimbursement paradigm, the financial drivers of the healthcare system will change. Analysts estimate that by the turn of the century, 70 percent of the payment throughout the entire healthcare system will be prepaid at-risk capitation.

The key to a capitation system of payment is control of healthcare costs. Utilizing primary physicians as the leaders in care management is critical. Trained to view the total needs of the patient, both physically and cognitively, and not from a single dominant perspective, they will control the continuity of care. Capitated systems use primary care physicians as gatekeepers for any care a patient requires. Through prevention, early access to care, and aggressive utilization, capitated systems can result in the lower inpatient hospital and specialty service utilization, with enormous savings to the system.

When physicians are given a financial incentive to stay within a budget, they will change from being providers of care to being "managers" of care. They will utilize cost-effective services, prevent unnecessary hospitalization and treatments, and seek volume discounts and practice pattern changes from the specialist physicians with whom they contract. Obviously, a physician visit costing $100 is significantly lower than a single-day hospital stay at $1,000. The lowest-cost settings and every efficiency in the system will be utilized, but the potential controllers of the system will change.

Current statistics show that the lowest-cost integrated healthcare systems are led by primary physicians under global capitation. For example, physician groups can use prevention methods to aggressively manage many patient populations, like asthmatics and diabetics, thus avoiding unnecessary hospital care. Primary physician groups will become the gatekeepers or care managers of the new service delivery systems. This means that the primary care physicians (family practice, internists, pediatricians) will serve as the contact for any and all services their patients require. Any specialist procedures will have to be referred by the primary physicians, who will then monitor all services delivered.

Independent capitated primary physician groups will be the drivers of the system because they will offer high-quality service with the lowest premiums to the purchasers of healthcare. Aggressive managed care will compress the expenses and profits of the healthcare system, and the savings will be passed through to the purchasers of healthcare.

The most important relationship is between the patient and the physician. It is certainly a more tangible and critical relationship than one a physician may have with an insurance plan. Patients trust their physicians as knowledgeable, professional advisors on the subject of healthcare. This relationship is going to drive the system.

In the past, hospitals were dominated by specialists who performed procedures and provided care in the hospital setting. Referrals from hospitals were primarily controlled by the specialists rather than primary care physicians. In the future that will change. Subacute providers will have to refocus their marketing efforts to target primary care physicians instead of specialists.

Attitude Adjustment

For healthcare "the times they are a changin'." Healthcare has been, except for service innovation, a very slowly evolving field. Planning for hospitals used 10-year projections, and marketing healthcare services was unknown. The industry was exceptionally stable, and thinking past six months was considered fortune-telling.

Many individuals in the field are having difficulty understanding the changes and dealing with the ambiguities. Suffice it to say, healthcare needs are not going away; and if services are not provided in one setting, they will be provided in another. Opportunities for entrepreneurs will be exceptional. Individuals who are willing to take risks will be like the providers that assume capitated rates: they will thrive and be very successful.

Index

About the Author

Since 1991 Marshall W. Kelly has been the president of Rehab Partners, a consulting firm specializing in mergers and acquisitions and subacute and rehabilitation development. In addition to writing extensively, during the last three years he has spoken on the subject of subacute development in public forums and has given many internal presentations to organizations. His other areas of interest are physician group development, disease carve-out operations, and niche HMOs. He regularly attends Wall Street healthcare conferences and works with healthcare investment analysts. Previous to this he was a CEO of a chain of subacute centers and a national marketing director of a large chain of rehabilitation centers. He started his 15-year career in healthcare working for 6 years at Stanford University's teaching hospital.

Also available from Irwin Professional Publishing

SUBACUTE CARE
Redefining Healthcare

Laura Z. Hyatt

ISBN: 1-55738-630-7